T0318495

ROUTLEDGE LIBRARY EDITIONS:
ECONOMETRICS

Volume 5

INPUT–OUTPUT IN
THE UNITED KINGDOM

INPUT–OUTPUT IN THE UNITED KINGDOM

Proceedings of the 1968
Manchester Conference

Edited by
W. F. GOSSLING

Routledge
Taylor & Francis Group

LONDON AND NEW YORK

First published in 1970 by Frank Cass and Company Limited

This edition first published in 2018
by Routledge
4 Park Square, Milton Park, Abingdon, Oxon OX14 4RN

and by Routledge
605 Third Avenue, New York, NY 10017

Routledge is an imprint of the Taylor & Francis Group, an informa business

Copyright © 1970 Taylor & Francis.

British Library Cataloguing in Publication Data
A catalogue record for this book is available from the British Library

ISBN: 978-0-8153-9640-6 (Set)
ISBN: 978-1-351-14012-6 (Set) (ebk)
ISBN: 978-0-8153-5437-6 (Volume 5) (hbk)
ISBN: 978-0-8153-5495-6 (Volume 5) (pbk)
ISBN: 978-1-351-13127-8 (Volume 5) (ebk)

Publisher's Note
The publisher has gone to great lengths to ensure the quality of this reprint but points out that some imperfections in the original copies may be apparent.

Disclaimer
The publisher has made every effort to trace copyright holders and would welcome correspondence from those they have been unable to trace.

Input – Output
in the
United Kingdom

Proceedings of the 1968 Manchester Conference

Edited by
Dr. W. F. GOSSLING

FRANK CASS & CO. LTD.
1970

First published in 1970 by
FRANK CASS AND COMPANY LIMITED
67 Great Russell Street, London, W.C.1

©

Printed in Great Britain by
Billing & Sons Limited, Guildford and London

CONTENTS

SESSION V

SPECIAL SESSION

SESSION VI

SESSION VII

LIST OF FIGURES

LIST OF TABLES

ACKNOWLEDGEMENTS

The Conference took place under the auspices of the Econometrics Department (Faculty of Economic and Social Studies), the Department of Extra-Mural Studies, and the Manchester Business School, of and within the University of Manchester. I am grateful for the encouragement of Professor Johnston and members of the Faculty, and for the excellent advice of Professor Wedell and Professor McClelland and the help of their staffs during the preparations for the Conference, and I am also indebted to Professor J. A. C. Brown of Bristol, Professor M. McManus of Birmingham, and Professor Richard Stone and Mr. Owen Hooker of Cambridge for many useful suggestions, and to the Operational Research Society and the Business Economists' Group for notifying their members about the Conference. Several participants who wrote afterwards wish to join me in expressing our appreciation of the fine hospitality provided by the Warden, Mr. Garside, and the staff of Holly Royde College, University of Manchester. Acknowledgement is due to H.M. Stationery Office and the editors of *Statistical News* for permission to reprint Mr. L. S. Berman's paper "Developments in Input–Output Statistics" which was first printed in *Statistical News* 3, November 1968, and to the editors and publishers of *The Manchester School* for permission to reproduce my "Note on User Cost". Finally, a vote of thanks is due to members of certain British companies and government offices who provided material help with the Conference papers, to Dr. H. Neudecker of the University of Birmingham for a final reading of the typescript, and to Mr. R. E. Crum for compiling the subject index.

Norwich,
November 1969   W. F. G.

INTRODUCTION

Among other things, the 1968 Manchester Conference was held to discuss the construction and uses of input–output tables of inter-industry current flows. Tables of interindustry (priced, physical) capital flows on replacement and extension accounts, and of capital stocks of fixed and inventory capitals, by industry of origin and use, were mentioned in the discussion but were not dealt with formally in any of the papers. Such capital tables are another (and more difficult) set of economic matrix-statistics.

Simultaneity is a characteristic feature of input–output, and thus it was natural to open the Conference (Session I) with an illustration of its presence in a multi-product firm, at the same time giving the participants a systematic view, in the small, of the flows between interdependent activities as a working analogy of the "semi-macro" flows between the interdependent industries in the economy. This latter topic was the chief subject of the next paper (Session II) which began with a review of past input–output tables for the United Kingdom (the first was for the year 1935) and went on to cover recent, present, and proposed future work by the Central Statistical Office and the Board of Trade on such tables. The connection of the indus-trial firm with the economy via its industry was a topic common to three of the ensuing four sessions (including the Special Session) which provoked a substantial amount of discussion. The papers given in Sessions V and VI allow one to see how the input–output table enters the scheme of a model for the entire economy, international trade included.

Input–output or interindustry economics has its origins in the writings of eighteenth-century economists. Implicitly, it is a seven-dimensional subject: we are concerned with firms, commodities, and geography, both on the buying and the selling sides, plus also the channels of trade. Explicitly, it is two-dimensional: we view the transactions either between industries, aggregates of firms, or alternatively the production of commodities by means of commodi-ties, pressed out flat on to a two-dimensional matrix, or tableau. In these two-dimensional forms we have abstracted from the geography of firms and households, from the extremely complex network of trade channels, and from (or out of) joint production. We can recon-sider these abstractions by trying to remove them: bring back geography, and we need an interregional block matrix of input–output matrices; review the channels of trade, and ponder whether the trade and transport charges on an industry's *outputs* or on its *inputs* should be charged to its trade and transport outlays—that is, whether the input–output table should be set up in purchasers' or producers' prices: the latter is, for good reasons, preferable. Moreover, reintroduce joint production, and look at the two-floored halfway house which contains the commodities-into-industries (absorption) and commodities-out-of-industries (make) matrices—respectively related to the (a_{ij}) and (b_{ij}) matrices in von Neumann's Model of General Economic Equilibrium. This is the model with which I open my paper ("Some Comments on Linear Models") which was given as the Foreword to the Conference, prior to Session I.

Having run through seven movements of the suite at speeds varying from *andante* to *allegrissimo*, the conference ended with a Theme and Variations: the current and proposed input–output research by British companies, and in British universities. I am particularly grateful to the speakers at this final session (VII) for their succinct and illuminating contributions.

Various "programme notes" are included: a list of participants, an index of speakers, an index of subjects, and a list of general references. Critics of recorded music occasionally protest that a symphony sounds too perfect to be real because the recording comprises many pieces of judiciously spliced tape; I must apologise if I have erred too far in this direction in editing the recorded discussions of the Conference papers.

W. F. Gossling

Econometrics, Manchester,
June 1969

LIST OF PARTICIPANTS

Mr. R. M. Adelson, University of Lancaster
Dr. R. Agarwala, The London Graduate School of Business Studies
Mr. S. Z. Al-Saadi, The University of Birmingham
Mr. A. Armstrong, Department of Applied Economics, Cambridge
Mr. M. Asaadi, The University of Birmingham
Mr. B. Asher, Standard Telephones and Cables Limited
Mr. G. Bain, The Dunlop Company Limited
Mr. J. M. Barber, H.M. Treasury
Mr. T. S. Barker, Department of Applied Economics, Cambridge
Mr. R. W. Bayliss, The University of Birmingham
Mr. L. S. Berman, Central Statistical Office
Professor C. Blake, The University, Dundee
Mr. F. D. Boggis, Dundee College of Technology
Mr. R. F. Bond, I.C.I. Limited
Mr. T. A. Broadbent, Centre for Environmental Studies
Mr. B. C. Brown, Ministry of Housing and Local Government (*late*
    D.E.A.)
Mr. A. Cigno, The University of Birmingham
Mr. J. T. Climpson, The United Steel Companies Limited
Mr. J. R. Cole, Fisons Limited
Miss F. Conway, University of Salford
Mr. A. Crowther, National Economic Development Office
Mrs. J. Curtis, I.C.I. Limited
Mr. L. Curtis, Hoare & Company
Mr. R. W. Daniels, University of Lancaster
Mr. D. B. Drage, The English Electric Company Limited
Mr. P. D. Dworkin, Board of Trade
Mr. J. R. Eaton, The London Graduate School of Business Studies
Mr. F. Edmondson, Leigh Edmondson & Company Limited
Mr. T. E. Gambling, The University of Birmingham
Miss M. Gellner, British Steel Corporation
Mr. S. J. Gielnik, Unilever Limited
Mr. R. W. Goodsman, British Steel Corporation
Dr. W. F. Gossling, University of East Anglia (*late* University of
    Manchester)
Mr. R. L. Harrington, University of Manchester
Mr. J. T. Harwood, Mullard Limited
Mr. D. F. Heathfield, The University, Southampton
Mr. D. M. Heeley, Turner & Newall Limited
Dr. G. R. Hext, Ministry of Power

Mr. J. Hey, Hoare & Company
Mr. T. E. Heywood, I.C.I. Limited
Professor T. P. Hill, University of East Anglia
Mr. K. Hilton, The University, Southampton
Mr. A. D. Insull, White Fish Authority
Mr. N. J. Ireland, University of Kent
Mr. A. M. Irving, The University of Birmingham
Mr. J. R. C. Lecomber, Department of Applied Economics, Cambridge
Mr. D. Liggins, The University of Birmingham
Mr. P. D. Lowe, The University of Birmingham (*late* The University, Sheffield)
Mr. B. G. Luker, I.C.I. Limited
Mr. D. A. Lury, University of Kent
Miss S. Mason, The London Graduate School of Business Studies (*late* Morgan Grenfell)
Mr. R. Morley, University of Durham
Wing-Cmdr. R. Morris, Ministry of Defence
Professor M. McManus, The University of Birmingham
Mr. Carl W. Nelson, Boston University (*late* Manchester Business School)
Dr. H. Neudecker, The University of Birmingham
Professor E. T. Nevin, University College of Wales, Swansea
Mr. R. Outred, Esso Chemical Limited
Dr. F. T. Pearce, W. & T. Avery Limited
Mr. F. G. Pelling, The Dunlop Company Limited
Mr. J. N. Robinson, The University of Reading
Mr. A. R. Roe, Department of Applied Economics, Cambridge
Dr. D. Simpson, University of Sterling (*late* University College London)
Mr. R. Skinner, The British Aluminium Company Limited
Mr. A. Sluce, Building Research Station
Dr. I. Steedman, University of Manchester
Professor I. G. Stewart, University of Edinburgh
Mr. J. D. Sugden, Building Research Station
Mr. J. Tzoannos, G.C.M.S., The University of Birmingham
Mr. D. C. Upton, Central Statistical Office
Mr. R. van Noorden, Department of Economic Affairs
Mr. K. Vernon, Hoare & Company
Mr. K. J. Wigley, Department of Applied Economics, Cambridge
Mr. R. O. C. Wolfram, Economic Consultants Limited
Mr. M. B. Yates, English China Clays, Lovering Pochin & Company Limited

Some Comments on Linear Models

by

W. F. GOSSLING

Research Fellow in Economic Statistics, University of Manchester

(Foreword to the Conference)

I have to make a quick survey of the economic models and special devices employed in the papers given at this conference. We start at the beginning with the von Neumann model (1937; translated into English and published in the *Review of Economic Studies* 1945–6) which is central to the whole discussion. On the first two pages of the *Review* paper one has all the statements one needs for the really basic input–output accounting. If we aggregate up from the von Neumann model, we can arrive at the Leontief model. These models differ: the chief difference is that von Neumann allows joint production and sells all his fixed capital goods out at the end of the period whether they are new or secondhand; Leontief rules out joint production and expresses these fixed capital goods as capital stocks which turn over at their own specific rates. So if one has a family of processes in von Neumann's (expanding) model which use working capital turning over in a year and a family-specific five-year-lived capital good that is "fixed", one also has a timeless characteristic distribution of quantities of fixed-capital stocks—shaped like the wing of a grand piano. From this exponential distribution one can see the relative proportions of the pieces of fixed capital in this family of von Neumann processes each of which is working with the proper amount of working capital. Now in the Leontief model, these processes are all glued together into an "industry", and dividing all their fixed capital by their aggregated output gives one a Leontief capital-output coefficient; a Leontief input–output coefficient is computed similarly. But that is a very simple case of how one gets from von Neumann to Leontief; it can, of course, be much more complicated.

Then, connected with the Leontief model, we branch out into the theory of the firm and the economy, the subject which Mr. Cigno (from the University of Birmingham) is speaking on in Session III. At a more familiar level to some of us, I thought we should go inside the firm; Mr. Carl Nelson (from the Manchester Business School) is giving, in Session I, a paper on the subject of the multi-activity firm.

The Leontief model also connects with the General Theory of Employment Interest and Money. This, as everyone knows, is short period; and I should add that the matrix is not the multiplier: Keynes used the method of residuals, with aggregation, so that inter-industry flows were washed out. We have worked on this recently at Manchester, and I have given out this paper entitled "A Note on User Cost". The national accounts, disaggregated by industry, form a companion set of statistics to go with the input–output matrix of interindustry current flows. On combining the national accounts and the input–output matrix we have a more comprehensive scheme which, I believe, is the one that is basic to Chapter 6 of Keynes' General Theory; more detail on this point is found in my "Note on User Cost".[1] Keynesian theory, dealing only with Gross National Product and Gross National Income, does of course abstract from the interindustry, or better, interfirm, flows and thereby such theory is endangered if its expositors wish to go beyond the "short period".

Aggregating to industries rather than to the whole economy, then, we can look at the industries in the context of the economy. This is a more aggregate step than in Mr. Cigno's paper, which covers firms in their industries as well, but it does allow us to connect such subjects as macro-economics, increasing returns, and input–output, and to consider whether these can be worked together into a growth model.

We must move to some further problems: the von Neumann model is solved for a unique, maximum *common* growth rate: the problem is to find a model with growth *rates*, more than one growth rate, or better, with flexible growth rates. Some progress towards the growth-rates model has been made at Cambridge, and the next step is to deal with flexible growth rates of commodities in final consumption. For example, if one has a change in the growth rate, say from zero to a positive growth rate, one does run into a replacement-of-capital difficulty, and this crops up, unstated and unsolved in several of what I call "The Cambridge Models", and elsewhere. So we need to know more about "writhy growth".

The foregoing discussion has been about macro-economics with aggregation as far as industries. But one might be interested, if one is an industrialist, in looking at the pieces of other industries, besides all of one's own industry, which are essential to produce the whole of the gross output of one's own industry; this is the approach that

[1] Appended to this paper.

I used for my study of the American agricultural sector. This joins up with the first of the Cambridge models, the Sraffa model (in Mr. Sraffa's *Production of Commodities by means of Commodities*), which is a long-run, stationary, static-technology model that is needed in the search for a standard commodity and a solution for prices. In Appendix A of his book, Mr. Sraffa looks for a subsystem for each commodity in final demand, and as it happens this is a useful approach if one has a multi-product firm—of the sort that Mr. Nelson has studied—and wants to look at the profits for a particular commodity that it produces, as opposed to the profits of the activity principally producing that commodity.

Mr. Sraffa, in his search for a standard commodity[2] and a solution for prices, discovered the standard system. It can have three vectors: the bill of goods for interindustry flows or "means of production", the bill of goods for profits-consumption, and the bill of goods for wage-consumption. These vectors are all scalar multiples of a standard bill of goods, so all three are standard. Professor Robinson's model in *The Accumulation of Capital* has only two pieces of standard commodity: extension-investment and wage-consumption, together comprising net national product (the interindustry flows are not in). For the Stone and Brown Model (*Review of Economic Studies*, June 1962) with *one* growth rate, there is but final consumption as a standard commodity *which stays so over time*; with multiple growth rates the standardness of final consumption vanishes as it moves from period nought to all later periods. So we move away from the rather abstract standard-commodity world (which beats the price index-number problem) to the above model of Stone and Brown, and the Stone (1963 Colston conference, and later) models which approach the "real world".

There have been some other contributions which extend the Stone and Brown paper: Mathur's (*Review of Economic Studies*, January 1964) on growing subsystems, each subsystem growing at its own specific rate; and, in parallel with that, Dr. Pasinetti presented a very long paper in *The Econometrics of Development Planning* (North Holland, 1965).

A few other remarks: we come into this problem, this qualitative problem (which we shall get into from our 20×20 game[3]) of the

---

[2] That is, a list, or vector, of specific commodities in certain fixed proportions.

[3] Participants at the Conference from 20 distinct industries in the United Kingdom were asked to state from which of *these* industries their company or institution bought inputs. The resulting 20×20 matrix proved to be irreducible (and indecomposable, of course).

matrix structure, and we shall determine whether this 20×20 system is, for instance, decomposable into blocks, and things akin to that. This is linked up with Mr. Sraffa's standard-commodity system (see my note,[4] *Review of Economic Studies*, October 1967) and a section of the Session I paper.

For some further developments from Stone's "British Economic Balances in 1970", we have had papers by Mr. Wigley, by Barker and Lecomber, and by Lecomber and Barker. The second of these is the "Ports Study"; the last one "Foreign Trade Functions in an Input–Output Model of the British Economy" is the precursor to Mr. Lecomber's paper in Session V. All this is related to *A Programme for Growth*, Volume III and what is called the Yellow Book, the *1954 Input–output tables* published by the Central Statistical Office and the Board of Trade. Mr. B. C. Brown's paper in Session VI is similar in that it is about a national model, the one set up by the D.E.A.

This takes us up towards the research going into the the tables for 1963 and later years; it is hoped that input–output tables for 1963 and later years will be forthcoming. Mr. Berman is giving a paper on this, in Session II.

In winding up this survey, I should recombine its components by going to the Leontief closed model where, formally, there is no final demand sector: final demand is input into an industry called "Households", and the whole model is closed. Then one can start with an $(n+1)$ by $(n+1)$ matrix, $\mathbf{M}$, including households; on adding every row (postmultiply by $\mathbf{i}$, the unit or summation vector) one obtains $\mathbf{x}$, the total gross outputs vector (of industries (1) to $(n+1)$):

$$\mathbf{Mi} = \mathbf{x} \tag{1}$$

One can then take the matrix of coefficients, $(n+1)$ by $(n+1)$, $\mathbf{A}$, and postmultiply by $\hat{\mathbf{x}}$ ($\mathbf{x}$ diagonalised) which will give what one started with:

$$\mathbf{A}\hat{\mathbf{x}} = \mathbf{M} \tag{2}$$

the flow matrix $\mathbf{M}$. Then we have the expression:

$$\mathbf{Ax} = \mathbf{x} = \mathbf{Ix} \tag{3}$$

so that we can write:

$$[\mathbf{I} - \mathbf{Ax}] = \mathbf{0} \tag{4}$$

Our last step is to alter that slightly and to put:

$$[\lambda \mathbf{I} - \mathbf{A}]\mathbf{x} = \mathbf{0} \tag{5}$$

with $\lambda = 1$. This is stating the Leontief model crudely, in character-

---

[4] With G. R. Blakley.

istic-equation form. It gives us a field over which non-negative technologies and outputs, respectively **A** and **x**, may lie. Suppose we make a change in **M**: for example, if we alter the fuel requirements of industries (taking the electricity row across the table) there will be a change in **x**, and also, usually, a change in **A**, the input–output coefficient matrix for the closed model. As another example, consider an upward change in **x**, concomitantly raising $x_{(n+1)}$; this is a change, from under-employment towards full employment, which, if it is short-period, is well known to readers of the *General Theory*.

There are obviously other possibilities with this "general equilibrium" type of approach which it might be useful to investigate numerically. If we have data after 1963 for the United Kingdom, there is this possibility: we can look at the geometry—all the projections that one can draw out of the input–output table—and obtain qualitative information from classifying the geometrical shapes of curves projected from a complex model of this sort. (Mr. Lecomber is providing an example of something like this, with his graph of balance-of-payments *versus* home unit costs). Geometrical shapes of this sort can be obtained by systematic numerical exploration; they are, I think, an interesting field for macro-economic research.

So much for this introduction: from the subjects of the papers mentioned the aim is, primarily, to discuss the progress of empirical research using input–output. It is a subject that is profitably used *inside* the large multi-product firm; inside the *economy*, it can be used by a firm, in a particular industry, which wants to compare the distribution of its sales (across industries and final buyers) with that of all firms in this industry taken together, and likewise to reappraise its input structure, including purchases from other industries than its own. This empirical research is a subject which we would like to reach in informal discussion. I hope that we shall be able to come to tentative decisions on input–output research during the closing sessions of this conference.

APPENDIX
A NOTE ON USER COST[5]

This is written in the hope that Keynesian economists and readers of the *General Theory* [G.T.] may see that that theory shares some common ground with Leontief's "input–output". I believe I have unearthed one of the larger difficulties that might prevent persons

---

[5] Reprinted by kind permission of the Editor of the *Manchester School*.

from seeing the relevance of input–output even to the *General Theory*, let alone a particular economy.

The principal difficulty is with user cost: [G.T.], Chapters 3, 4, and 6. On Keynes's definitions the user cost of the *firm* is the *difference* between the entrepreneur's purchases of finished output from other entrepreneurs, A_1, and the entrepreneur's current investment, I([G.T.], p. 66); because it is defined as a difference, it has a slightly awkward feel to it. More explicitly, there are four quantities in its computation ([G.T.], pp. 52–53): G', what the entrepreneur's capital stock would have been worth at the end of an accounting period, "if he had decided *not* to use it to produce output", provided also that a "certain optimum sum" B' would have been spent "on its maintenance and improvement"; if the entrepreneur had used his capital to produce output he would have ended up with "a capital equipment . . . having a value G". "He will also have spent a certain sum, designated by A_1, on purchasing finished output from other entrepreneurs." User cost, U, is then defined as:

$$U = (G' - B') - (G - A_1) = A_1 - (G - (G' - B')) = A_1 - I$$

where "$G - (G' - B')$, namely the increment in the value of the entrepreneur's equipment beyond the net value which he has inherited from the previous period, represents the entrepreneur's current investment in his equipment and can be written I" ([G.T.], p. 66). Apart from peculiar capital involved in commercial biological processes, it is usual to assume non-negative time depreciation T of an entrepreneur's capital stock; then T must include fixed-technology depreciation and can include changing-technology obsolescence. Now suppose that his stock "which he has inherited from the previous period" has a net value G_0 at the beginning of the current period. Then the expenditure, B', on the maintenance and improvement of the stock should be such that $(G' - B')$ just approaches equality with $(G_0 - T)$. Assuming that this is so, user cost can then be written:

$$U = A_1 - (G - (G_0 - T)) = A_1 + (G_0 - G) - T$$

so that user cost could comprise the purchases of finished output from other entrepreneurs, the running-down (positive) or up (negative) of capital stock through use, minus time depreciation. We must now see whether, and how, this fits in with Keynes's other definitions. As a start, we are told "call the depreciation of the equipment, which is involuntary but not unexpected, i.e. the excess of the expected depreciation over the user cost, the *supplementary cost*, which will be written V" ([G.T.], p. 56). Writing D for expected depreciation, we have:

$$D - U = V \quad \text{or,} \quad U + V = D$$

But we can also write:

$$U + V = A_1 - I + V = A_1 - (G - G_0) - T + V$$

and assuming that V is equal to T, which follows from the discussion in [G.T.], p. 56, then:

$$D = A_1 - (G - G_0) = G_0 - G + A_1 = G_0 - (G - A_1)$$

an equation that is self-evidently correct, confirming the foregoing assumption.

Taking the definition of the firm's current investment:

$$I = G - (G' - B')(= G - G_0 + T)$$

one can subdivide I into extension, and replacement, investment, respectively ${}^{\varepsilon}S$ and ${}^{\delta}S$; one is then tempted to equate ${}^{\varepsilon}S$ with $(G - G_0)$ and ${}^{\delta}S$ with T.

It then follows that $\Sigma(A_1 - U)$ is the (gross) investment of the economy and that $\Sigma(A_1 - U - V)$ is the formula for its net investment, the summation, Σ, being over all the economy's firms. The reader is invited to test out this interpretation of Keynes's definitions by re-reading his appendix on user cost ([G.T.], pp. 66–73) as well as Ch. 6 ([G.T.] pp. 52–65).

It is convenient to consider a closed economy of n firms in which there is at least some interdependence between firms for "the desirability of providing in a generalised way for the case of a non-integrated system of production" ([G.T.], p. 55). Suppose X is the n by n matrix of intra- and inter-firm current flows, ${}^{\varepsilon}S$ and ${}^{\delta}S$ are respectively n by n matrices of intra- and inter-firm outlays on capital extensions and replacements, and that we use the sign $\hat{\ }$ to mean the main diagonal of a matrix, other entries zero, and $\check{\ }$ to mean all entries except the main-diagonal ones—which latter are all noughts. Then $\check{X}$, ${}^{\varepsilon}\check{S}$, and ${}^{\delta}\check{S}$ refer to inter-firm outlays, while $\hat{X}$, ${}^{\varepsilon}\hat{S}$, and ${}^{\delta}\hat{S}$ are intra-firm ones. We now need an n by n matrix U whose column sums give the user costs of the economy's n firms:

$$U = [\check{X} + {}^{\varepsilon}\check{S} + {}^{\delta}\check{S}] - [{}^{\varepsilon}S + {}^{\delta}S] = [\check{X} - {}^{\varepsilon}\hat{S} - {}^{\delta}\hat{S}]$$

where $[\check{X} + {}^{\varepsilon}\check{S} + {}^{\delta}\check{S}] = A_1$, A_1 being a matrix each of whose columns gives a firm's purchases of finished output from other firms, and, $[{}^{\varepsilon}S + {}^{\delta}S] = C$, C being the matrix of gross investment by supplying and purchasing firms; its column sums give the gross investment of firms $1, 2, \cdots n$.

Now let us define a column n-vector $\bar{a}$, the entries of which give the "finished output" sold "to consumers or to other entrepreneurs" during an accounting period; this quantity for the firm is designated as A (in [G.T.], p. 52). Then add the n-vectors of intra-firm current flows $\hat{X}i$, intra-firm capital extensions $^{\varepsilon}\hat{S}i$, and intra-firm capital replacements $^{\delta}\hat{S}i$ to $\bar{a}$ giving an n-vector a. Gross national product is:

$$i'[\bar{a} - Ui] = i'[\bar{a} - \check{X}i + {}^{\varepsilon}\hat{S}i + {}^{\delta}\hat{S}i + \hat{X}i - \hat{X}i] = i'[a - Xi]$$

that is to say, the sum of firms' total productions $i'a$ minus all intra- and inter-firms' current flows $i'Xi$. (For the benefit of readers who follow matrix algebra with difficulty, if an array, such as X above, is post-multiplied by i the column n-vector of 1's, the result is an n-vector the elements of which are the row sums of X; if an n-vector, like a above, is pre-multiplied by i' the row n-vector of 1's, the result is the summation of all entries in a. With X pre- and post-multiplied respectively by i' and i, the result is the summation of all entries in X.)

Gross national product can be split into two parts, consumption, and investment. Consumption is:

$$i'[\bar{a} - A_1 i] = i'[\bar{a} - \check{X}i - {}^{\varepsilon}\check{S}i - {}^{\delta}\check{S}i]$$
$$= i'[\bar{a} - \check{X}i - {}^{\varepsilon}\check{S}i - {}^{\delta}\check{S}i + \hat{X}i + {}^{\varepsilon}\hat{S}i + {}^{\delta}\hat{S}i - \hat{X}i - {}^{\varepsilon}\hat{S}i - {}^{\delta}\hat{S}i]$$
$$= i'[a - Xi - {}^{\varepsilon}Si - {}^{\delta}Si]$$

that is to say, the sum of firms' total productions, minus not only all intra- and inter-firm current flows but also all intra- and inter-firm outlays on capital extensions and replacements. Investment is (gross):

$$i'A_1 i - i'Ui = i'Ci = i'[{}^{\varepsilon}Si + {}^{\delta}Si]$$

(If the accountants have calculated firm's supplementary costs, ΣV, correctly, this should be sufficient to finance all their capital replacements $i'^{\delta}Si$. Net investment is simply $i'[A_1 - U - {}^{\delta}S]i = i'^{\varepsilon}Si$. Net national product is $i'[a - Xi - {}^{\delta}S]i)$.

This is all that need be said. Except this. Re-reading the *General Theory* against the above set of definitions for the aggregate quantities just as Keynes thought of them *in terms of intra- and inter-firm flows* (and thus, with some grouping, in terms of intra- and inter-industry flows) is a truly rewarding experience.

SESSION I

Input–Output Applications for the Multi-activity Firm

by

CARL W. NELSON

*Visiting Lecturer in Operational Research
at the Manchester Business School*

I. OBJECTIVES OF THE PAPER

Since its inception, Professor Leontief's input–output analysis has apparently received only cursory attention as an analytical tool appropriate to problems within the individual firm. The objectives of this paper are:

1. To review briefly the assumptions and methodology of the input–output approach.
2. To illustrate the procedures based on an actual industrial situation and thereby specify the management functions and production systems where the method might be successfully implemented.
3. To connect and compare procedures actually used in a multi-activity firm with the corresponding "academic" approaches.

II. ASSUMPTIONS AND METHODOLOGY

A typical multi-product firm involving final sales to customers (or other sections of the same company) at various stages of the production process can be depicted by a "linear graph", a node of which is drawn in Figure 1. Flows from node to node may either be in terms of physical quantities or cash equivalents, and resources are "inputted" to the first and subsequent nodes according to technological requirements.[1]

If we let:

x_i = value of production of cost centre i

x_{ij} = value of production of cost centre i "sold" to cost centre j.

[1] These nodes are synonymous with the concept of a manufacturing cost centre if one, and only one, product is produced at the cost centre. Joint production is ruled out.

1

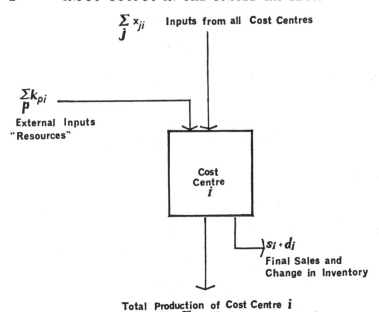

Figure 1. Inputs and Outputs of a Cost Centre

Then

$\Sigma_j x_{ij}$ = total "sales" to other cost centres from cost centre i.

$\Sigma_j x_{ji}$ = value of inputs to cost centre i from all cost centres.

And furthermore if we let

k_{pi} = value of input of p-th external resource (labour, raw materials, etc.) to cost centre i.

s_i = value of change in inventory requirement of cost centre i's products.

d_i = value of demand for cost centre i's output from final sales to customers.

Then

$$x_i = s_i + d_i + \Sigma_j x_{ij} \quad = \quad \Sigma_j x_{ji} + \Sigma_p k_{p^i} \tag{1}$$

Now, if we make the strong assumptions of constant returns to scale,

i.e.
$$a_{ij} = \frac{x_{ij}}{x_j}$$

then the first equality in equation (1) may be written in matrix [1] terminology as

$$x = Ax + s + d \qquad (2)$$

and the solution easily determined by matrix inversion as[2]

$$x = (I - A)^{-1} \cdot (s + d) \qquad (3)$$

For a given technology (A matrix) we are therefore able to find gross outputs (x vector) given a vector of forecasted or proposed final demand and change in inventory.

Now if we can make the similar strong assumption of constant returns to scale for each of the external resource inputs

i.e.
$$b_{pj} = \frac{k_{pj}}{x_j}$$

then the total cost vector c for each of the external factors can be determined by[3]

$$c = Bx, \qquad (4)$$

where B is the matrix of external resource input coefficients: the b_{pj}'s above.

Then from (3) and (4) we have

$$c = B(I - A)^{-1}(s + d) \qquad (5)$$

III. ILLUSTRATIONS

The interdepartmental flow matrices and corresponding flow charts of two chemical processes are set out in Figures 2 and 3 and

---

[2] This can be seen another way: To produce $s + d$ we need intermediate input $A \cdot (s + d)$; to produce such intermediate input we need $A \cdot A(s + d)$ or $A^2(s + d)$ which in turn needs $A^3(s + d)$ and so on *ad infinitum*. Summing all these requirements to $s + d$ gives the total output requirement

$$(I + A + A^2 + A^3 + \ldots)(s + d)$$

Now, since each of the columns of A sum to less than unity this power series in A converges, isomorphically to the well-known geometric progression $(I + r + r^2 + \ldots)$, to $(I - A)^{-1}$; *cf* $(I - r)^{-1}$. The convergence is usually quite rapid.

[3] If previous cost centre profit figures were available and the strong assumptions of the b_{ij} coefficients held here for profits as well, then it would be possible to include this information directly in the B matrix.

Table 1. Flow Matrix 13×13: Inorganic Chemicals

Inputs \ To						Cost Centres								Sales	Total Outputs
	1	2	3	4	5	6	7	8	9	10	11	12	13		
1	0	·35	·35	5·6	2·1	0	0	0	0	0	0	0	0	0	8·4
2	0	0	0	0	0	0	·6	0	0	0	0	0	0	0	·6
3	0	0	0	0	0	·45	0	0	0	0	0	0	0	0	·45
4	0	0	0	0	0	0	·3	1·2	2·592	1·8	0	0	1·5	0	7·392
5	0	0	0	0	0	4·8	0	0	0	0	0	0	0	0	4·8
6	0	0	0	0	0	0	0	0	0	0	0	0	0	7	7
7	0	0	0	0	0	0	0	1·8	0	0	·012	0	0	0	1·812
8	0	0	0	0	0	0	0	0	0	0	0	0	0	5	5
9	0	0	0	0	0	0	0	0	0	5·04	0	0	0	0	5·04
10	0	0	0	0	0	0	0	0	0	0	0	12	0	0	12
11	0	0	0	0	0	0	0	0	0	0	0	·024	0	0	·024
12	0	0	0	0	0	0	0	0	0	0	0	0	0	18	18
13	0	0	0	0	0	0	0	0	0	0	0	0	0	5	5

All figures are in £ millions

Table 2. Flow Matrix 24×24: Organic Chemicals

Inputs \ To	1	2	3	4	5	6	7	8	9	10	11	12	13	14	15	16	17	18	19	20	21	22	23	24	Sales	Total Outputs
1	0	0	1·7	·48	·26	8·4	0	0	0	0	0	0	0	0	0	0	0	0	0	0	0	0	0	0	0	10·84
2	0	0	·003	·004	·006	·003	0	0	0	0	0	0	0	0	0	0	0	0	0	0	0	0	0	0	0	·016
3	0	0	0	0	0	0	0	0	0	0	0	0	0	0	0	0	0	0	0	0	0	0	0	0	2	2
4	0	0	0	0	0	0	0	·64	0	·014	0	0	0	0	0	0	0	0	0	0	0	0	0	0	0	·654
5	0	0	0	0	0	0	0	0	0	0	1	0	0	0	0	0	0	0	0	0	·35	0	0	0	0	1·35
6	0	0	0	0	0	0	0	0	0	0	0	24	0	0	0	0	0	0	0	0	0	0	0	0	0	24
7	0	0	0	0	0	0	0	4·56	0	·078	3	0	0	0	0	0	0	0	0	0	0	0	0	0	0	7·638
8	0	0	0	0	0	0	0	0	0	0	0	0	15·6	0	0	0	0	0	0	0	0	0	0	0	0	15·6
9	0	0	0	0	0	0	0	0	0	0	0	0	2·275	·9	·003	0	0	0	0	0	0	0	0	0	0	3·178
10	0	0	0	0	0	0	0	0	0	0	0	0	0	·96	·05	0	0	0	0	0	0	0	0	0	0	1·01
11	0	0	0	0	0	0	0	0	0	0	0	0	0	0	0	0	0	0	0	3	0	0	0	0	3	6
12	0	0	0	0	0	0	0	0	0	0	0	0	0	0	0	0	0	0	0	0	0	0	0	0	30	30
13	0	0	0	0	0	0	0	0	0	0	0	0	0	0	0	40	0	0	0	0	0	0	0	0	0	40
14	0	0	0	0	0	0	0	0	0	0	0	0	0	0	0	0	·6	0	2·4	0	0	0	0	0	0	3
15	0	0	0	0	0	0	0	0	0	0	0	0	0	0	0	0	0	0	·24	0	0	0	0	0	·8	1·04
16	0	0	0	0	0	0	0	0	0	0	0	0	0	0	0	0	58	0	0	0	0	0	0	0	0	58
17	0	0	0	0	0	0	0	0	0	0	0	0	0	0	0	0	0	·1	0	0	0	0	0	0	96	96·1
18	0	0	0	0	0	0	0	0	0	0	0	0	0	0	0	0	0	0	0	0	0	0	·16	0	0	·16
19	0	0	0	0	0	0	0	0	0	0	0	0	0	0	0	0	0	0	0	0	0	0	0	0	8·2	8·2
20	0	0	0	0	0	0	0	0	0	0	0	0	0	0	0	0	0	0	0	0	0	0	0	0	5	5
21	0	0	0	0	0	0	0	0	0	0	0	0	0	0	0	0	0	0	0	0	0	·5	0	0	0	·5
22	0	0	0	0	0	0	0	0	0	0	0	0	0	0	0	0	0	0	0	0	0	0	0	0	1·25	1·25
23	0	0	0	0	0	0	0	0	0	0	0	0	0	0	0	·2	0	0	0	0	0	0	0	0	0	·2
24	0	0	0	0	0	0	0	0	0	0	0	0	0	0	·002	0	0	0	0	0	0	0	0	0	0	·002

Cost Centres

All figures are in £ millions

Table 3. Inverse Matrix 13 × 13: Inorganic Chemicals

Rows	Columns													External Sales Vector	Total Production Vector
	1	2	3	4	5	6	7	8	9	10	11	12	13		
1	1	·583333	·777778	·757576	·4375	·35	·318583	·296508	·38961	·277273	·159292	·185061	·227273	0	8·4
2	0	1	0	0	0	0	·331126	·119205	0	0	·165563	2·20751 E-4	0	0	·6
3	0	0	1	0	0	6·42857 E-2	0	0	0	0	0	0	0	0	·45
4	0	0	0	1	0	0	·165563	·299603	·514286	·366	8·27815 E-2	·2441	·3	0	7·392
5	0	0	0	0	1	·685714	0	0	0	0	0	0	0	0	4·8
6	0	0	0	0	0	1	0	0	0	0	0	0	0	7	7
7	0	0	0	0	0	0	1	·36	0	0	·5	6·66667 E-4	0	0	1·812
8	0	0	0	0	0	0	0	1	0	0	0	0	0	5	5
9	0	0	0	0	0	0	0	0	1	·42	0	·28	0	0	5·04
10	0	0	0	0	0	0	0	0	0	1	0	·666667	0	0	12
11	0	0	0	0	0	0	0	0	0	0	1	1·33333 E-3	0	0	·024
12	0	0	0	0	0	0	0	0	0	0	0	1	0	18	18
13	0	0	0	0	0	0	0	0	0	0	0	0	1	5	5

Note: For E-J, where J is an integer, read "times 10^{-J}".

Tables 1 and 2. Although simplified for expository purposes,[4] both the 13×13 flow matrix for all the inorganic processes and the 24×24 flow matrices for the organic system typify two general production schemes [3], [6], [7]. The set of inorganic processes comprise merely a "straight-line" production system while the organic processes include "recycling". Earlier and later stages of the processes may be identified in straight-line production while recycling recalls Leontief's concept of "whirlpools" of production. Having assured ourselves of constant returns to scale we may compute $(I - A)^{-1}$ for both of these systems retaining the results for analysis in equation (3) or (5) when necessary.

Needless to say $(I - A)^{-1}$ post multiplied by the original external sales vector should yield the original total production vector. Where matrix inversion programmes force an economy of storage space this check provides evidence of the validity of the inversion procedure. The matrix inversion and post-multiplication by the external sales vector is shown in Tables 3 and 4 for the two sets of processes.

IV. SOME FURTHER CONSIDERATIONS

A. *Upper Triangularity*

One may argue that production systems in which there is no recycling obviate the need for a matrix inversion approach: thus if we examine any straight line interdepartmental flow matrix closely enough we will observe that it is upper triangular, and the corresponding equations may be solved seriatim. Developing the necessary data processing software to systematically accomplish these gymnastics may be another matter however, and for this reason the inversion process seems generally desirable.

B. *Non-negative Square Matrices*

One of the practical limitations of input–output analysis in the firm is the extraordinary size[5] that the flow matrix may take, thereby frustrating all attempts at inversion unless something can be done to reduce the system to one of manageable proportions.

Since a firm's interdepartmental flow matrix is both non-negative and square (Gantmacher [4]) a reasonable way out of the size

---

[4] Inventory requirements (s vector) and cost information (B matrix) are not included. While of extreme importance to the firm their inclusion is analytically and computationally trivial at this point.

[5] Of the order of thousands or tens of thousands.

Table 4. Inverse Matrix 24 × 24: Organic Chemicals

Rows ↓ \ Columns →	1	2	3	4	5	6	7	8	9	10	11	12	13	14	15
1	1	0	·85	·733945	·192593	·35	0	3·01106 E-2	0	1·01735 E-2	3·20988 E-2	·28	1·17431 E-2	3·25552 E-3	3·80327 E-4
2	0	1	·0015	6·11621 E-3	4·44444 E-3	·000125	0	2·50921 E-4	0	8·47791 E-5	7·40741 E-4	·0001	9·78593 E-5	2·71293 E-5	3·16939 E-6
3	0	0	1	0	0	0	0	0	0	0	0	0	0	0	0
4	0	0	0	1	0	0	0	4·10256 E-2	0	1·38614 E-2	·166667	0	·016	4·43564 E-3	5·18196 E-4
5	0	0	0	0	1	0	0	0	0	0	0	0	0	0	0
6	0	0	0	0	0	1	0	·292308	0	7·72277 E-2	·5	0	·114	0	0
7	0	0	0	0	0	0	1	0	0	0	0	·8	·39	2·47129 E-2	2·88709 E-3
8	0	0	0	0	0	0	0	1	0	0	0	0	·056875	0	0
9	0	0	0	0	0	0	0	0	1	0	0	0	0	·3	2·30437 E-3
10	0	0	0	0	0	0	0	0	0	1	0	0	0	·32	3·73841 E-2
11	0	0	0	0	0	0	0	0	0	0	1	0	0	0	0
12	0	0	0	0	0	0	0	0	0	0	0	1	0	0	0
13	0	0	0	0	0	0	0	0	0	0	0	0	1	0	0
14	0	0	0	0	0	0	0	0	0	0	0	0	0	1	1·00002
15	0	0	0	0	0	0	0	0	0	0	0	0	0	0	0
16	0	0	0	0	0	0	0	0	0	0	0	0	0	0	0
17	0	0	0	0	0	0	0	0	0	0	0	0	0	0	0
18	0	0	0	0	0	0	0	0	0	0	0	0	0	0	7·46285 E-4
19	0	0	0	0	0	0	0	0	0	0	0	0	0	0	0
20	0	0	0	0	0	0	0	0	0	0	0	0	0	0	0
21	0	0	0	0	0	0	0	0	0	0	0	0	0	0	0
22	0	0	0	0	0	0	0	0	0	0	0	0	0	0	0
23	0	0	0	0	0	0	0	0	0	0	0	0	0	0	0
24	0	0	0	0	0	0	0	0	0	0	0	0	0	0	1·49257 E-3

Note: For E-J, where J is an integer, read "times 10^{-J}".

Table 4. Inverse Matrix 24×24: Organic Chemicals (continued)

Rows	Columns 16	17	18	19	20	21	22	23	24	External Sales Vector	Total Production Vector
1	8·10717 E-3	4·91331 E-3	3·07082 E-3	9·63849 E-4	1·92593 E-2	·134815	5·40172 E-2	2·45666 E-3	4·81924 E-4	0	10·84
2	6·75598 E-5	4·09443 E-5	2·55902 E-5	8·03207 E-6	4·44444 E-4	3·11111 E-3	1·24521 E-3	2·04721 E-5	4·01604 E-6	0	·016
3	0	0	0	0	0	0	0	0	0	2	2
4	·011046	6·69439 E-3	4·18399 E-3	1·31324 E-3	0	0	1·24367 E-4	3·34719 E-3	6·56622 E-4	0	·654
5	0	0	0	0	·1	·7	·28	0	0	0	1·35
6	0	0	0	0	0	0	0	0	0	0	24
7	7·87029 E-2	4·76545 E-2	·029784	7·31664 E-3	·3	0	6·92902 E-2	2·38272 E-2	3·65832 E-3	0	7·638
8	·269246	·1625	·1018	0	0	0	0	·08125	0	0	15·6
9	3·92682 E-2	2·55729 E-2	1·59831 E-2	8·78616 E-2	0	0	5·53050 E-4	1·27865 E-2	4·39308 E-2	0	3·178
10	3·44828 E-6	·002	·00125	9·47412 E-2	·6	0	8·97219 E-3	·001	4·73706 E-2	0	1·01
11	0	0	0	0	0	0	0	0	0	3	6
12	0	0	0	0	0	0	0	0	0	30	30
13	·690374	·416667	·260417	0	0	0	0	·208333	0	0	40
14	1·07759 E-5	·00625	3·90625 E-3	·292654	0	0	5·24156 E-5	·003125	0	0	3
15	0	0	0	2·92654 E-2	0	0	0	0	1·46327 E-2	·8	1·04
16	1·00104	·604167	·377604	0	0	0	0	·302083	0	0	58
17	1·72593 E-3	1·00104	·625651	0	0	0	0	·500521	0	96	96·1
18	2·76149 E-3	1·66667 E-3	1·00104	0	0	0	0	·800833	0	0	·16
19	0	0	0	1·000	0	0	1·79108 E-4	0	·50011	8·2	8·201
20	0	0	0	0	1	0	·4	0	0	5	5
21	0	0	0	0	0	1	0	0	0	0	·5
22	0	0	0	0	0	0	1	0	0	1·25	1·25
23	3·45187 E-3	2·08333 E-3	1·30208 E-3	0	0	0	0	1·00104	0	0	·2
24	0	0	0	4·36796 E-5	0	0	3·58217 E-4	0	1·00002	0	·002

Note: for E-J, where J is a integer, read "times 10^{-J}".

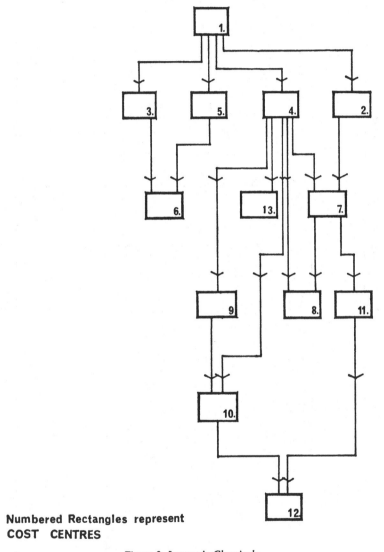

Numbered Rectangles represent
COST CENTRES

Figure 2. Inorganic Chemicals

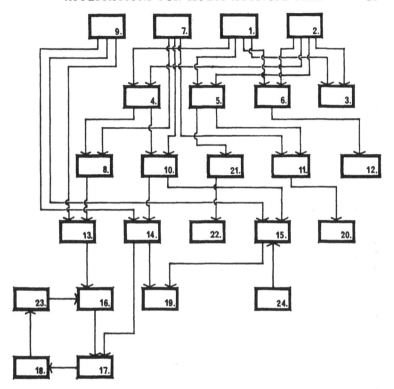

Numbered Rectangles represent COST CENTRES

Figure 3. Organic Chemicals

dilemma is to see whether the matrix is decomposable or reducible [2], [4]. These ideas can be pictorially represented as in Figure 4. Letters that are boxed in indicate square matrices and plain letters non-square matrices. A zero means that that segment of the partitioned matrix is composed entirely of zeros.[6]

Subject to any necessary permutation applied to both rows and columns of the coefficient matrix, the *decomposable* case can be thought of as representing two systems of equations which can be solved independently of one another, while the *reducible but indecom-*

---

[6] Before one may classify a given flow matrix row and column transformations by permutation matrices may be desirable. An algorithm to accomplish this systematically could be included in an input–output computer package.

C

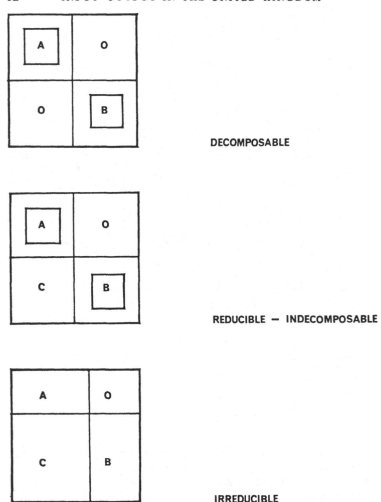

DECOMPOSABLE

REDUCIBLE — INDECOMPOSABLE

IRREDUCIBLE

Figure 4. Classification of Non-negative Square Matrices

posable case is one in which one system of equations may be solved outright and these results then incorporated into the solution of the remaining system of equations, and finally, the *irreducible* case does *not* permit further simplification.

The 24 × 24 matrix, upon inspection, can be shown to be reducible to an upper left-hand matrix of 14 × 14 and a lower right-hand matrix of 10×10. It should be clear from this example that the extent of reducibility in a given interdepartmental flow matrix is reflected by the number of nodes not included in any recycle process.

C. *Subsystems for each final sale[7] and each "total" sale[8]*

This approach might be of interest to the sales-minded accountant. We can solve for any particular flow into final demand, for instance $(s_j + d_j)$. To do this we only need to post-multiply our inverse matrix by a vector in which all elements are zero except for the j-th: $(s_j + d_j)$. Call this vector $\mathbf{f}^{(j)}$.

$$\mathbf{f}^{(j)} = \begin{bmatrix} 0 \\ \vdots \\ 0 \\ (s_j + d_j) \\ 0 \\ \vdots \\ 0 \end{bmatrix}$$

Call $\mathbf{x}^{(j)}$ the production vector for the "*j-th subsystem*". Then $\mathbf{x}^{(j)} = [\mathbf{I} - \mathbf{A}]^{-1} \mathbf{f}^{(j)}$ and of course $\sum_j \mathbf{x}^{(j)} = \mathbf{x}$, that is the subsystems add up exactly to the entire system. From section II we had

$$\mathbf{c} = \mathbf{B}[\mathbf{I} - \mathbf{A}]^{-1}(\mathbf{s} + \mathbf{d})$$

and we can define the cost (primary-input) vector $\mathbf{c}^{(j)}$ for the j-th subsystem:
$$\mathbf{c}^{(j)} = \mathbf{B}[\mathbf{I} - \mathbf{A}]^{-1} \mathbf{f}^{(j)}$$

We are interested in the profit for each subsystem. This is the element $c_\pi^{(j)}$ in $\mathbf{c}^{(j)}$.
$$c_\pi^{(j)} = \mathbf{B}_\pi [\mathbf{I} - \mathbf{A}]^{-1} \mathbf{f}^{(j)}$$

where $\mathbf{B}_\pi$ is the profit *row* for the n activities. In general, $c_\pi^{(j)} \neq [\mathbf{B}_\pi]_j$ the j-th element of $\mathbf{B}_\pi$, unless all activities never buy from each other in which case the subsystem and activity making a particular final output are identical.

For a given profit-by-activity vector, profits by activity are com-

---

[7] See Sraffa [8] Appendix A.

[8] See Gossling [5]. This approach of activity subsystems, one for each "total" sale, may be of interest to a person chiefly concerned with the profitability of a whole activity.

pared with profits by subsystem in Table 5. Note that if a whole row in the entire tableau of flows is scaled by a positive number reflecting a change in market price, the subsystems are always unaffected; under such a change, a subsystem profit can only change if one of the $B_{\pi j}$'s change.

This seemingly academic approach is, in fact, being employed to a suitable degree of approximation by industrial accountants carrying out a "break-back" analysis for each final sale in the whole firm. This analysis multiplies out, for example, $A . f^{(j)}$ giving intermediate inputs needed for the manufacture of the final sale of product j; next these inputs are summed as outputs and *their* necessary intermediate inputs are then $A^2 . f^{(j)}$, (as mentioned in footnote 2, page 3) and so on. Since $A + A^2 + A^3 + \cdots$ converges quite rapidly, $[I - A]^{-1} f^{(j)}$ may be suitably approximated after five or six "rounds", giving $x^{(j)}$, which in turn allows the break-back to be taken through to external resource inputs, the usual objective of such analysis.

Table 5. *Comparison of Profit by Activity versus Profit by Sub-system: An Example*

Activity	Profit by Activity (£mn.)	Profit by Sub-system (£mn.)
1	0	0
2	0	0
3	·2	·2
4	0	0
5	0	0
6	0	0
7	0	0
8	0	0
9	0	0
10	0	0
11	−·09	−·045
12	3·5	3·5
13	0	0
14	0	0
15	·07	·04188
16	0	0
17	15·02	15·02
18	0	0
19	1·21	1·22241
20	·62	·575
21	0	0
22	−·13	−·114295
23	0	0
24	0	0

POSTSCRIPT

Although not explicitly stated, it should be clear that input–output analysis gives no thought to feasibility or optimality. In this sense it is of limited usefulness as a short-term production planning technique. As with the "break-back" approach applied to every final sale (cumulating results), the Leontief input–output approach allows the computation of external resource inputs for some new vector of final sales in one go, once we have $[I - A]^{-1}$. By either path one may identify whether the requirement of any "external" resource input exceeds available supplies, thereby indicating a "bottle-neck" situation, or infeasible production schedule. In the industrial examples discussed, "external" resource inputs include such "non-current" inputs as the firm's labour force and usual supplies of raw materials. By computing x, the total outputs of activities in the firm, and comparing each x_i with its activity's capacity output, we can determine whether a bottle-neck has arisen in the firm's plant *per se*. We would then turn to linear programming or some other optimising technique to see whether and how these bottle-necks might be removed or side-stepped; alternatively some minor changes in processes might have the same effect.

The principal benefit of input–output analysis to the firm, as this paper has attempted to show, is in the area of financial and resource planning and control, especially where production systems involve recycling. Moreover, a joint benefit lies in the concomitant systemisation of a firm's standard costing procedures.

In conclusion one could argue that if more firms used input–output analysis internally and made their *aggregated* accounting information available to the government, then the particular task of modifying the national input–output table to suit the needs of any one firm would be greatly simplified.

REFERENCES

(1) Bellman, R., *Introduction to Matrix Analysis.* New York: McGraw-Hill, 1960.
(2) Blakley, G. R. and Gossling, W. F., "The Existence, Uniqueness and Stability of the Standard System", *The Review of Economic Studies*, 4 (1967), 427–430.
(3) Farag, S. M., "A Planning Model for the Divisionalised Enterprise", *The Accounting Review*, 2 (1968), 312–320.
(4) Gantmacher, F. R., *The Theory of Matrices*, Vol. II. New York: Chelsea, 1960.
(5) Gossling, W. F. and Dovring, F., "Labour Productivity Measurement: The Use of Sub-systems in the Inter-industry Approach, and some Approxi-

mating Alternatives", *Journal of Farm Economics*, Vol. 48, No. 2, May, 1966.

(6) ICIRI, Y., "An Application of Input–Output Analysis to Some Problems in Cost Accounting", *Management Accounting*, Section 1, 8 (1968), 49–61.

(7) NOBLE, A. S., *Input–Output Cost Models and their Uses for Financial Planning and Control*, I.C.I. Management Services, Wilmslow, Cheshire, England.

(8) SRAFFA, P., *Production of Commodities by Means of Commodities*. Cambridge University Press, 1960.

SESSION I: DISCUSSION OF MR. NELSON'S PAPER

Chairman: PROFESSOR C. BLAKE (DUNDEE)

QUESTION:

You might like to mention how many American firms are involved in input–output studies?

MR. NELSON

As far as I know, there may be one firm, in the U.S., building input–output models, and there are a certain number of firms who, like I.C.I., are interested in using the technique.

MR. BERMAN (C.S.O.)

I was wondering how in practice one could produce input–output tables for a firm. The transactions in the table relate to the transactions between one branch and another, or, one division and another within the firm. How does one value these transactions? The values placed on each of these transactions would, of course, determine the profit earned by each of the branches (or divisions) within the firm. How does the accountant go about filling in the table?

MR. NELSON

Well, certainly, disentangling joint production, disentangling the production of the various divisions within a company is very crucial, but the matrix for a company, such as the one presented in my paper, is a chemical conundrum that involves technological constraints resulting in a relatively stable matrix. A firm would need to organise its accounting and valuation procedures in such a way that we could get over these very knotty problems. But since I am not a qualified accountant, perhaps there is someone on the floor who would like to comment on this.

MR. HEYWOOD (I.C.I.)

The questioner is presumably especially concerned with processes having more than one output.

There are three or four standard methods of evaluating joint production, but no answer to the problem which will give real satisfaction. We can allocate the costs *pro-rata* to the output on any basis you like, providing you remember what you do. Another popular method is to use the market price (particularly the world market price for products in the oil business) for say three out of four joint products leaving the largest to take a net cost. A third is to credit net scrap or selling prices for surplus minor materials to the main product; but in the first case all four then move on to other stages at the price or cost according to whichever valuation is given.

In the case of joint production which recycles back and is used again as a raw material it will take the price of the raw material it replaces.

A fourth method is used where there is a recycle (or "by-product") which goes back in the process and replaces an intermediate. In this case it is the usual practice to equate the value of the recovered product to the value cost of the intermediate that is replaced.

The reason I stressed the point about remembering what is done in case 1 is that if the problem is one of a linear programme containing over 8,000 constraints then you've got to use rule-of-thumb methods until somebody devises a method of completing an optimising model of this size.

What we do then, if a decision is to be made on one of the end products arising from joint (interdependent) production, is to use a break-back table to find out what will be the effect (on the other end products) of the joint (interdependent) costs and what bottle-neck(s) will arise. Really you can't do it without a computer; we prepare manual break-back tables from standard costs up to about 100 products at any one time, but once you get beyond this you are in difficulties.

MR. WIGLEY (Cambridge)

I'm rather surprised that this paper makes no mention of linear programming which is used in a great number of firms, both in this country and elsewhere. The use of a rigid input–output matrix which allows one activity—one method of achieving each aim—is completely demand-oriented and ignores any capacity limits. Firms who have maximised a linear programme are able to construct the input–output matrix at the optimum point which they could then supply as data to government centres and collecting agencies.

On the point of decomposition one could certainly learn a lot by drawing up a network in matrix form and, by rearrangement, study its structure. I'd be interested to hear just how far computing problems arise in practice with the computers now available.

I should like to ask the speaker just how exactly he intends to use his subsystem approach for financial planning. I recognise that in the presentation of his paper he was assuming constant returns to scale. In the vector he used, which had all elements equal to zero apart from one, there must be a very great temptation, instead of taking the actual level of sales plus inventory changes for this element, to try to work out the marginal profit of a small increment in demand, principally for one particular product. This is particularly dangerous when all the coefficients are average. This after all is one of the principal problems in financial planning—how to increase the capacity in your firm—a marginal decision and not an average one. It is here that the shadow prices calculated in a linear programme may be useful because they refer to marginal movements away from the optimum position.

DR. GOSSLING (Manchester)

I just wish to make a reference to the problem of jointness: it has been solved by Bates and Bacharach at Cambridge; this is in *A Programme for Growth, Volume III*, and this is a very brilliant paper which should have received more academic acclaim. Their approach involves the von Neumann matrices, the "absorption" matrix for inputs and the "make" matrix for outputs. By doing certain operations on these two matrices you can get from these two matrices for joint production to a purified commodity–commodity (single-product) system (like Leontief's or Sraffa's), or, alternatively, to an industry–industry system. There is a further paper on the efforts by the Canadian input–output analysts who also go into this problem of getting rid of jointness by matrix methods: that is Professor Rosenbluth's paper (Input–Output Analysis: A Critique) which he gave at the A.U.T.E. meeting at York in April 1968 while visiting L.S.E. from the University of British Columbia.

With respect to subsystems, I am coming to Mr. Nelson's rescue here because we have been working on these together. This *is* an average technique—as the last speaker said. What we want to do though is to focus on, get an answer for, a particular commodity;

because sometimes, in a multi-product, multi-activity firm, you are running some processes at current prices at a loss, and you want to know whether you should drop them. Well, if you drop them you have to buy from outside: you lose control. So you have a choice here between the devil and the deep sea, and if you look at the subsystem answers, the profit margin on the activity may be negative while the profit margin on the subsystem for this commodity may be positive. Now if you go from a "profit and/or loss" vector for *activities* (with some losses), and find that the subsystems give all-positive profits, then the loss-making activity is not a problem here; it evens out; the loss all comes out in the wash, so to speak. Obviously, though, you can't have too many loss-making activities in the firm, nor for that matter loss-making industries in the economy.

MR. HEYWOOD

If I might describe a real-life situation; one of our major problems is that a division—making, say, oil products—may have 150 products and does deal with these by linear programming, specifically because it has variable inputs and variable outputs in individual production stages as is well known. The trouble is that these products then pass on through maybe two divisions with very large numbers of products, passing through what we might call single-product cost stages, and then from this they move on to the divisions which sell from stock, for example, dyestuffs, paints, and explosives. The result is a great increase in the total number of constraints. The divisions are separated by man-made boundaries on the basis that each divisional chairman should be responsible for his own profits. This can be a major headache. The trouble is that once you get into the end-of-chain selling organisations you are running into cost models of large size. One already approaches $13,000^2$ and we could have divisional models of $50,000^2$. (But this isn't very big in comparison to such a model for an engineering firm.) So you have considerable data-gathering problems and considerable computational problems; actually we have about five different computer methods, ranging from simple data-processing of straight line production to the type of models that have been described, plus one or two of our own design.

(At this point Mr. Nelson moved a vote of thanks to the industrial firms which had assisted with his paper.)

MR. NELSON

There are some other industries for which this analysis might be applicable, outside the chemical industries and the oil industries: there is a possibility for the use of input–output analysis in the steel industry, in which the recycling is in terms of a tremendous amount of scrap: I understand that because of scrappage, up to 30 per cent of the flow is recycled.

MR. GAMBLING (Birmingham)

Actually my question is just a simple one, and I wish it had been possible to stand up at the back and say "Hey, what is this?" I was a little uncertain—I think my colleagues beside me were a little uncertain—about precisely what your definition of an activity was, and precisely what a subsystem was, you know, under the activities. I'm pretty certain it's something you know that we talk about in different terms. I can't quite understand what an activity is.

MR. NELSON

By an activity we are referring to the production of an identifiable product in the production system. By a subsystem (I think this is maybe a poor word) we are looking at the system in terms of (if I may use a psychological concept) a gestalt, as it were; we are concerned with it not only in terms of individual activities, but in terms of all of the flows. Does that make it clearer?

QUESTION

Is a subsystem a special form of an input–output system?

MR. NELSON

Yes: It is just that the word subsystem has been used before in the economic literature; so I have repeated it.

QUESTION

Should the profits summed by activity and by subsystem be the same?

MR. NELSON

Yes, they should be the same; there is just a very small rounding error involved in my computations.

DR. HEXT (Ministry of Power)

First a couple of quick comments, if I may. On large linear programming systems there is a firm recently started up in London, S.I.A. Ltd. (23 Lower Belgrave Street, London, S.W.1, very near Victoria Station). They have a new CDC 6600 computer, and are using software developed in Paris. They claim that their linear programming system will handle 10,000 rows with ease, and up to about 20,000 maximum.

Another quick comment. I don't scan the literature on this regularly but I did spot, in the papers presented to last year's O.R. conference down at Exeter, a report by one steel company on the development and use that they have made of input–output methods ("An economic model of an integrated steelworks" by M. T. Johnston and D. A. Cameron, of Richard Thomas and Baldwins Ltd.).

I am now taking up the Chairman's invitation and trying to cast myself in the role of, say, the manager of the procylan red plant: I am wondering; I see in the list that my profit by activity is 5, my profit by subsystem is only 2.8; how would this be explained to me?

MR. NELSON

With any operational research technique, we need to sell the idea to management, and the conclusions that one can reach from these ideas are sometimes difficult to put across—I'm not sure whether you're bringing up the question of rivalry between divisional managers or whether it's just a question of mathematical explanation or economic explanation. We can explain the discrepancy, and I've tried to explain why the two figures are different in the paper. I am not sure whether you are bringing in another angle.

PROFESSOR BLAKE (Dundee)

Well, if I may intrude here, I think the questioner was asking you how you would put this in non-theoretical language: it's a question of exposition rather than analysis.

MR. NELSON

Your activity, that is the department of procylan red, while showing an activity profit of 5, only shows a subsystem profit of 2.8 because production from procylan red is dependent on, and goes to, other production within the system, and our profit by activity differs from the profit by the subsystem because other activities are making a different profit on the basis of the flows from our individual cost centres.

DR. GOSSLING

I think I should clarify this just a bit further. The point is that procylan red is dependent on various other activities (you can say interdependent with all other activities). Suppose you have a 3-activity table, and activity 1 is procylan red which is dependent on the second and third activities. Suppose we know the other flows in this table; then we can work out the fractions of activities 1, 2 and 3, which are directly and indirectly supporting the production of procylan red for final external use. We might find that this *subsystem* consisted of 0·7 of activity 1, 0·5 of activity 2, and 0·2 of activity 3; then we would pick up 0·7 of the profit from procylan red (of 0·5), which would give us 0·35 (all this is a separate example from Mr. Nelson's), then 0·5 of the loss on activity 2 (of minus 2·0) so that gives us minus 1·0 here, and 0·2 of the profit on activity 3 (plus 0·8), which gives us 0·16. We add that up and we get 0·35 minus 1·0, plus 0·16, and that is a loss of 0·49. Now the subsystem we can see as a part of column 1, point seven of column 1, plus 0·5 of column 2, plus 0·2 of column 3, plus the sales of activity 1 to the external market. Now you have got a subsystem: it is all the above pieces of your $(n+1)$ by $(n+1)$ tableau for the n-activity system (with $n = 3$). So you can either see your subsystem as one of a set of independent subsystems (which will together add up to the original complete system) or you can see your procylan red as an industrial activity: as one of the set of interdependent activities of the system.

PROFESSOR HILL (East Anglia)

I am not sure whether my question should be addressed to the speaker or to Mr. Berman who is speaking this evening. It seems to me that there is a close or identical formal similarity here between the comparison of profit by activity versus profit by subsystem and, for example, the comparison of the direct import requirements of an entire industry versus the total (direct plus indirect) import requirements for the final output of that industry.

MR. BARKER (Cambridge)

I have two comments to make. The first is that I think you could introduce purchases of commodities from other industries or from abroad quite easily into the analysis (and this would also get round the problem mentioned by Mr. Wigley of constraints of production: since you might be able to produce only so much naphtha, you could obviously import it instead). The second is that the input–output technique has been contrasted with linear programming;

but it seems to me that linear programming is a much more powerful technique. It would tell you, if you are going to maximise profits, what you should be selling, whereas input–output tells you what you have to produce if you give it the sales you are going to make and the stock building you want to do. Linear programming seems to be a much more complicated procedure for doing alternative calculations as compared with input–output. So I'd like to ask you what your opinion is on the question of linear programming versus input–output as a technique for use by a company.

MR. NELSON

I would argue that linear programming certainly is of value in terms of investment decisions, in terms of pricing decisions, in terms of any short-run fluctuations that you wish to examine: but in terms of the accounts and accounting and the financial bases of a firm I feel that input–output analysis has much to offer here that linear programming does not. It is not an optimal-seeking technique as is linear programming, but it has benefits on the financial planning and control side. We may use the techniques of input–output analysis to identify potential bottle-necks and then proceed with linear programming to determine the optimal level, as suggested by Mr. Heywood.

MR. WIGLEY (Cambridge)

I should like to ask the speaker to distinguish carefully between the uses of the technique which he has described; to distinguish firstly the allocation of costs between either activities or subsystems in an accounting sense (that is to say in an average sense) from financial policies which relate to actual financing decisions, i.e. to investment decisions. He has made the claim that this method helps in financial policy, and I should like to ask him to explain what exactly he means by that.

MR. NELSON

On the basis of a proposed change in inventory or sales policy, one can draw up a budget for the individual firm in the ensuing year, and this is one of the financial techniques in which input–output analysis would be helpful. Also, in keeping track of the firm's accounts there is a strong similarity between the accounting information which is kept in matrix form and that of keeping the accounting information in double entry book-keeping form. The introduction and operation of standard costing procedures can be facilitated by the implementation of an input–output model.

SESSION II

Developments in Input–Output Statistics

by

L. S. BERMAN

Assistant Director, Central Statistical Office

Note: This paper is also published in *Statistical News*, No. 3, November 1968 (H.M.S.O.).

I. BACKGROUND

The United Kingdom was among the first of the countries to produce input–output tables and to use them for analytical purposes. They have been produced by private investigators, research institutions and by government departments. Detailed tables, with thirty or more industries, have been published for the years 1935, 1948, 1954 and 1960 and the Central Statistical Office is now in the process of producing a set of detailed tables for the year 1963.

The first official table appeared in the first National Income Blue Book in 1952. This was a "summary" table consisting of only eight industry groups. Somewhat larger summary tables have appeared in subsequent Blue Books. The first really detailed official input–output table, relating to 1954, was published early in 1961 in *Input–Output Tables for the United Kingdom*, 1954. This consisted of forty-six industry groups. The first "inverted" input–output table for the United Kingdom was published in the National Income Blue Book in 1955.

It should be noted that in order to produce a firmly based input–output table it is necessary to have a census of production, which provides detailed information about both sales and purchases for the manufacturing industries and for the mining and quarrying, construction, and the gas, electricity and water industries. Such censuses have been taken in respect of the years 1948, 1954 and 1963. Detailed censuses have also been taken for the years 1951 and 1958, but these asked firms to provide detailed figures of their outputs and not of their inputs. When the census of production for 1958 was being planned in the mid-1950s an important consideration was to cut down the burden of form filling. At that time a considerable

24

effort was being made to develop the quarterly national income accounts, and private industry and trade were being called upon to make new quarterly returns of their fixed capital expenditure, stock-building and trading profits. Industrial firms find it particularly difficult to provide detailed figures of their purchases of goods and services, and it was thought that it would be sufficient to ask for this kind of information in every other detailed census of production. Furthermore, there was no demand for detailed input–output tables for use within the government service or elsewhere. (In contrast, considerable use has always been made of the summary input–output tables pioneered by the Central Statistical Office.) Looking back now, I think it is unfortunate that firms were not asked to provide details of their purchases in the census for 1958.

Towards the end of 1962, Professor Stone and others of the Department of Applied Economics, Cambridge, published an up-dated table for the year 1960, consisting of thirty-one industry groups. (An up-dated input–output table is one which is not based on detailed information about industrial inputs for the year in question, but on projections from a firmly based table—in this case 1954—for an earlier period.) This up-dated table provided the statistical basis for the input–output tables used in the national plan.

The most up-to-date input–output tables relate to the year 1963 and consist of twenty-eight industry groups. They appeared in an article by Mr. D. C. Upton, Central Statistical Office, published in the August 1968 issue of *Economic Trends*.

II. THE INPUT–OUTPUT TABLES FOR 1963

Plans for producing a detailed set of input–output tables for 1963 were laid down as soon as the tables for 1954 were completed in 1961. The design of the census of production for 1963 took account of the needs of input–output analysis. Firms were asked to provide details of their purchases of commodities (including fuel) and also of certain other business expenses, such as expenditure on repairs and maintenance, rates, market research and advertising. Questions about these business expenses were not included in the census of production for 1954. Unfortunately, the timetable for producing the input–output tables has been upset because processing the basic census of production results by the Board of Trade Census Office has been delayed by computer problems and programming difficulties. However, these have now been sorted out and the bulk of the census of production results will be available before the end of this year.

Because of these difficulties, we have taken, as it were, several bites at producing the input–output tables. In the August 1966 issue of *Economic Trends*, we published a small input–output table for 1963 consisting of fifteen industry groups. This was based partly on the provisional summary results of the census of production and on other information relating to 1963, but for the most part is represented an up-dated version of the detailed table produced for 1954. Its purpose was to help bridge the gap between the taking of the census and the completion of the detailed input–output analysis. In the August 1968 issue of *Economic Trends*, this provisional analysis was carried further and a "stretched" version of the up-dated table with twenty-eight industry groups was published. The transactions matrix is reproduced at the end of this paper in Table 1. An important feature of this somewhat larger table is that it provides a disaggregation of the services industry group which until then had always appeared as a single row and column in the tables produced by the Central Statistical Office. In this new table Road transport, Rail transport, Other transport, Communications, Distribution and Other services are shown as separate industries.

Another new feature of the table is that an import matrix is superimposed on the interindustry matrix. This import matrix provides a classification of imports by commodity group analysed according to consuming industries and final demand. The estimates are provisional until the results of the census of production are fully analysed and must, in any case, be very approximate. But despite this limitation they have been published in response to numerous requests.

The detailed input–output tables which are being compiled for 1963 consist of about seventy industry and commodity groups. A list of these is given at the end of this paper in Table 2. The list is based on the Standard Industrial Classification, which is essentially a classification of statistical units by principal product or process. We hope that the classification will satisfy most users; but we recognise that it cannot satisfy them all. In particular, it will not meet the needs of those who are interested in a purpose, or functional, classification of activities, for example, those who are interested in sales and purchases of fuel, packaging materials, advertising, entertainment, durable goods, capital goods and so on. These functional headings straddle a number of quite different industry groups. For example, packaging materials are produced, *inter alia*, by the paper, timber, glass, metal and plastics industry groups. Furthermore, within each of these industries, factories manufacturing packaging materials (e.g. paper bags and wrapping paper) also manufacture other products (e.g. tissues). To attempt to meet the needs of all possible users of input–output tables, the industry classification adopted needs to be very fine; not so much because there might be an interest in each of the very large number of separate industries specified (these could number several hundred) but to permit the user to regroup the data to meet his own particular needs.

We propose to compile two basic input–output tables consisting of about seventy industry/commodity groups for the year 1963. The first of these is a matrix providing a classification by commodity group of the output of each industry group and of imports. This table will be similar to Table C of *Input–Output Tables 1954*. It will show for each commodity group how much is produced by the industry group for which they are principal products, how much is produced as secondary products by each of the other industries and how much is imported. The second basic table is the "absorption matrix", which provides a classification by commodity group of each industry group's purchases. In this matrix no distinction will be made between whether the commodity purchased is home-produced or imported, or whether it is purchased from the industry producing it as a principal product or as a secondary product. This table will be similar to Table B of the *Input–Output Tables 1954*.

In addition to these two basic tables, three other flow (or transactions) tables will be compiled. First, an import matrix providing a commodity classification of imports purchased by each industry group and by each component of final demand. To make this table more useful, it is proposed to divide the commodity classification of imports into more that seventy groups in order to distinguish the more important agricultural and mining products which do not have a counterpart in U.K. production or, which are for the most part, imported. Examples are imports of tobacco, raw cotton, raw wool crude oil. The second and third matrices are the industry/industry and the commodity/commodity flow tables.

The industry/industry table is the traditional interindustry transactions table, which sets out the pattern of sales and purchases of each of the different industry groups, and will follow the lines of tables previously published by the Central Statistical Office (e.g. Table A of *Input–Output Tables (1954)*. This table can be used for assessing the relationship between the outputs and inputs of different industry groups, for calculating the primary input contents (e.g. the import content and the labour cost content) of the outputs of different industries and of various forms of final expenditure, for tracing the effects of price changes in one industry on other industries and

D

for considering the manpower requirements of different industries, and so on. The commodity/commodity flow table is considered by many to be more suitable for projection work at a detailed level because it is said that the technical coefficients are more stable. Commodity matrices of this kind were used in compiling the national plan.

In addition to these matrices of seventy industry and commodity groups, it is intended to produce a commodity classification by seventy groups of the inputs into each of the 119 separate manufacturing industries distinguished in the census of production for 1963. This rectangular matrix should be compiled fairly readily from the worksheets used in producing the seventy industry square matrix. However, expanding the seventy industry matrix into a larger one in which each of the separate industries distinguished in the census are shown separately—in other words, into a square matrix of the order of 130 separate industry groups—is a problem of a different order of magnitude. Only limited resources are available for this kind of work in the Central Statistical Office and it is not certain whether constructing this very large table should be given priority over other input–output work discussed below.

In the "stretched" twenty-eight industry matrix published in the August 1968 issue of *Economic Trends* the services industries (other than Public administration, etc.) were divided into six separate categories. It is hoped to do the same thing again when the seventy industry table is compiled, but until the work is further advanced it is not yet certain whether it can be done. Although interest in the various services industries in the United Kingdom economy is steadily increasing, the information available about their purchases of goods and services and on the allocation of their sales is generally inadequate. Although very rough estimates of expenditure by the twenty-eight broad industry groups on road, rail and other transport have been made, it is not certain whether existing information really justifies the extention of these estimates to cover as many as seventy industry groups. One difficulty is that in the census of production the valuation of goods sold is not uniform. The sales value is essentially the invoiced value—the amount charged to the customer— which can be either the delivered price, including transport paid by the manufacturer, or the ex-works price where the transport is paid for by the purchaser. In the case of exports the delivered price would be the f.o.b. value. From the point of view of each reporting establishment this is the most sensible treatment, but from the point of view of input–output analysis it is not. Another difficulty is that, in the census, firms are not asked to distinguish the amounts they pay for the different kinds of transport.

Work on compiling the detailed tables for 1963 is now going ahead rapidly, but a great deal remains to be done. At the end of September one-third of the census industry reports had still to be analysed, and when this is completed the important problem of balancing estimates of the total supply of each commodity group against the estimated total demand on the commodity group will have to be tackled. A major difficulty is that so little is known about distributive channels and margins, particularly on interindustry transactions. If we find we are unsuccessful in matching total demand against supplies we will have to consider introducing an "unallocated" column into the transaction tables, but we would prefer not to do so. Experience in compiling the 1954 tables suggests that this process of balancing could take two or three months of concentrated effort. If all goes well we expect to complete the detailed input–output tables by the middle of next year.

III. MORE UP-TO-DATE TABLES

The next detailed census of production will relate to the year 1968. In this census the number of separate census industries to be distinguished will be 154 compared with 128 for 1963, as some of the census industries are to be subdivided. For example, metal furniture, metal holloware and manufactured stationery will be distinguished as separate census industries. Past experience suggests that detailed input–output tables based on the census are unlikely to become available before 1972. We recognise that a delay of four years between the year of the census and the year when the full results of the input–output work become available is too great for most purposes. To overcome this we intend to produce up-dated tables projected forward from the latest basic detailed table, which up to 1972 will relate to 1963. Once the detailed tables for 1963 have been compiled we propose to up-date them to the year 1966 or 1967. We hope that the up-dated tables will consist of something like seventy industry groups corresponding to the basic table for 1963. But it is not certain how much work this would involve, whether they would be sufficiently reliable and whether such detailed tables are really required. What may be done is to produce the information in two stages. First an up-dated table consisting of something like thirty to forty industry groups and, at a later stage, the more detailed tables with up to seventy industry groups. An important consideration here is how successful we will be in constructing a reasonably reliable seventy industry matrix for 1963 to provide the jumping-off point for the up-dated tables for subsequent years. A difficult problem to be faced is the reconciliation of the detailed figures of final expenditure given in the National Income Blue Book, which are based mainly on surveys of expenditure, with the detailed figures of final output, based on output data, which will emerge from the input–output exercise.

We[1] propose to publish classification converters for each of the main items of final expenditure (e.g. consumers' expenditure, public authorities' current expenditure on goods and services, gross domestic fixed capital formation, etc.) which will show the relation between the functional classifications of final expenditure given in the national income accounts and the commodity classifications used in the input–output tables.

The[2] gradual introduction of a new system of production statistics following the census of production for 1968 will greatly facilitate the calculation of up-dated tables. A description of the proposed scheme was given in an article by Mr. J. Stafford (Director of Statistics, Board of Trade) in the first issue of *Statistical News*. The intention is that the new Business Statistics Office, which will be developed out of the existing Board of Trade Census Office, will collect detailed information on sales by manufacturing industries on a quarterly basis. This will be supplemented by annual inquiries which will collect information on total sales and purchases, changes in stocks and work in progress, wages and salaries and certain other data necessary to compile census net output and gross output. The quarterly inquiries will produce up-to-date figures of sales by different industry groups which, when combined with the annual information, will provide the kind of information which is now only obtained in a full and detailed census of production. Under the proposed new arrangements the detailed results will become available very much more quickly than hitherto. In addition to this regular information, it is intended to collect from industry, at periodic intervals (perhaps once every three or four years) detailed information about goods and services purchased. For the years in which this information is collected, it will be possible to produce firmly based detailed input–output tables, which in turn will provide the benchmarks from which more up-to-date tables can be derived.

IV. FURTHER WORK ON INPUT–OUTPUT ANALYSIS

Input–output analysis is potentially a very powerful tool and, if

---

[1] Para. 17 referred to in Discussion.   [2] Para. 18 referred to in Discussion.

it is to be exploited to the full, a considerable amount of research and analysis needs to be done. Among the first things to look at are the technical coefficients to see whether they have changed between 1954 and 1963, the two years for which we will have firmly based tables.

Comparing the technical coefficients (or the input–output relationships) in 1963 with those in 1954 can be done broadly speaking in two different ways. First, what may be called the superficial approach could be adopted. Using this approach, the 1963 input–output flow table would be reduced in size and made as far as possible comparable to the table for 1954. (It will be remembered that the 1954 table comprises forty-six industry groups whereas the 1963 table will consist of about seventy industry groups.) This procedure is not as simple as it may look at first sight. The first problem is to convert the two tables to the same price basis, which means that each cell will have to be revalued by the price index appropriate for the transaction. A major snag with this calculation is that the errors involved may be large in relation to the changes in technical coefficients which the analysis is seeking to measure. There are other problems. For example, the 1954 tables were based on the old 1948 Standard Industrial Classification, whereas the 1963 tables will be based on the 1958 Classification. A further difficulty is that sales of merchanted goods were largely excluded from the census of production for 1954, whereas in the 1958 and 1963 censuses they are specifically included and shown separately. In the 1963 input–output analysis these distributive activities are being treated systematically as secondary output, whereas in the 1954 tables they were not. Furthermore, in order to get the tables out as quickly as possible, the input–output analysis for 1954 concentrated on the flows between the industries covered by the census of production leaving the services industries to be shown as one large aggregate. This meant that the estimates of purchases and sales by the Services industry group were obtained in many cases as residuals. In compiling the 1963 tables a more thorough analysis of the services industries has been carried out and, even though the results obtained so far are provisional, it is becoming clear that some of the estimates of inputs into the services industries shown for 1954 may be too high. Another difficulty is that since the tables for 1954 were compiled, the estimates of national income and expenditure to which they are related have been revised, which means that the published tables for 1954 need to be adjusted before valid comparisons can be made with 1963. There is also the very important human element to be considered. The people compiling the 1963 tables are not the same as those who constructed the 1954 tables. Inevitably, different assumptions and estimates will have been made in the two exercises.

It should be clear from this that any comparison of the two tables using this superficial method will certainly be subject to doubt. Also, it is arguable whether any useful conclusions about changes in technical coefficients can be drawn from considering input–ouput tables with as few as forty or so industry groups. For many purposes these industry groups are rather wide and apparent changes in technical coefficients may reflect shifts in the product mix within the industry groups. A further point is that 1954 and 1963 are two isolated years on different points in the business cycle. It is statistically unsatisfactory to attempt to derive a trend from two observations.

The alternative approach is to carry out a detailed systematic analysis of changes in technical coefficients by analysing the original material which is being published in the 1963 census of production industry reports. These give an analysis of materials and fuel purchased by establishments employing twenty-five or more persons in 1963 with comparable figure for 1954. However, a detailed and comprehensive comparison of the input–output coefficients in the two years would mean virtually reconstructing the 1954 input–output matrix from scratch. Maybe this is what should be done; I do not know. But it would certainly use up a large amount of resources. If the comparison were to be carried out by research workers outside the Central Statistical Office who did not have access to the worksheets used in compiling the 1963 tables, it is quite likely that they would make different assumptions and take different decisions and they could very well end up with different results. Any detailed work on comparing the 1954 and 1963 data needs to be done in consultation with the Central Statistical Office. It is clear that to make useful comparisons of the input–output relationships in 1963 and 1954 will require a major effort.

It might be useful to carry out an intensive study of a limited number of industries from the published material given in the census of production. In this case it is for consideration whether the analysis of purchases of goods and services should be valued at purchasers' prices and not at sellers' prices, which is the usual and most useful way of recording transactions in input–output tables. If we are concerned only with the purchases of an industry in two different periods, I think it would be more appropriate to consider the actual prices paid rather than the prices at which the goods and services were sold.

Another approach would be to make a cross-section study of the variations in technical coefficients by size of establishment within a number of selected industries. This analysis might throw some light on the rate of technical progress and efficiency in the various industries. To carry out such an analysis, detailed tabulations of inputs for establishments grouped by size would need to be made available from the census. Another line of approach would be to make comparisons of individual establishments making returns in both the 1963 and 1954 censuses. Naturally, much of the work would have to be done within the Board of Trade Census Office in order to avoid disclosing the activities of particular firms.

I have the impression that in macro-economic work and in building micro-economic models of the national economy, input–output tables of much less than seventy industry groups are required. For these purposes input–output tables of the order of thirty or forty industry groups are considered adequate. But in view of the developments in other countries, in particular in the United States, careful consideration needs to be given to the construction and to the use of very large matrices consisting perhaps of three or four hundred industry groups. This is the kind of detail which many large firms seem to require for their management and market research purposes. If this is the case, the information made available for each census industry would need to be expanded. We would need to have details of inputs and outputs for the various subdivisions of each census industry. Such information would permit the user to consider and investigate rather narrowly defined industries and also groups of industries'which straddle across the Standard Industrial Classification.

Careful consideration needs to be given to the problem of up-dating, a subject which has been touched upon already. Some people believe that annual input–output tables should be prepared by up-dating the benchmark data for a previous year. But if they are interested in measuring changes in technical coefficients, there would seem to be little purpose in providing annual up-dated tables with say thirty industries. On the other hand, an annual up-dating of a more detailed table of the order of seventy industries would require relatively large resources and pose considerable data problems.

The signs are that the business world is becoming interested in input–output analysis. This interest will almost certainly increase as more and more people become familiar with the technique and with its possibilities. There are also signs that research workers at the universities and research institutions are wishing to carry out more input–output studies. In order to avoid the possible duplication of research on input–output, the Central Statistical Office has undertaken the responsibility for co-ordinating this work.

Table 1. Summary Input–

Sales by	d/i	Agriculture (1)	Forestry and fishing (2)	Coal mining (3)	Other mining and quarrying (4)	Food (5)	Drink and tobacco (6)	Mineral oil refining (7)	Other Chemicals, etc. (8)	Metal manufacture (9)	Ship building (10)	Motor vehicles (11)	Aircraft (12)	Other vehicles (13)	Other engineering (14)
1 Agriculture	d	—	—	—	—	423	23	97	—	—	—	—	—	—	—
	i	62	—	—	—	155	—	—	55	—	—	—	—	—	—
2 Forestry and fishing	d	—	—	5	—	11	—	—	—	—	—	—	—	—	—
	i	—	—	—	—	19	—	—	—	—	—	—	—	—	—
3 Coal mining	d	1	—	—	1	9	5	—	156	12	—	3	1	1	9
	i	—	—	—	—	—	—	—	—	—	—	—	—	—	—
4 Other mining and quarrying	d	—	—	—	—	3	—	2	9	24	—	—	—	—	13
	i	10	—	—	—	—	—	—	360	100	—	—	—	—	11
5 Food	d	262	—	—	—	—	—	17	—	32	—	—	—	—	—
	i	17	—	—	—	—	242	5	—	4	—	—	—	—	—
6 Drink and tobacco	d	5	—	—	—	6	—	—	3	—	—	—	—	—	—
	i	—	—	—	—	—	6	—	—	—	—	—	—	—	—
7 Mineral oil refining	d	15	4	1	1	6	3	—	78	20	1	3	1	1	14
	i	8	2	1	1	3	2	—	12	12	1	2	1	—	8
8 Other chemicals, etc.	d	122	—	9	14	116	9	48	—	110	5	57	3	2	117
	i	60	—	—	1	31	—	—	132	—	1	1	—	—	5
9 Metal manufacture	d	—	—	48	1	6	2	—	28	—	39	272	33	32	757
	i	—	—	—	—	—	—	—	5	213	—	21	5	2	63
10 Shipbuilding	d	—	6	—	—	—	—	—	—	—	—	—	—	—	—
	i	—	—	—	—	—	—	—	—	—	—	—	—	—	—
11 Motor vehicles	d	4	—	1	2	3	1	—	2	4	1	—	—	13	31
	i	2	—	—	—	—	—	—	—	—	—	9	—	—	—
12 Aircraft	d	—	—	—	—	—	—	—	—	—	—	—	—	—	—
	i	—	—	—	—	—	—	—	—	—	—	—	4	—	—
13 Other vehicles	d	—	—	—	—	—	—	—	—	7	—	4	1	—	9
	i	—	—	—	—	—	—	—	—	—	—	1	—	—	—
14 Other engineering	d	26	—	42	15	64	27	2	82	124	56	397	54	19	—
	i	—	—	—	—	—	—	—	21	—	6	8	3	3	65
15 Textiles	d	—	6	6	—	10	—	—	8	1	1	14	2	1	26
	i	—	—	—	—	1	—	—	—	—	—	—	—	—	—
16 Leather and clothing	d	4	—	2	—	1	—	—	2	1	1	10	1	—	7
	i	—	—	—	—	—	—	—	—	—	—	—	—	—	—
17 Other manufacturing	d	42	—	49	7	87	42	12	85	29	12	177	11	9	267
	i	—	—	4	—	—	3	—	3	1	—	—	—	—	3
18 Construction	d	29	1	18	—	6	6	—	11	8	2	5	3	1	22
	i	—	—	—	—	—	—	—	—	—	—	—	—	—	—
19 Gas	d	—	—	—	—	7	—	—	23	18	1	5	1	1	26
	i	—	—	—	—	—	—	—	—	—	—	—	—	—	—
20 Electricity	d	16	—	25	3	19	5	5	32	37	4	16	5	2	60
	i	—	—	—	—	—	—	—	—	—	—	—	—	—	—
21 Water	d	—	—	—	—	6	5	—	5	5	—	4	—	—	7
	i	—	—	—	—	—	—	—	—	—	—	—	—	—	—
22 Road transport	d	8	—	—	23	14	39	—	26	23	—	7	1	—	82
	i	—	—	—	—	—	—	—	—	—	—	—	—	—	—
23 Rail transport	d	—	—	—	—	10	3	1	25	24	—	3	—	—	5
	i	—	—	—	—	—	—	—	—	—	—	—	—	—	—
24 Other transport	d	10	7	—	—	29	7	76	10	25	1	1	—	1	11
	i	—	—	—	—	—	—	—	—	—	—	—	—	—	—
25 Communication	d	5	—	2	1	6	9	—	14	7	1	9	4	1	53
	i	—	—	—	—	—	—	—	—	—	—	—	—	—	—
26 Distribution	d	118	3	4	6	18	7	1	15	7	4	24	2	4	50
	i	—	—	—	—	—	—	—	—	—	—	—	—	—	—
27 Other services	d	125	5	34	14	75	54	6	134	106	31	93	46	13	434
	i	—	—	—	—	—	—	—	—	—	—	—	—	—	—
28 Public administration, etc.[a]	d	—	—	—	—	—	—	—	—	—	—	—	—	—	—
	i	—	—	—	—	—	—	—	—	—	—	—	—	—	—
29 Imports															
(i) Total goods net c.i.f.		159	2	5	1	451	113	360	256	327	7	42	13	5	157
(ii) Services, re-exports and valuation adjustments		-10	—	—	2	-37	4	-76	29	-32	2	31	2	2	80
(iii) Total goods and services		149	2	5	3	414	117	284	285	295	9	73	15	7	237
30 Sales by final buyers[b]		—	—	—	1	5	3	—	5	48	1	5	15	1	22
31 Total goods and services (1 to 30)		941	34	251	92	1,354	384	437	1,070	935	171	1,182	212	96	2,219
32 Taxes on expenditure less subsidies		-246	-6	9	10	38	21	7	32	37	5	19	5	2	70
33 Income from employment		320	33	535	47	387	159	25	388	502	167	417	222	84	1,877
34 Gross profits and other trading income[c]		576	24	117	34	236	238	29	312	249	16	152	70	7	686
35 Total input (31 to 34)		1,591	85	912	183	2,015	802	498	1,802	1,723	359	1,770	509	189	4,852

[1] A matrix of net imports of goods, rows labelled d, valued c.i.f. is superimposed on the matrix of domestic transactions, rows labelled i. The total imports of goods and services row is, however, valued on a balance of payments basis.
[2] Public administration and defence, public health and educational services, ownership of dwellings, domestic services to households and services to private non-profit-making bodies serving persons.

transactions Matrix 1963

£ million

	Other nd vth-bng 16	Other manu-factur-bng 17	Con-struc-tion 18	Gas 19	Elec-tricity 20	Water 21	Transport Road 22	Rail 23	Other 24	Com-munica-tion 25	Distri-bution 26	Other services 27	Public adminis-tration etc.[b] 28	Total inter-mediate output (1 to 28) 29	Personal sector 30	Public authori-ties 31	Gross domestic capital formation Fixed 32	Stocks 33	Exports 34	Total final output (30 to 34) 35	Total output (29 to 35) 36	
	28	36	—	—	—	—	—	—	4	—	—	—	—	482 667	1,040 455	14 —	9 —	5 26	41 —	1,109 481	1,591 1,148	1
	5 —	—	—	—	—	—	—	—	—	—	—	—	—	21 19	43 19	— —	— —	19 —	2 —	64 19	85 38	2
	51 —	—	112	232	1 —	—	29	1	1 —	3	3 —	—	—	647 208	208 26	— 21	— −23	33 —	265 —	912 —	3
	60 22	52 —	—	—	—	—	—	—	1	1 —	—	—	—	165 527	— —	— —	— —	18 —	18 —	183 527	4
	2 6	—	—	—	—	—	—	7	—	—	29 —	—	—	351 274	1,436 494	49 —	— —	48 —	131 —	1,664 495	2,015 769	5
	1 —	—	—	—	—	—	—	—	—	—	40 —	—	—	55 6	628 47	— —	— —	7 —	112 —	747 47	802 53	6
1	18 10	20 11	9 6	20 11	1 —	15 9	7 4	19 13	1 1	14 8	8 4	—	—	287 133	61 31	15 11	8 —	2 —	125 —	211 42	498 175	7
2	151 37	90 2	12 —	8 —	2 —	5 —	14 —	3 —	—	9 1	109 —	—	—	1,049 285	247 13	135 —	— −19 −6	390 —	753 7	1,802 292	8
	22 4	139 12	17 —	3 —	9 —	—	14 —	—	—	—	—	—	—	1,424 327	—	5 —	40 —	−27 −8	281 —	299 −8	1,723 319	9
	—	—	—	—	—	—	—	—	57 —	—	—	—	—	63 —	—	—	150 —	93 6	−1 —	54 —	296 6	399 6	10
	9 —	9 —	1 —	1 —	—	73 —	—	2 —	2 —	9 —	115 —	—	—	286 11	475 19	62 —	294 5	34 —	619 —	1,484 24	1,770 35	11
	—	—	—	—	—	—	—	11 9	—	—	—	—	—	11 13	—	352 —	10 17	34 —	102 —	498 17	509 30	12
	1 —	2 —	—	—	—	69 —	—	—	—	—	7 —	—	—	100 1	9 6	—	40 —	−1 —	40 —	89 6	189 7	13
	129 23	194 24	10 —	56 1	2 —	—	12 —	10 —	15 —	37 8	123 —	—	—	1,549 167	354 53	317 10	1,305 205	70 —	1,257 —	3,303 268	4,852 435	14
35	89 5	3 —	—	—	—	—	2 —	1 —	2 —	6 2	6 —	—	—	417 134	446 45	13 —	— —	−5 −1	365 —	819 44	1,236 178	15
24	9 —	3 —	—	—	—	—	1 —	—	—	3 —	6 —	—	—	55 24	699 84	24 —	— —	18 —	108 —	849 84	904 108	16
3	341 —	486 109	3 —	15 —	8 —	51 —	18 2	20 —	11 1	148 4	355 —	—	—	1,999 475	640 90	151 —	42 3	14 1	318 —	1,165 96	3,164 571	17
	14 —	—	8 —	5 —	2 —	11 —	2 —	7 —	5 —	53 —	34 —	—	—	260 —	386 —	303 —	2,170 —	21 —	10 —	2,890 —	3,150 —	18
	14 —	—	—	—	—	—	—	—	17 —	61 —	—	—	—	177 —	207 —	13 —	19 —	—	4 —	243 —	420 —	19
	63 —	9 —	4 —	—	5 1	9 —	10 —	3 —	6 —	70 —	48 —	—	—	484 1	394 —	63 —	127 —	—	—	584 —	1,068 —	20
	6 —	—	—	—	—	—	—	—	5 —	7 —	—	—	—	55 —	52 —	5 —	12 —	—	—	69 —	124 —	21
	82 —	18 —	1 —	7 —	—	—	—	30 —	3 —	107 —	29 —	—	—	475 —	374 —	46 —	— —	20 —	—	440 —	915 —	22
	22 —	6 —	12 —	20 —	—	—	—	—	26 —	124 —	28 —	—	—	312 —	147 —	29 —	17 —	—	14 —	207 —	519 —	23
	30 —	8 —	5 —	12 —	—	—	—	17 —	212 —	25 —	—	—	—	515 —	181 —	40 —	7 1	—	734 —	963 —	1,478 —	24
	46 —	23 —	4 —	3 —	1 —	2 —	—	3 —	—	86 —	103 —	—	—	403 —	166 —	41 —	27 —	—	17 —	251 —	654 —	25
	15 3	72 —	8 —	2 —	—	17 —	—	—	2 —	—	103 —	—	—	488 3	3,679 14	101 —	197 —	—	311 —	4,288 14	4,776 17	26
	204 —	41 —	28 —	47 —	—	20 —	2 —	36 —	11 —	378 —	—	11 —	—	2,018 11	2,362 —	506 —	181 —	1 —	371 —	3,421 1	5,439 27	27
	—	—	—	—	—	—	—	—	—	—	—	—	—	—	1,478 —	2,732 —	—	—	—	—	4,210 —	4,210 —	28
93	487 —	158 —	6 —	13 —	—	9 —	6 —	22 —	2 —	15 —	23 —	—	—	3,078 —	1,371 —	21 —	236 —	15 —	—	1,643 —	4,721 —	(i)
−3	−40 —	−12 —	—	—	—	—	—	549 —	16 —	20 —	15 —	—	—	516 —	270 —	168 —	14 —	−1 —	262 —	713 —	1,329 —	(ii)
90	447 —	146 —	6 —	13 —	—	9 —	6 —	571 —	18 —	35 —	38 —	—	—	3,594 —	1,641 —	189 —	250 —	14 —	262 —	2,356 —	5,950 —	(iii)
	13 —	—	—	—	—	2 —	1 —	2 —	2 —	29 —	36 —	—	—	199 —	194 —	−393 —	−75 —	—	75 —	−199 —	—	30
	1,507	1,323	240	444	31	214	187	787	123	1,346	1,313	—	—	17,941	17,547	4,989	4,794	212	5,814	33,356	51,297	31
	70	55	10	48	11	62	−124	15	10	258	191	—	—	637	2,648	91	112	—	—	2,851	3,488	32
	1,169	1,364	112	222	40	455	348	414	386	1,924	2,717	3,075	18,160	—	—	—	—	—	—	—	18,160	33
	418	408	58	354	42	184	108	262	135	1,248	1,218[a]	1,135	8,609	—	—	—	—	—	—	—	8,609	34
	3,164	3,150	430	1,068	124	915	519	1,478	654	4,776	5,439	4,210	45,347	20,195	5,080	4,906	212	5,814	36,207	81,554	35

m sales by final buyers consist of scrap materials and fees and charges for government services. These
are not the output of any industry in 1963 and are therefore treated as primary inputs.
fore providing for depreciation, but after deducting stock appreciation.
cludes the 'residual error' in the national income accounts amounting to £28 million.
easured free from duplication.

Extract from *Economic Trends*, August, 1968

Table 2. Classification of Industry and Commodity Groups for the Input–Output Tables, 1963

Industry or commodity group	Standard Industrial Classification 1958 Minimum List heading	Net output (£m.)	
		Census[1]	National Income[2]
1. Agriculture	001		896
2. Forestry and fishing	002, 003		57
3. Coal mining	101	655	
4. Other mining and quarrying	102, 103, 109	117	
5. Grain milling	211	81	
6. Other cereal foodstuffs	212, 213, 219	296	
7. Sugar	216	37	
8. Cocoa, chocolate and sugar confectionery	217	117	
9. Other food	214, 215, 218, 229	283	
10. Drink	231, 239	346	
11. Tobacco	240	110	
12. Mineral oil refining	262	64	
13. Paint and printing ink	274	80	
14. Coke ovens	261	28	
15. Pharmaceutical and toilet preparations	272	174	
16. Soap, oils and fats	275	82	
17. Synthetic resin and plastics materials	276	77	
18. Other chemicals and allied industries	263, 271, 273, 277	542	
19. Iron and steel	311 to 313	627	
20. Light metals	321	80	
21. Other non-ferrous metals	322	123	
22. Agricultural machinery	331	32	
23. Machine tools	332	100	
24. Engineers' small tools	333	74	
25. Industrial engines	334	62	
26. Textile machinery	335	65	
27. Contractors' plant and mechanical handling equipment	336, 337	122	
28. Office machinery	338	35	
29. Other non-electrical machinery	339	409	
30. Industrial plant and steel work	341	180	

[1] Net output as defined in the census of production.

[2] The industry group's contribution to the gross domestic product, which is rather more narrowly defined.

Table 2—continued

Industry or commodity group	Standard Industrial Classification 1958 Minimum List heading	Net output (£m.)	
		Census	National Income
31. Other mechanical engineering (including machinery repair)	342, 349	306	
32. Scientific instruments, etc.	351, 352	165	
33. Electrical machinery	361	227	
34. Insulated wires and cables	362	80	
35. Radio and telecommunications	363, 364	417	
36. Other electrical goods	365, 369	239	
37. Cans and metal boxes	395	30	
38. Other metal goods	391, 392, 393, 394, 396, 399	588	
39. Shipbuilding and marine-engineering	370	214	
40. Motor vehicles (including tractors)	381	733	
41. Aircraft	383	322	
42. Other vehicles	382, 384, 385, 389	99	
43. Production of man-made fibres	411	109	
44. Cotton, etc., spinning and weaving	412, 413	163	
45. Wool	414	185	
46. Hosiery and lace	417, 418	127	
47. Textile finishing	423	66	
48. Other textiles	415, 416, 419, 421, 422, 429	153	
49. Leather, leather goods and fur	431 to 433	59	
50. Clothing	441 to 446, 449	285	
51. Footwear	450	97	
52. Cement	464	41	
53. Other building materials, etc.	461, 469	231	
54. Pottery and glass	462, 463	147	
55. Furniture, etc.	472, 473	123	
56. Timber, and miscellaneous wood manufactures	471, 474, 475, 479	176	
57. Paper and board	481	145	
58. Paper products	482, 483	173	
59. Printing and publishing	486, 489	540	
60. Rubber	491	172	
61. Other manufacturing (including plastics mouldings, etc.)	492 to 496, 499	223	

Table 2—continued

Industry or commodity group	Standard Industrial Classification 1958 Minimum List heading	Net output (£m.)	
		Census	National Income
62. Construction	500	1,857	
63. Gas	601	216	
64. Electricity	602	670	
65. Water	603	96	
66. Railways	701		456
67. Road transport	702, 703		639
68. Other transport	704, 705, 706, 709		676
69. Communication	707		521
70. Distributive trades	801, 802, 831, 832		3,172
71. Miscellaneous services, including	871, parts of 872 and 874 873, 875, 879, 881 to 889 and parts of 891 and 899		
Insurance, banking and finance	860 part		3,935
72. Public administration and defence and public health and educational services	901, 906 and part of 872, 874		2,732
73. Domestic services to house- holds, Private non-profit making organisations serving households	891 part 899 part		343
74. Ownership of dwellings	860 part		1,135

SESSION II: DISCUSSION OF MR. BERMAN'S PAPER

Chairman: PROFESSOR I. G. STEWART (EDINBURGH)

QUESTION

Might it be possible to produce a table larger than 70 × 70?

MR. BERMAN (C.S.O.)

The number of industry groups to be shown in the 1963 tables is intended to be a compromise. A much larger table would take a very much longer time to produce. As I said, there is a possibility of expanding the 70 × 70 to a 130 × 130 table. But we don't know yet whether we will be able to do this. However, we will produce the rectangular table, which I think will be very useful, showing for each of the 120 manufacturing industries a commodity analysis (by seventy groups) of its purchases. On the detail used for model building, I just have the impression, from the macro-economic models I have seen, that no more than thirty or forty industry groups are generally shown separately. SAM is based on thirty, and most other models are based on thirty or forty. Input–output is just one part of a macro-economic model, an essential part of course, but only one part. I understand that the computing capacity isn't generally available to handle anything very much larger, but I may be wrong on this.

MR. WIGLEY (Cambridge)

Mr. Berman has mentioned a number of hurdles which he and the members of his department face in the work before them, and I am sure we all wish them well in overcoming these. He has mentioned three broad areas which have proved difficult. The first is resources in government; clearly there are limitations in manpower, necessitating priorities to be given to the most pressing problems. It is my feeling that for too long the government has ignored long-term problems in order to concentrate on short-term ones.

The second problem area he has mentioned is confidentiality, and, of course, he works strictly within the confines of legislation on trade statistics. Presumably businessmen are not willing to give readily more statistics unless they can see some profit, some additional information in return; on the other hand little information can be given in return until more detailed statistics are collected.

The third area is the lack of actual statistics themselves, and Mr. Berman has recognised this, particularly in paragraph 18 of his paper. He indicates that information collected in a quarterly basis by the new Business Statistics Office will be supplemented by annual enquiries which will collect information on total sales and purchases, changes in stocks, work in progress, wages and salaries, and, *certain other data*. The actual suggestions I have for the certain other data are as follows:

One item comprises labour inputs: wages and salaries are certainly very important statistics to collect, but so are detailed labour inputs, in particular hours of work and details of part-time working.

Secondly, price movements: I appreciate that great detail on the prices of individual outputs and individual inputs may involve difficulty and might well be dealt with once every three or four years. I'm thinking here, rather, of price movements of principal outputs and principal inputs; these may be limited to perhaps three or four principal items per industry group, or individual firm. Even that would be a significant improvement on the price data we have at the moment.

The third area is investment, and here I would welcome information both on the actual value of the investment goods put in place, and, separately, the cash flows for the period. In the statistics we have at the moment, the definition of investment is very confused; one is never quite sure whether the investment figure one is using refers to a cash flow or an estimate of the capital work done. It makes a good deal of difference in matching up the financing of investment with the balancing of the commodity account for investment goods.

The fourth suggestion I have refers to marginal changes in capacity, and this is a piece of statistics which we do not collect at the moment. I appreciate the difficulties of definition here but surely we can get some rough measure of the capacity which was used during that quarter, but not used in the quarter before, and the capacity which was *not* used this quarter but *was* used in a quarter before. In other words, the capacity which has been brought into use during that period, and the capacity which has been retired or scrapped during that period possibly in percentage terms. Ideally, of course, we would like to know the relationship between the investment put in place and the capacity output, but I won't press that further at the moment.

PROFESSOR STEWART (Edinburgh)

I'm sure that every time an input–output table is drawn up, and every time there is a meeting of the minds on what ought to go in, we are over the horns of a dilemma: that we would like to have a lot more information but at the same time recognise that there are difficulties in obtaining it quickly; and I wonder if Mr. Berman would like to say a word about these very cogent observations.

MR. BERMAN

Well, it is quite obvious from what we have heard that Mr. Wigley is a user of statistics and not a producer! He reads tables and doesn't fill in forms. Shortage of manpower—I can't say anything about that. Confidentiality—here we are bound by the Statistics of Trade Act. On the question about statistics I can make some contribution. Questions about labour inputs will continue to be asked, either by the Board of Trade or by the D.E.P. Under the arrangements which we are working towards, instead of two different departments asking the same question, we will have one department asking the question on behalf of all government departments. We do think quite a bit about the form-fillers as well as the users. On price movements: in the U.K. we have very good information on the price movements; I think the Board of Trade have got as much information as you want. If you cannot get what you want write to me and I will see what I can do to help. If they can't provide you with what you want, it is probably because the industry providing the information regards the particular series as confidential. They may not want it published because it might give information to their competitors abroad. This links up with your second point about confidentiality where we are in the hands of the providers of information. On investment, the story is really very simple. Our figures of investment relate to expenditure charged to capital account. On the stock of capital and on capacity, these are difficult items to ask firms to provide. It might be worth your while carrying out a private enquiry on this yourself.

PROFESSOR HILL (East Anglia)

The first question is: are you in fact proposing to produce a constant-price table for 1963, I mean at 1954 prices? Are you, yourselves, proposing to do that?

MR. BERMAN

Well, there is no point in producing a table for 1963 at 1954 prices, unless we have a table for 1954 according to 1963 classifications.

PROFESSOR HILL

Well, I think that answers the immediate question. If you'd said yes, I wouldn't have followed up with a second one.

MR. BERMAN

Supposing I had said yes?

PROFESSOR HILL

The reason I ask this is because there is another use for a constant price table quite apart from the stability of the individual input–output coefficients. Some of us, for instance, are interested in growth measures for individual industries, and in particular to compare, say, the growth of the gross output of an industry with a measure of the growth of its value added that would be obtained by using double deflation. The difference between the two growth measures only involves the stability of the input–output coefficients at a very aggregative level. Nevertheless, analysing the growth rates of individual industries does provide another source of demand for constant price input–output tables.

MR. BERMAN

Well, I think my answer is whether we should be forward looking or backward looking? Once we have completed the tables for 1963, should we start comparing them with 1954 and put a lot of resources into this work? This would be a very big job. Or, should we say let us leave this to the academics and instead concentrate on producing up-to-date input–output tables regularly. I don't think we can do both. This is what I should like to know: where do you think we should go? I'm not saying that we can decide tonight, but it would be very useful to me to know where you as users think we should go. As I said there is a choice between starting with the 1961 tables and up-dating them to 1966 or 1967 and then following this up by a double deflation process on changes between 1963 and 1966, and 1967 and 1968; and of going back to make comparisons with 1954. Also, I would like to know how much detail you want.

MR. HEYWOOD (I.C.I.)

In response to the last question by the speaker I'd like to see a $1,000^2$ table of U.K. input–output, since you asked that question. It seems to me that Mr. Berman's talk——

MR. BERMAN

Are you speaking on behalf of I.C.I. there? Can I say when I get back to London, that I.C.I. want a 1,000-industry table, or do I say that just Mr. Heywood wants it?

MR. HEYWOOD

You can say that this would be welcomed by the I.C.I. people who would like to work in this field.

MR. BERMAN

Very good! Thank you.

MR. LUKER (I.C.I.)

My colleague on my right is not a provider of statistics [*laughter*].

MR. HEYWOOD

Correction. . . . if we were to get the data from a $1,000^2$ model we would be.

I have another point. It seems to me that this is a catalogue of difficulties of getting data, and having had some experience of data raising, I think it is a bit pathetic that the Americans can get a 200^2 model for a population as large as 200 million, and all we can do, with a population of 50 million is perhaps a table of about forty-five sectors, several of which are tied up with government controls anyway and the whole of which is not directly useful. This is not big enough nor is it produced often enough. In the last year an American consultant has offered to up-date at least fifteen of these sectors for the princely sum of £120,000. We turned them down because when they'd finished, it would still have not been useful; we are already in on all those sectors now, and what we want to know is which sectors we are not in—that is the first question: where is there some more business which we can pick up; you just can't tell from the current table.

On a further point, I have here some blank forms of the Census of Production: this one happens to be for pharmaceuticals, and as far as I can tell, there are only two S.I.C.s[1] in it, plus the usual statistical information on purchases and sales; I can't see from the paper any direct connections between inputs and outputs; it asks for an analysis of inputs over a number of headings, and analysis of sales over a number of headings; there is no technical connection between the two on this questionnaire, although you may ask for it separately. I wonder what happens in practice with the people who actually fill these up. I wonder what kind of response you get.

A third question is: I wonder if you prorated the purchases to the sales; if so you could be entirely wrong technically. Would you also prorate the profits to sales—because I presume that somewhere at the end of the table on the right-hand side you split the gross national product between home consumption and overseas sales. Now the ratio of volume that is needed to produce, say, £100 of overseas sales compared with £100 of home sales could be two-and-a-half times. These are the difficulties with not using internal technical coefficients;

---

[1] Standard Industrial Classification.

E

you could be wrong in using the indirect coefficients from the tables for forecasting changes in production volume.

MR. BERMAN

The first question as I understand it is that, in the census of production, firms are asked to provide details of inputs, details of sales, details of outputs, and you can't really relate particular inputs to particular outputs. Well, this is right. In the census of production, each establishment, which is more or less a factory, or perhaps a group of related factories, is asked to fill in a census form. In the real world no establishment is a single-product establishment; they produce a wide range of goods. You can't go to a firm and say, "You produce this particular commodity (paper bags); what are your inputs corresponding to that?" You can't do that. You can go to the establishment in the paper-products industry and say "What are all your sales and what are all your inputs?" This is a problem with input–output. Product-mixes differ and the pattern of inputs differ. One is dealing with the average position for the average establishment within the particular industry group. However finely an industry is defined, there will always be a spread of product-mixes within the industry group. I think I said this somewhere in the paper. You can't really relate particular outputs to particular inputs unless you ask technical experts within the firm to supply the technological information. Input–output tables are based on accounting data, provided for each establishment by accountants.

One could go to firms and say "Let's have all your technical coefficients"; let's look at this particular firm, making pharmaceutical products; or take a firm making just aspirins, I'm sure it doesn't exist, because a firm makes more than aspirins.

MR. HEYWOOD

Yes, but what if your firm is dealing with a largish number of sectors?

MR. BERMAN

Well, even if one did it for 400 it still would be difficult to get down to say, paper bags.

MR. HEYWOOD

A finer division of input–output would be helpful.

MR. BERMAN

Agreed!

PROFESSOR STEWART

Well, I think the point is taken, isn't it?

MR. BERMAN

No, I disagree. I think that you just can't do it, not in the real world.

MR. HEYWOOD

What are the obstacles to such an input–output table?

MR. BERMAN

One could compile an input–output table for 1,000 commodity groups, based not on accounting data, but by going out to firms and saying, "Look, for this particular product group, whatever it is, aspirins, penicillin (I'm sure you shouldn't combine them, but one has to combine something), what are the corresponding inputs?" If you are going to show a product like aspirins separately, you will need a million commodity headings. I.C.I. might be able to provide these, but the other 129,000 establishments in manufacturing could not.

MR. HEYWOOD

But I could illustrate this—any firm with standard costing could give you that information.

MR. BERMAN

May be.

The second is, what does one do about profit margin? Firms often make smaller profit margins on exports than on sales on the home market. This is the trouble with input–output analysis; when one uses it, one assumes that the profit margin is the same on all sales; for example when one inverts the matrix and works out the primary input content and the profit element in the final demand. To this extent input–output goes wrong, but this is not a fault of the tables we produce, it is the fault of the way they are used. Input–output tables set out only the average relationships in the year.

DR. GOSSLING (Manchester)

I think it is true that in the research being done in America there are people who are concerned with disaggregating a particular row and column of the 80 × 80 table, and, I think what they are trying to do is to run a consulting service which is mostly done by academics but is joined in to the U.S. Department of Commerce (who produce the 80 × 80 table). In this way the sort of question Mr. Heywood was asking just now can be answered, at least to some extent, both on the sales side "across the board", and possibly on the inputs side.

This is one of the research subjects we should perhaps discuss: how to have a means of changing, so to speak, from top gear (the C.S.O. table) down to second or third or even bottom (an I.C.I. table).

MR. WIGLEY

In connection with this last point that has been raised, we have a submodel for the fuel and power industry at Cambridge which has a separate calculation for the five fuel rows and the five fuel columns and contains more detail of the individual processes for producing gas and electricity, although not, I must admit, on the scale which Mr. Heywood from I.C.I. has mentioned. We are publishing, in Volume 8 of *A Programme for Growth*, an illustration of an input–output calculation in which a detailed submodel for a group of commodities and a group of production activities for these commodities is integrated into input–output calculations as an iterative process and which gives results which can be compared immediately with the forecasts being given by official sources.

In connection with my suggestions for additional data for collection, I thank the speaker for explaining that labour inputs will be collected at the same time as other infomation from individual establishments. I think all of us will welcome this step because there has in the past been a rather poor correspondence between the Ministry of Labour's classification of industry sectors and that of the Census of Production. On prices, yes, it is true that Board of Trade has individual price movements, I understand, for as many as 7,000 commodities, but they are not collected at the same time as additional data from the individual establishments and the problem with these prices is that it is difficult to get weights for combining the individual prices into price index movements for groups of establishments within an industrial sector. If these prices could be collected at the same time as the gross output of the sector or establishment concerned then at least we would be able to combine these individual commodity prices together, with appropriate weights for calculating price-index movements for groups of establishments.

The suggestion given by the speaker that a small research group should conduct its own sample survey on investment and changes in capacity I do not find very convincing. It seems to me that these are two pieces of information which are vitally important for understanding the growth of the economy in the medium term; it is significant that this was the area which was totally lacking in the national plan. After all, the level of investment and the net increase of capacity are absolutely basic to an increased rate of growth, and I must say I am very sorry to hear a representative of the Central Statistical Office suggesting that these very important pieces of data should be left to a private sample survey.

MR. GAMBLING (Birmingham)

Actually, I was really going back to the point Mr. Heywood was raising with Mr. Berman here; it is something that has struck me throughout both this paper and the last one, that really there is a complete failure of communication on this point; in which people are completely at cross-purposes, it seems to me, about what is meant by a technical coefficient. Input–output models can be built in two ways: it seems to me they can be built from the top downwards from quite highly aggregated accounting data, or they can be built from the bottom upwards from standard-costing data; Mr. Heywood, of course, is talking of building from the bottom upwards; Mr. Berman must be talking of building it from the top downwards, and hopefully, they will meet in the middle in some sort of average; though this is by no means certain or useful.

MR. BERMAN

May I just say something about Mr. Wigley's remarks. On capacity: the thought at the back of my mind which I obviously expressed very badly, was that capacity is something which is a very difficult thing to measure and before one asks firms to give figures of capacity one has to work out exactly what one is trying to measure and what firms can provide. What one ought to do first of all is have a talk with people in industry, and ask them if they can produce answers to these questions. I am no expert on this subject, but I guess these are questions which are very difficult to answer, and I thought as part of the Cambridge Research Project (which is so interested in relating investment to output and seeing what makes the economy tick) that this is a basic question. Why don't you go to two or three firms and ask them if they can answer such questions, and try to work out the kind of questions which would be practicable for government to ask; and if you should come up with some positive results, then of course, we could follow them up. Although you might say the government ought to do this, there are so many things the government is trying to do; may be we have got our priorities wrong; I don't know. We are not thinking of this one at the moment. I believe the C.B.I. does something on the utilisation of capacity; maybe theirs is the right approach. But it is only useful, I think, for short-term forecasting, for watching the short-term movements in the economy and not for medium- or long-term planning.

On these questions of top and bottom. When we compile an input–output table we compile it on the basis of returns provided by establishments' accounting data; this is *all* we can do. There is this alternative technological approach and I suppose the two could meet, but they could only meet when you get down to an establishment which makes only one product: and this doesn't exist. If you can find an establishment which makes one product then in that particular case the two will meet, but if an establishment makes a whole range of products the two approaches cannot meet.

MR. HILTON (Southampton)

We have been doing some work at Southampton attempting to use input–output tables, so I present myself purely as a user. Mr. Berman asked us to say what we thought of the proposal of up-dating the tables for 1963 and later years and whether or not such tables would be of interest to users. One thing we would like to know before we can sensibly answer this question is: how does C.S.O. up-date and propose up-dating the tables, for we do not know precisely how they up-dated the 1963 table. I imagine they propose using some sort of "R-A-S" system to up-date the tables, but from where do they get all their data? This is not made clear in the official publications. And from where will they get the output data for 1964 and later years? Until we know all these facts we cannot say whether the tables would be of any use.

Can I make a second point? Mr. Berman has been suggesting that academics should be doing more work on, for instance, double-deflating the 1954 table; Professor Hill also asked about this. We have been doing some very crude work by double-deflating the 1963 (thirteen industry) table in order to compare it with the 1954 table. Some of our estimates have been very crude because we have had to construct price indices ourselves, but our results are available to those who are interested.

MR. BERMAN

I will make two comments on that. I think it is unfair to say that the C.S.O. have not given a description of the way in which we compiled the input–output tables for 1963. A description was given in the August 1966 issue of *Economic Trends* and it was repeated in the August 1968 issue of *Economic Trends*. The precise method is set out there.

PROFESSOR STEWART

I think Mr. Hilton has a point. If I have understood the August 1968 issue article of *Economic Trends* I am very much in sympathy with the question, because it appears to suggest that the coefficients, if they may be called such, at any rate the elements in the matrix of interindustry flows for 1963 are in fact derived by taking first of all gross output and net output control totals at the end of the row and in the columns and then working back by a sort of process of residuals, which you test against the 1954 figures *pro rata*—or, that's not quite strictly accurate, but you use a *pro rata* method for what you can't obtain by residuals. Now this seems to me to leave Mr. Hilton's question wide open, because I think if we are going to answer the question whether we would like to see up-dated tables (and I think this is a rather important question), whether we would like to see up-dated tables or benchmarked tables every so often at more frequent intervals, then we really do have to apply ourselves a little bit more conscientiously to this problem of what method we use. I hope I have not misunderstood you, Mr. Hilton, is that really the point you are making?

MR. HILTON

In fact it is! It was the point I was making.

PROFESSOR STEWART

Yes, the first point; but the other?

MR. HILTON

The principal point I was trying to make is, how does one up-date these matrices when there are, in fact, no Census of Production outputs for post-1963?

MR. UPTON (C.S.O.)

The gross outputs used for up-dating 1963 were the provisional results of the Census of Production for that year. This was, in fact, explained in the 1966 article, not in the 1968 one—we didn't repeat this in the 1968 article because people would have read it before. The inputs were up-dated in the same way as in the S.A.M. project at Cambridge, or almost the same way—you must be familiar with that.

For up-dating forwards from 1963 the gross outputs would be obtained from the new industrial statistics that are being collected.

MR. BERMAN

I think the simple answer to your question is that when we produce the detailed table, the benchmark table for 1963, we will up-date to 1966 or 1967. We won't do it for the intermediate years, we will go straight to 1966 or 1967 so that the users will have a more up-to-date version of the benchmark data. We would extrapolate, by using all available indices of production and prices. As you say, there is no census of production for any year between 1963 and 1968. This will provide provisional results which can serve until the full results of the 1968 Census are available. Maybe we will up-date again and produce something for 1970. As you say, the figures of gross outputs and inputs are not available from the census of production although I would hope that by 1971 we would have the new annual enquiries going. The exact date when these new enquiries will begin has not been decided. It may be 1970 or 1971, it depends again on the resources problem. The introduction of the new system of production statistics—the quarterly enquiries into deliveries and the annual enquiries into the main aggregates, like gross outputs and net outputs—will be introduced gradually over a period. It can't be done straight away, it has to be done in co-operation with industry.

MR. LECOMBER (Cambridge)

I'm very glad that this stress is being laid on the up-dating problem, and I want to make one or two comments. The importance of up-dating arises of course from the fact that input–output coefficients change over time (whether these are "technical" changes or just changes in product-mix is another question). This not only means that a table for 1954, say, has got very out of date even as an estimate of what is going on now; but also in, for instance, projecting into the future, the rate of change of coefficients is important; the five-year increase in the output of some industry like chemicals will be as much due to the rising coefficients as to the rise in user outputs. This is very important in projection work. It will be a useful start, of course, to compare 1954 with 1963; this is something that we would all welcome. Mr. Berman, however, stressed some of the difficulties: one of them is getting comparable data (for two reasons—both mentioned by him—one is cyclical differences between the years, the other is that there may be statistical discrepancies, particularly when you have price-deflated one of the years). Now this suggests that one wants to link this with a more systematic time series analysis of some sort or other, in order to distinguish trends from short term aberrations and errors. We did a little work on this, when I was in the D.E.A.

We started from a single table and used the coefficients in this year to estimate a time series of industry using the relation:

$$\overset{*}{q}_{it} = \sum_{j} a_{ij0}\, q_{jt} + f_{it} \qquad (1)$$

where q_{jt} is the actual output of the j-th industry in year t.

f_{it} is the actual final demand for products of the i-th industry in year t (including net exports).

a_{ij0} is the typical input–output coefficient in the base year.

We computed and plotted the discrepancies between estimated and actual outputs (d_{it}):

$$d_{it} = \overset{*}{q}_{it} - q_{it} \qquad (2)$$

Strong cyclical effects emerged for many industries, notably iron and steel and non-ferrous metals, illustrating the dangers of a simple comparison of two years. Many of the discrepancy series contained strong trends which could be projected. A scheme like this could be modified to take into account having two base years by using, in place of a_{ij0} in equation (1), something like a weighted average of the two coefficients in the two base years. It seems to me that something like this needs doing.

The other point I wanted to make is connected and concerns the size of the tables. We have had, on the one hand, the comment that for many purposes you need very detailed tables, but, on the other hand, if tables become too large some of us have computational difficulties and all of us have *data* difficulties in getting the stuff *on* the computer. For general economic work, smaller tables are quite useful, with seventy, thirty, or even thirteen industries; it does seem to me that we ought not to be deterred from doing these vital up-dating exercises and comparisons of 1954 with 1963, by the fact that we can't do these at the full seventy-industry detail. It is true that we will obscure technical-coefficient changes and product-mix changes. But this is, to some extent, true whatever degree of aggregation we are working at; certainly it is true if one is working at seventy industries (for instance, other chemicals—a terrible product-mix problem); the value of very detailed tables is lost if, because of resource limitations, they cannot be brought up-to-date or projected; it is more useful, certainly for projection purposes, to work at a more aggregative level and allow for changes in coefficients through time, even if this does not allow product-mix effects and technical changes to be disentangled.

Finally, one other small point. You did mention getting out gross-output movements, and I am very delighted to hear that because it seems to me something that is terribly important for input–output work. We work mostly in terms of gross outputs and the index of industrial production is very inadequate for this purpose; for, although it starts with gross output series, on the whole it weights them together with net-output weights. In this computer age, re-weighting the basic series with gross-output weights should not prove impossible.

MR. LURY (Kent)

I wonder whether it might help the comparison of coefficients if you took the existing 1963 table, which is in effect the 1954 coefficients up-dated to 1963, and compared it with the final 1963 table which is being produced?

MR. BERMAN

May I just say that Mr. Lecomber's remarks are very interesting as always and there are a lot of useful points there to follow up; but I'm not quite sure where the division of labour should be between the C.S.O. and the research institutions. I have a general feeling that researchers don't let us know what they have been doing and find out from us what we're doing. You could always ring us up or write a letter or come and see us to find out what we in the C.S.O. are doing. We are inundated with visitors, but we are always willing to spare half-an-hour or an hour with someone; even though there are only a few of us.

MR. HILTON

I don't want to criticise the C.S.O.: for we all know the great job they do. But there are two reasons for our failure to contact the C.S.O. One is that we wished to educate ourselves with published information before wasting government officials' time. Second, when we have contacted the C.S.O. in the past it has taken three or four months and a great deal of effort to obtain even limited information.

MR. BERMAN

There ought to be more close contact, and this is one point of having this seminar, to have a bit more contact between the producers and the users so that the two can get together and see one another's problems. Mr. Lury, is it? made a suggestion about the 1963 tables. I don't think this is quite right because, although we start off with the coefficients for 1954, they are adapted, as one prorates up and down and across to know totals for the year 1963; so I don't think one would really get anything out of comparing our provisional figures for 1963 with what will finally emerge next year. If some of the figures come out the same I will be very happy, but we shall not be surprised if a lot of them don't.

MR. B. C. BROWN (D.E.A.)

I would just like to raise one point which really hasn't been raised, and I think it would be useful if Mr. Berman could say something about it. It is the extent to which, in drawing up the tables, an analysis (a commodity analysis in effect), will be made of the various components of final demand. Some sort of analysis of this sort will clearly be made, but if in fact it is applied only to a limited number of components (total consumers' expenditure, total fixed capital formation and so on); it may be that something will be lost which could have been got out of the work; clearly, for model-building purposes, very probably we shall have to get out and do some classification converters. We've suggested, for example, a classification converter between the ordinary functional analysis of consumers' expenditure and the commodity analysis in the input–output table. Now I have reason to believe that in fact, in the process of allocating consumers' expenditure among commodities, something could be done and probably is being done, but I think all of us would like an assurance on this, and it's not only in this field, the same sort of thing may be possible in the field of public expenditure and investment as well.

MR. BERMAN

It is said in paragraph 17 of the paper that we propose to publish some classification converters to go from the functional classifications of final demand shown in the Blue Book to the commodity classifications which are shown in the input–output tables. The big problem is that in our national income accounts, unlike almost every other country, we base our figures of final expenditure on surveys—surveys of investment, surveys of stock-building and surveys of consumers' expenditure, or retail sales—whereas when we produce our input–output tables we will get independent estimates of goods and services coming forward to final demand. We will have a problem matching the two—the output estimates got from the commodity flow approach and the expenditure estimates which we use at the moment. And maybe one should spend a whole year trying to reconcile these two sets of data and perhaps rebasing the national income estimates, but I am sure you wouldn't want us to take that long. So I am not quite sure what the answer would be; we will just keep our fingers crossed and when we come to the crunch we hope that the two sets of figures will match, but there is a big problem here.

MR. VAN NOORDEN (D.E.A.)

In paragraph 24, I think it was, you raised the question of comparing the technical coefficients of small firms and large firms in selected industries as an indication of technical progress over time, as some guide, that is, when comparing the 1954 and 1963 coefficients. I should just like to make a point about that on a detail, and then use it as a basis for a larger point. There is often a clear difference in kind between the small firms classified to a particular industry and the large firms classified to the same industry. Your suggested comparison, on a cross-section basis for one year, would not therefore tell you very much about any progress of technical development. And I do not think the 1954 to 1963 time-series studies that I think you may have suggested, looking at individual small and large firms over time, would be much use to you either. Of course, large firms might give more useful replies than small firms (this having been found, I think, in C.B.I. surveys), but this is not of relevance to your particular comparison.

MR. BERMAN

It was meant to be a cross-section analysis in one year.

MR. VAN NOORDEN

Yes. Well, from a cross-sectional analysis in one year you cannot deduce that the small firms would become like the large firms in their technical coefficients when they are in fact small firms getting larger over time. There is a difference in concept. If it is a question of technical progress over time there must be assumptions made about economies of scale, so it is dangerous to talk simply about changes of input per unit of output. I do not think this sort of economic study could be done. The larger point was that when we were discussing the detail of the input–output tables, 70^2 or $1,000^2$ whatever the number of sectors was to be, it seemed that the C.S.O. was going to move into the Market Research field; my point is that the C.S.O. should not try to sell input–output to industry by saying that it is a substitute for Market Research. And I do not think it could be used, as your particular study suggested, as a guide to economies of scale or what happens to small firms when they are growing. I think that as the decisions that come from studying input–output tables will be concerned with changing the pattern of flows between industries, or with the effects of macro-changes on the industry pattern, this is therefore the sort of area in which the C.S.O. should work, not in the area of Market Research or on detailed economic studies.

MR. BERMAN

May I just say that for this cross-section study or seeing what happens to an establishment over time, this is the kind of thing which can only be done within the government. It would have to be done largely by the Board of Trade Census office, because it involves confidential information; but it wouldn't involve very much work. One could get the information out fairly quickly from the computer and from the detailed returns. Anyway, I am interested to know that you think it is a waste of time.

One other thing: the C.S.O. has no intention of entering the Market Research game. The thought at the back of my mind was that under the new system of production statistics, industry is being asked to provide at considerable expense details of sales and purchases and the least the government can do, in my opinion, is to repackage this information and give it back to industry in the form of detailed tables, *if they want it*. If they don't want it we won't do it, but if they want it I think we ought to do it. Only the government can produce these tables as far as I can see, and *then* it is up to the Market Research people to use them; and if they don't want them then we won't do it; but American experience suggests that this is the kind of thing that some of the big firms in this country will want, but if they don't want it then there is no reason why we should produce big tables. The government is not interested in very big tables for its own purposes.

MISS GELLNER (British Steel Corporation)

I wondered about the international context, and what work is being done in other countries, and whether you were thinking about comparability.

MR. BERMAN

Well, I feel it is difficult enough to compare input–output tables over time in any country. It must be more difficult to make comparisons between countries. The Common Market countries have done quite a lot; you might have seen their studies. They have uniform tables and all the Common Market countries have produced tables for a particular year; I think Mr. Upton knows more about this than I do, but I do have a feeling that our seventy-industry table would be more or less comparable with the kind of tables produced in the Common Market countries, in Canada, and in the United States.

DR. SIMPSON (University College, London)

Well, first of all I would like to say that I have always found the C.S.O. extremely helpful on input–output questions. Secondly, I think that if input–output is going to develop in this country or anywhere at all, it must develop as a practical tool and therefore it means that it must be intelligible to businessmen; in other words, we must have more detail until the level at which the statisticians are working down from the top meets the level that businessmen and operations researchers are working from below. This means we must be thinking in terms of detail, at least to the order of a hundred or even two hundred sectors; and I must say I find the idea that there is something attractive about small tables completely extraordinary, because this just means that you have less information; and we cannot be satisfied with less information. Now obviously there is some constraint in terms of resources, but what I should like to do is to ask Mr. Berman how we, as users, can most effectively lobby, not for one form or another of choice within the present resources, but how we can lobby for far more statistical resources being devoted to providing more detailed tables more frequently.

MR. BERMAN

I don't think I should *answer* the last question.

PROFESSOR STEWART

Not today, anyway.

MR. BERMAN

No.

PROFESSOR STEWART

I think that the paper has generated a lot of very interesting discussion: particularly on the kind of information which ought to be assembled and presented; the question of the physical relationship between the inputs and outputs; the very important point that has been made about the attempt to build a bridge from our standard-costing data and the technological data in the establishment to the national-accounting approach which starts from the more aggregated information. These, together with the discussion of up-dating, seem to represent a series of very good basic problems that will, no doubt, continue to occupy us at our future sessions and I would like therefore to invite you to thank Mr. Berman for a very stimulating paper.

SESSION III

A Linear Model of Production, Distribution and Growth

by

A. CIGNO[1]

Lecturer in the Department of Mathematical Economics,
University of Birmingham

(Summary)

The model of economic growth proposed in this paper closely resembles Schumpeter's "vision" of the development process [9]. The basic assumption is that only one or a few firms in each industry are capable of adjusting their production plans, in time, with respect to changes in technical know-how, consumers' preferences, and supplies of original factors. These leading firms make profits, which are used to finance innovatory investments, while the other firms make losses, which force them, after a while, to modify their production plans or go out of business.

The general model is built up step by step. The first section of this paper describes a recursive programming model of the profit-maximising firm. In the second section the individual models are aggregated at the industry level and an exact definition of "industry" is provided; the solution of the aggregate model is *not* the sum of the component firms' optimal solutions, because some of the firms are not optimising. In the third section the analysis is extended to the whole economic system: prices and income distribution are determined within a general-equilibrium setting and profits appear as the remuneration of a very special factor of production, "entrepreneurship", which becomes "scarce" only in times of change.

The programming approach adopted makes the model suitable for empirical application. The model can be used to forecast output, prices and technical change for a whole economic system or for a

---

[1] I am indebted to Professor M. McManus, A. Heesterman, L. Mendelson, and several other colleagues of Birmingham University, for their helpful comments and criticisms on an earlier draft of this paper.

section of it. With minor modifications, the model can also be converted into a decision model for economic planning.

I. A DYNAMIC MODEL OF THE PROFIT MAXIMISING FIRM

Let us assume, in the first place, that all entrepreneurs make or revise their production plans at regular intervals, so that the continuous flow of time can be subdivided into finite periods, each period being defined as the length of time that elapses between any two production decisions. Then consider the case of any particular firm: at the beginning of period t, the entrepreneur disposes of a collection of inventories and capital goods purchased or produced in the course of period $t - 1$. Capital goods of the same nature but of different age can be regarded as different commodities and I shall refer indifferently to all these factors of production as the capital stocks of the firm in period t.

The entrepreneur knows that by combining the factors of production already available with others that he can buy on the market, according to certain fixed proportions dictated by his technical knowledge, he *can* produce certain fixed combinations of goods. He also knows that the same combination of outputs can be obtained by a finite number of techniques, i.e. different combinations of inputs. I shall call "process" the act of producing—in the widest sense of the word, so as to include such activities as buying, selling, transporting and storing—a determined combination of commodities with a particular combination of inputs.[2] Two processes might then differ only in that the output is sold during the current period in one process, while it is stored in the other, which produces inventories instead of current output. Similarly two processes might differ only in that they use capital goods of the same nature but of different age.[3] Processes using capital goods as inputs "produce" either capital goods of the same nature but one period older, or scrap.

We can then describe all the production possibilities open to an entrepreneur as a collection of processes. These are not necessarily all that exist, because not all processes are known to the entrepreneur, neither are all those known to him within his reach. Given this description of the firm's technology, technical change can be defined

[2] Joint production is regarded, here, as the general case: single production is a special case where all outputs but one are equal to zero.

[3] Differences in the age of the capital stocks are reflected by differences in the other input and output coefficients. Besides, if there is a "gestation period" the current inputs and outputs of processes using new capital goods will be null or very small.

F

in the simplest possible way: as the addition of new, more efficient processes to the collection.

Suppose that, at the beginning of period t, our entrepreneur can choose among J processes. Let

$x_j^t \geqq 0 \, (j = 1, ..., J)$ denote the level of operation of the j-th process during period t;

$a_{kj} \geqq 0 \, (k = 1, ..., K)$ denote the k-th capital input of the j-th process;

$c_{kj} \geqq 0 \, (k = 1, ..., K)$ denote the k-th capital output of the j-th process;

$s_{hj} \geqq 0 \, (h = 1, ..., H)$ denote the input of services of the h-th original productive factor (labour, land or other natural resources) of the j-th process;

$q_{ij} \lessgtr 0 \, (i = 1, ..., I)$ denote the i-th current output $(q_{ij} > 0)$ or input $(q_{ij} < 0)$ of the j-th process.

Here the difference between "current" and "capital" goods does not lie in their nature of durability—capital goods have been defined in such a way that they can only last for a period—but in whether they are the outcome of decisions taken during the current period or in the past.[4] All inputs and outputs are expressed per unit of one particular input or output, chosen arbitrarily.

Now let us assume that *all markets are large enough for our entrepreneur to regard himself as a price taker*, and suppose, for the moment, that *our particular entrepreneur is a profit-maximiser and, furthermore, all current prices are known to him from the beginning of the period*. When formulating this production plan for period t, our entrepreneur has in mind both current and future revenues. Therefore he attempts to maximise concurrently the difference between current receipts and outlays, and the productive capacity of the firm at the end of the period, i.e. the expected value of the capital stocks made available for period $t+1$.

Let

$p_i^t \geqq 0 \, (i = 1, ..., I)$ denote the market price of the i-th current good in period t;

$w_h^t \geqq 0 \, (h = 1, ..., H)$ denote the market price of the h-th original factor service in period t.

---

[4] Thus the act of scrapping a machine or selling a stock of inventories transforms a capital input into a current output.

$v_k^t \geqq 0$ $(k = 1, ..., K)$ denote the imputed value (or shadow-price) of the k-th capital stock in period t.

$\hat{v}_k^{t+1} \geqq 0$ $(k = 1, ..., K)$ denote the expected value of the k-th capital stock in period $t+1$.

The entrepreneur chooses non-negative process levels x_j^t so that

$$\sum_{j=1}^{J} \left(\sum_{i=1}^{I} p_i^t q_{ij} - \sum_{h=1}^{H} w_h^t s_{hj} + \sum_{k=1}^{K} \hat{v}_k^{t+1} c_{kj} \right) x_j^t = \max. \tag{1}$$

subject to K capital constraints

$$\sum_{j=1}^{J} a_{kj} x_j^t \leqq \sum_{j=1}^{J} c_{kj} x_j^{t-1} \tag{2}$$

The surplus over the cost of current inputs realised during period t is imputed to the capital stocks available at the beginning of the period. This problem of imputation is the "dual" of problem (1)–(2) and consists of finding non-negative capital stock shadow-prices v_k^t so that

$$\sum_{k=1}^{K} \sum_{j=1}^{J} (c_{kj} x_j^{t-1}) v_k^t = \min. \tag{3}$$

subject to

$$\sum_{k=1}^{K} v_k^t a_{kj} \geqq \sum_{i=1}^{I} p_i^t q_{ij} - \sum_{h=1}^{H} w_h^t s_{hj} + \sum_{k=1}^{K} \hat{v}_k^{t+1} c_{kj}. \tag{4}$$

A shadow-price v_k^t is thus defined as the value imputed to a capital stock available *at the beginning* of period t, and it is equal to the sum of the rental accruing to the stock *during* period t, plus the expected value $\hat{v}_k^{t+1}$ of the same stock at the beginning of period $t+1$, i.e. *at the end* of period t.

How this model works is best explained by a simple example. Suppose that

(a) There is only one finished product, which is not storable.
(b) There is only one type of machine which lasts only two periods.
(c) There is a market for used machines but not for scrap.
(d) No inputs other than the machine are required to obtain the finished product.

Let us examine the case of a firm that, at the beginning of period t, owns a used machine. Four courses of action or "processes" (see Table 1) are then possible

(1) To use the old machine until it wears out.

(2) To sell the old machine right away.
(3) To buy additional used machines.
(4) To buy new machines.

Table 1. Production and Investment Possibilities of a Hypothetical Firm in Period t

Processes→	Input and output coefficients				Shadow Prices and Market Prices
	1	2	3	4	
Capital input: used machines	1	1	0	0	v_u^t (unknown)
Capital output: used machines	0	0	0	1	$\hat{v}_u^{t+1}$ (expected)
Current inputs and outputs:					
used machines	0	1	−1	0	p_u^t (known)
new machines	0	0	0	−1	p_n^t (known)
finished product	q_u	0	q	q	p^t (known)

If we denote by z_j^t the coefficient of x_j^t in equation (1), we get in this case:

$$z_1^t = p^t q_u$$
$$z_2^t = p_u^t$$
$$z_3^t = p^t q_u - p_u^t$$
$$z_4^t = p^t q_n - p_n^t + \hat{v}_u^{t+1}$$

The firm will buy an additional machine or keep one ready in hand only if its market price is less than the sum of the rental that would accrue to the machine during period t, plus the expected value of the machine at the end of the period. Thus, the firm will buy used machines and keep the one available only if

$$p_u^t < p^t q_u,$$

and will buy new machines only if

$$p_n^t < p^t q_n + \hat{v}_u^{t+1}.$$

For this simple case it is easy to calculate the value or shadow-price imputed to the machine available at the beginning of period t: v_u^t will be equal to either z_1^t or z_2^t, whichever is the largest.

We are now left with the problem of determining the ϑ_k^{t+1}, i.e. of translating the past experience of the entrepreneur into expectations. I shall assume that:

$$\vartheta_k^{t+1} = v_k^{t-1}$$

which is the same as saying that the entrepreneur expects the value of a capital good at the end of the current period to be equal to that of capital goods of the same age and nature at the end of the last period (i.e. at the very date when he is formulating the production plan). Then, the model of the profit-maximising firm becomes:

$$\sum_{j=1}^{J} \left(\sum_{i=1}^{I} p_i^t q_{ij} - \sum_{h=1}^{H} w_h^t s_{hj} + \sum_{k=1}^{K} v_k^{t-1} c_{kj} \right) x_j^t = \max. \qquad (1')$$

$$\sum_{j=1}^{J} a_{kj} x_j^t \leqq \sum_{j=1}^{J} c_{kj} x_j^{t-1} \qquad (2)$$

$$\sum_{k=1}^{K} \sum_{j=1}^{J} \left(c_{kj} x_j^{t-1} \right) v_k^t = \min. \qquad (3)$$

$$\sum_{k=1}^{K} a_{kj} v_k^t \geqq \sum_{i=1}^{I} p_i^t q_{ij} - \sum_{h=1}^{H} w_h^t s_{hj} + \sum_{k=1}^{K} v_k^{t-1} c_{kj}. \qquad (4')$$

This is a dynamic model of production and investment in which the decisions of each period are conditioned by all past decisions and condition all future decisions. The economic life of the firm is thus determined by a never-ending sequence of choices, each resembling the solution of a linear programming problem. For every such problem the parameters of the primal objective-function and the right-hand-side coefficients of the dual constraints are calculated from the dual solution of the previous problem and from market prices. The parameters of the dual objective-function and the right-hand-side coefficients of the primal constraints are calculated from the previous problem's primal solution.

The same simplified example examined before can be used to show how the model works in the new formulation. As said before the firm buys used machines only if $p_u^t < p^t q_u$ and buys new machines only if $p_n^t < p^t q_n + \vartheta_u^{t+1}$. But now ϑ_u^{t+1} is assumed equal to v_u^{t-1} which, in its turn, could be equal to either $p^{t-1} q_u$ or p_u^{t-1}, according to whether process 1 or 2 were activated in period t-1. Thus the condition for the purchase of new machines could mean either:

$$p_n^t < p^t q_n + p^{t-1} q_u$$

or

$$p_n^t < p^t q_n + p_u^{t-1}$$

depending on the past history of the firm.

The decision to invest depends then on a comparison of the cost of the capital good with the sum of its expected yields, assumed equal to what they were at some point in the past. However, it could be argued that, in a simpler case like the one described in the example, the entrepreneur would attempt to base his estimates of future yields on forecasts of future prices rather than on past prices and, perhaps, would discount future yields as it is assumed in the neo-classical theory of capital. But, in a real-world firm with numerous processes and with capital goods lasting many periods, it would be impracticable to work out all the possible alternatives and likely outcomes for many periods ahead: the assumption I made that the entrepreneur uses the imputed values of his capital stocks as a guide to investment seems far more realistic.

II. THE BEHAVIOUR OF INDUSTRIES

A model of the whole economic system that attempted to consider each firm as an independent unit would be unmanageable; for this reason those larger units that we call "industries" need to be brought into the picture. But what exactly is an industry and what are the criteria for the aggregation of individual production models?

Before turning to these problems I shall set out the model described in the previous section more compactly using matrix notation. Let:

$$\mathbf{Q}_t = \begin{bmatrix} q_{11} \cdots\cdots\cdots\cdots q_{1J} \\ \\ \\ \\ q_{I1} \cdots\cdots\cdots\cdots q_{IJ} \end{bmatrix}_t \qquad \mathbf{p}_t = \begin{bmatrix} p_1^t \\ \\ \\ \\ p_I^t \end{bmatrix} \qquad \mathbf{x}_t = \begin{bmatrix} x_1^t \\ \\ \\ \\ \\ \\ \\ x_J^t \end{bmatrix}$$

$$\mathbf{S}_t = \begin{bmatrix} s_{11} \cdots\cdots\cdots\cdots s_{1J} \\ \\ \\ \\ s_{H1} \cdots\cdots\cdots\cdots s_{HJ} \end{bmatrix}_t \qquad \mathbf{w}_t = \begin{bmatrix} w_1^t \\ \\ \\ \\ \\ w_H^t \end{bmatrix}$$

$$C_t = \begin{bmatrix} c_{11} \cdots\cdots\cdots c_{1J} \\ \\ \\ \\ c_{K1} \cdots\cdots\cdots c_{KJ} \end{bmatrix}_t \qquad v_t = \begin{bmatrix} v_1^t \\ \\ \\ \\ v_K^t \end{bmatrix} \qquad z_t = \begin{bmatrix} z_1^t \\ \\ \\ \\ z_J^t \end{bmatrix}$$

$$A_t = \begin{bmatrix} a_{11} \cdots\cdots\cdots a_{1J} \\ \\ \\ \\ a_{K1} \cdots\cdots\cdots a_{KJ} \end{bmatrix}_t \qquad b_t = \begin{bmatrix} b_1^t \\ \\ \\ \\ b_K^t \end{bmatrix}$$

where

$$z_t' = p_t'Q_t - w_t'S_t + v_{t-1}'C_t \tag{5}$$

$$b_t = C_{t-1}x_{t-1} \tag{6}$$

All vectors and matrices refer to one particular period. In the case of the technology matrices Q_t, S_t, C_t and A_t, the time index means that they represent the technology of the firm only for period t: in period $t+1$ a new process might become available and another column added to all the matrices.

Now the dual problems (1')–(2') and (3')–(4') become those of finding $x_t \geqq 0$, $v_t \geqq 0$ so that

$$z_t'x_t = \text{max.} \tag{7}$$

$$A_t x_t \leqq b_t \tag{8}$$

and

$$b_t'v_t = \text{min.} \tag{9}$$

$$A_t'v_t \geqq z_t \tag{10}$$

Consider two firms, identified by superscripts (1) and (2), with identical technology,

$$A_t^{(1)} = A_t^{(2)} = A_t$$

and proportional variations in expected revenues[5] and capital stocks,

[5] I say "expected" revenues because they include the expected values of capital stocks at the end of period t.

$$z_t^{(2)} = \gamma z_t^{(1)}, \qquad \gamma > 0$$
$$b_t^{(2)} = \lambda b_t^{(1)}, \qquad \lambda > 0$$

where γ and λ are arbitrary scalars. Day [3] has proved the following *theorem:* "*If* $\mathbf{x}_t^{*(1)} \geqq 0$ *and* $\mathbf{v}_t^{*(1)} \geqq 0$ *are the solutions of the dual* (twin) *problems,*

$$z_t^{\prime(1)}\mathbf{x}_t^{(1)} = \text{max.} \qquad\qquad b_t^{\prime(1)}\mathbf{v}_t^{(1)} = \text{min.}$$
$$A_t\mathbf{x}_t^{(1)} \leqq b_t^{(1)} \qquad\qquad A_t'\mathbf{v}_t^{(1)} \geqq z_t^{(1)}$$

then the solutions of the dual (twin) *problems,*

$$z_t^{\prime(2)}\mathbf{x}_t^{(2)} = \text{max.} \qquad\qquad b_t^{\prime(2)}\mathbf{v}_t^{(2)} = \text{min.}$$
$$A_t\mathbf{x}_t^{(2)} \leqq b_t^{(2)} \qquad\qquad A_t'\mathbf{v}_t^{(2)} \geqq z_t^{(2)}$$
$$are\ \overset{*}{\mathbf{x}}_t^{(2)} = \lambda\overset{*}{\mathbf{x}}_t^{(1)} \qquad\qquad and\ \overset{*}{\mathbf{v}}_t^{(2)} = \gamma\overset{*}{\mathbf{v}}_t^{(1)},\text{''}\ \ ^6.$$

Thus the outputs of the two firms differ only for a factor of scale and the *relative* shadow-prices imputed to their capital stocks are the same. This is the customary result obtained when the firms have identical linear homogeneous production functions.

Consider now a group of M firms and denote by $A_t^{(m)}$, $b_t^{(m)}$, $z_t^{(m)}$ the capital-input matrix, capital-stock vector and expected revenue vector, respectively, of the m-th firm ($m = 1, ..., M$). Also let $\mathbf{x}_t^{*(m)}$, $\mathbf{v}_t^{*(m)}$ denote, respectively, the primal and dual solutions of the m-th

---

[6] The formal proof runs as follows: By hypothesis

$$A_t\overset{*}{\mathbf{x}}_t^{(1)} \leq b_t^{(1)}, \quad A_t'\overset{*}{\mathbf{v}}_t^{(1)} \geq z_t^{(1)}$$

thus

$$A_t\overset{*}{\mathbf{x}}_t^{(2)} = A_t[\lambda\overset{*}{\mathbf{x}}_t^{(1)}] \leq \lambda b_t^{(1)} = b_t^{(2)},$$
$$A_t'\overset{*}{\mathbf{v}}_t^{(2)} = A_t'[\gamma\overset{*}{\mathbf{v}}_t^{(1)}] \geq \gamma z_t^{(1)} = z_t^{(2)}.$$

This establishes the feasibility of $\overset{*}{\mathbf{x}}_t^{(2)}$ and $\overset{*}{\mathbf{v}}_t^{(2)}$. Also, by the "duality theorem" of Linear Programming [6],

$$z_t^{\prime(1)}\overset{*}{\mathbf{x}}_t^{(1)} = b_t^{\prime(1)}\overset{*}{\mathbf{v}}_t^{(1)},$$

so that

$$\gamma\lambda z_t^{\prime(1)}\overset{*}{\mathbf{x}}_t^{(1)} = \gamma\lambda b_t^{\prime(1)}\overset{*}{\mathbf{v}}_t^{(1)},$$

but

$$\gamma\lambda z_t^{\prime(1)}\overset{*}{\mathbf{x}}_t^{(1)} = [\gamma z_t^{(1)}]'[\lambda\overset{*}{\mathbf{x}}_t^{(1)}] = z_t^{\prime(2)}\overset{*}{\mathbf{x}}_t^{(2)},$$
$$\gamma\lambda b_t^{\prime(1)}\overset{*}{\mathbf{v}}_t^{(1)} = [\lambda b_t^{(1)}]'[\gamma\overset{*}{\mathbf{v}}_t^{(1)}] = b_t^{\prime(2)}\overset{*}{\mathbf{v}}_t^{(2)},$$

so that

$$z_t^{\prime(2)}\overset{*}{\mathbf{x}}_t^{(2)} = b_t^{\prime(2)}\overset{*}{\mathbf{v}}_t^{(2)}.$$

Thus, by the "duality theorem", $\overset{*}{\mathbf{x}}_t^{(2)}$ and $\overset{*}{\mathbf{v}}_t^{(2)}$ are the (optimal) solutions of the second firm's problem.

firm for period t. I shall say that this group of firms is "homogeneous" if the aggregate dual problems:

$$\mathbf{z}'_t\mathbf{x}_t = \text{max.} \qquad\qquad \mathbf{b}'_t\mathbf{v}_t = \text{min.}$$

$$\mathbf{A}_t\mathbf{x}_t \leqq \mathbf{b}_t \qquad\qquad \mathbf{A}'_t\mathbf{v}_t \geqq \mathbf{z}_t$$

where

$$\mathbf{b}_t = \sum_{m=1}^{M} \mathbf{b}_t^{(m)}, \qquad\qquad \mathbf{z}_t = \frac{1}{M}\sum_{m=1}^{M} \mathbf{z}_t^{(m)}$$

have (optimal) solutions:

$$\mathbf{x}_t^* = \sum_{m=1}^{M} \mathbf{x}_t^{*(m)}, \qquad\qquad \mathbf{v}_t^* = \frac{1}{M}\sum_{m=1}^{M} \mathbf{v}_t^{*(m)}.$$

From the above mentioned theorem it is intuitive that this group is "homogeneous" if all the firms have the same technology so that:

$$\mathbf{A}_t^{(m)} = \mathbf{A}_t, \text{ all } m,$$

and their capital stocks and revenue expectations are proportional:[7]

$$\mathbf{b}_t^{(m)} = \lambda^{(m)}\mathbf{b}_t, \quad \lambda^{(m)} > 0, \quad \sum_{m=1}^{M} \lambda^{(m)} = 1,$$

$$\mathbf{z}_t^{(m)} = \gamma^{(m)}\mathbf{z}_t, \quad \gamma^{(m)} > 0, \quad \sum_{m=1}^{M} \gamma^{(m)} = M.$$

This definition of homogeneity provides an exact criterion for aggregating individual firms into "industries" without incurring "aggregation bias". A homogeneous group can be then represented by a single model with capital stocks and expected revenues respectively equal to the sum and the mean of those of the constituent

---

[7] In fact, by the above theorem, we have:

$$\mathbf{x}_t^* = \frac{1}{\lambda^{(m)}}\mathbf{x}_t^{*(m)}, \quad \mathbf{v}_t^* = \frac{1}{\gamma^{(m)}}\mathbf{v}_t^{*(m)},$$

thus

$$\sum_{m=1}^{M} \mathbf{x}_t^{*(m)} = \mathbf{x}_t^* \sum_{m=1}^{M} \lambda^{(m)} = \mathbf{x}_t^*$$

and

$$\sum_{m=1}^{M} \mathbf{v}_t^{*(m)} = \mathbf{v}_t^* \sum_{m=1}^{M} \gamma^{(m)} = \mathbf{v}_t^*$$

so that

$$\frac{1}{M}\sum_{m=1}^{M} \mathbf{v}_t^{*(m)} = \mathbf{v}_t^*.$$

firms; the aggregate model generates a set of process levels and shadow-prices respectively equal to the sum and the mean of those generated by the individual models.

These conclusions rest on the assumptions that all entrepreneurs adjust promptly their production plans in response to changes in prices and technical know-how. But, as real industries are not entirely composed of keen innovators and successful maximisers, these assumptions must now be modified.

In the first place I shall drop the assumption that all entrepreneurs base their production plans on current prices: as all decisions are taken by definition at the beginning of each period, the knowledge of the prices of the incoming period requires perfect foresight. I shall suppose that *only a few outstanding entrepreneurs forecast correctly the new market prices and plan production accordingly; the others keep to the old plan until the change of market conditions has become manifest.*

In the second place, *when a scientific discovery or a technical improvement makes available a more efficient technique, the new process is not adopted automatically by all the firms that would draw some advantage from it.* On the contrary, it may take some time before an innovator, attracted by the prospect of higher returns, introduces the new process in his firm (or creates a new one), thus overcoming the force or inertia attached to the familiar methods of production and the risk aversion raised by the new one. Then, as the innovator starts to bid up the price of productive factors in order to enlarge his business, the other firms are gradually forced to adopt the innovation themselves or to go out of business.

These new features can be readily added to our aggregate model in the form of "flexibility" constraints on the industry's response to changes in prices and know-how. Let us define a vector of maximum process levels:

$$\mathbf{u}_t = \mathbf{u}(\mathbf{x}_{t-1}) = \begin{bmatrix} u_1(x_1^{t-1}) \\ \vdots \\ u_J(x_J^{t-1}) \end{bmatrix}$$

and a vector of minimum process levels,

$$\mathbf{l}_t = \mathbf{l}(\mathbf{x}_{t-1}) = \begin{bmatrix} l_1(x_1^{t-1}) \\ \vdots \\ \\ \\ \\ \\ l_J(x_J^{t-1}) \end{bmatrix}$$

for each period t, expressed as functions of the lagged process levels. The existence of these limits is accounted for by the fact that not all firms adopt the optimum production plan: in period t the processes that should be operated above the level of period $t-1$ find an upper bound in the productive capacity of the leading firms, while the processes that should contract find a lower bound in the productive capacity of the firms who do not change the plan to period $t-1$.[8]

Substituting equations (5) and (6) into problem (7)–(8) and introducing the flexibility constraints the aggregate "primal" problem is now finding $\mathbf{x}_t \geqq \mathbf{0}$, so that

$$[\mathbf{p}'_t\mathbf{Q}_t - \mathbf{w}'_t\mathbf{S}_t + \mathbf{v}'_{t-1}\mathbf{C}_t]\mathbf{x}_t = \text{max.} \tag{11}$$

$$\mathbf{A}_t\mathbf{x}_t \leqq \mathbf{C}_{t-1}\mathbf{x}_{t-1} \tag{12}$$

$$\mathbf{I}_t\mathbf{x}_t \leqq \mathbf{u}(\mathbf{x}_{t-1}) \tag{13}$$

$$-\mathbf{I}_t\mathbf{x}_t \leqq -\mathbf{l}(\mathbf{x}_{t-1}) \tag{14}$$

where $\mathbf{I}_t$ is a $(J \times J)$ identity matrix.

Unless the industry that we are considering operates in a completely stationary economy, it is obvious that now the value of the objective-function cannot be imputed entirely to the capital stocks, because some of the flexibility constraints are likely to be binding. If an upper bound comes into operation, the (positive) net revenue of the constrained process is imputed to that very special factor of production represented by the entrepreneur who correctly anticipated a price change or pioneered the use of an improved technique. Analogously, when a lower bound comes into operation, the (negative) net revenue of the constrained process is imputed to the entre-

[8] The functions $u_j(x_j^{t-1})$ and $l_j(x_j^{t-1})$, which determine the values of the upper and lower bounds, are behavioural relations. They can be estimated by regression analysis of time series or by interviews with businessmen. The use of "flexibility constraints" in empirical studies was first introduced by Henderson [7] and then by Day [2].

preneur who failed to foresee a price change or persisted in the use of an obsolete technique.

Thus, two new sets of dual variables make their appearance. Let

$$\phi_t = \begin{bmatrix} \phi\,_1^t \\ \\ \\ \\ \\ \\ \phi\,_j^t \end{bmatrix}$$

denote the vector of shadow-prices imputed to the upper flexibility constraints, and

$$\psi_t = \begin{bmatrix} \psi\,_1^t \\ \\ \\ \\ \\ \\ \psi\,_j^t \end{bmatrix}$$

denote the vector of shadow-prices imputed to the lower flexibility constraints. The "dual" of problem (11)–(12)–(13)–(14) consists in determining $\phi_t \geqq 0$ and $\psi_t \geqq 0$, as well as $\mathbf{v}_t \geqq 0$, so that:

$$[\mathbf{C}_{t-1}\mathbf{x}_{t-1}]'\mathbf{v}_t + \mathbf{u}(\mathbf{x}_{t-1})'\phi_t - \mathbf{l}(\mathbf{x}_{t-1})'\psi_t = \min. \tag{15}$$

$$\mathbf{A}_t'\mathbf{v}_t + \mathbf{I}_t'[\phi_t - \psi_t] \geqq \mathbf{Q}_t'\mathbf{p}_t - \mathbf{S}_t'\mathbf{w}_t + \mathbf{C}_t'\mathbf{v}_{t-1}. \tag{16}$$

Thus, the total value imputed to capital in each period t, $\mathbf{b}_t'\mathbf{v}_t$, may be greater or less than the sum of present and future revenues of the industry, $\mathbf{z}_t'\mathbf{x}_t$, according to whether the net value imputed to the entrepreneurial function, $[\mathbf{u}(\mathbf{x}_{t-1})'\phi_t - \mathbf{l}(\mathbf{x}_{t-1})'\psi_t]$, is negative or positive.

The dual problems (11)–(12)–(13)–(14) and (15)–(16) form a new model of production, aggregated at industry level, after the "perfect adjustment" assumptions have been relaxed.

III. GENERAL EQUILIBRIUM AND INCOME DISTRIBUTION

So far we have examined the behaviour of each firm or group of firms independently, considering market prices as constants. In this section I shall consider the problem of general economic equilibrium, that is the simultaneous determination, in a dynamic context, of prices and quantities exchanged.

Imagine an economic system composed of a number of firms, grouped into N industries (as defined in the last paragraph), and of a number of individuals. The latter can be classified into: (a) Workers and Landlords, who possess personal capacities, land and other natural resources, (b) Capitalists, who are the owners of money capital, and (c) Entrepreneurs who co-ordinate the productive activities of the firms. This is obviously a functional, not a personal, classification of individuals, as the same physical person can be and usually is classified under more than one heading at the same time.

Consider, firstly, a stationary economy, where no technical change has occurred for some time, and the supply of original factors of production and the demand for consumer goods do not vary. If this is the case, the market prices are the same in every period and the firms do not need to change their plans from period to period. Then the flexibility constraints are not binding in any of the industries and the value imputed to the capital stocks is equal in each period to the difference between the revenue from current sales and the cost of services and intermediate products. This residual value is used by the entrepreneur to repay with interest the money borrowed in the preceding period. Because of the competition among firms to secure adequate financing, we can expect the market rate of interest to be at such a level that the whole surplus over current costs is passed on to the capitalists.

In this case the entire value of all the "final" goods produced in the economy during a period is distributed to workers, landlords and capitalists, who spend part of it on purchasing current products and lend the rest to the entrepreneurs.

These loans, which come from personal saving, cover the cost of producing inventories and capital goods. However, as the demand for final goods and the supply of productive services are always the same, the entrepreneurs have no reason to increase the stocks of capital from one period to another: net investment is nil and the economy does not grow.[9]

[9] It must be noted that, having defined capital goods of different age as different commodities, the whole stock of capital is destroyed and reproduced in each period. Thus Investment and Investments (or Capital) are, in this model, the same thing and Net Investment (i.e. Gross Investment minus Depreciation) is equal to the difference between the capital output of one period and that of the last one. Similarly, I am supposing that all loans are repaid at the end of each period, so that also Saving and Savings are the same thing.

Now suppose that an entrepreneur adopts a new process that allows the production of more goods with the same amount of capital and current inputs. Then his firm realises a surplus over current cost larger than that of the other firms: the difference as we saw in the last paragraph, is imputed to the "entrepreneurial function" and remains inside the firm as a profit [9].

If nobody follows the example of the innovator, or the innovator manages to keep the secret of the new process, the profit becomes a permanent revenue, assuming the nature of a monopoly rent. Conversely, if the innovator is gradually imitated by the other entrepreneurs attracted by the prospect of making a profit, the innovation spreads through the whole industry and the profit is gradually washed out by the rising tide of wages, rents and interests or by decreases in consumer prices.

The other face of technical progress is obsolescence: the introduction of a more efficient process in the economic system makes one or several others obsolete. Once prices, wages, rents and the rate of interest have become adjusted to the new productivity standard, the entrepreneur who still persists in the use of the obsolete processes incurs a loss, that forces him to adopt the new process or go out of business altogether.

Changes in the size or composition of consumer demand and original factors' supply have the same effect of a technical advance. If the change consists in the appearance of a new factor of production —for example, a new source of energy—or in the demand for a new product, then the introduction of new processes is obviously necessary giving start to the sequence of events described above.[10] But also, the entrepreneur who anticipates an increase in the demand of a known product or a more abundant supply of a known factor's service and plans production accordingly realises a profit; conversely the entrepreneur who fails to anticipate a decrease in demand or the shortage of some factor's service incurs a loss.

If either of these kinds of change takes place, the stationary state is broken and net investment begins. The additional funds for capital production do not have to come from personal saving, which may not be affected at first, but from the reinvestment of net profits (i.e. the algebraic sum of the profits and losses of the individual firms).[11]

[10] If we assume, as Schumpeter [9] does, that the prime mover is always an entrepreneur and that even changes in the consumption pattern are induced by the fact that a new product has been put on the market, then change and innovation become synonymous.

[11] The assumption of profit reinvestment rests on the fact that profit is not a

As a result, income distributed will later increase and so will personal saving, thus contributing to finance additional investment. If no further change intervenes, the effect of the first change will eventually die out, profits will vanish[12] and the economy will settle at a higher stationary level.

Let us denote the flows of services that originate in each period t from the H original factors[13] by a vector function of calendar time:

$$\mathbf{f}_t = \mathbf{f}(t) = \begin{bmatrix} f_1(t) \\ \vdots \\ \\ \\ \\ f_H(t) \end{bmatrix}$$

and the consumers' demands[14] by a vector function of income distributed to capitalists, workers and landlords during the last period:[15]

---

permanent revenue. If it becomes permanent it is then distributed to capital and labour (including management).

[12] When all the firms have adjusted their production plans to the new market or technological situation (or have gone out of business), no further variation of process levels is required and the flexibility constraints cease to be binding. Then the source of net profit—the value imputed to the flexibility constraints— dries up.

[13] These include the various kinds of labour (including management), differentiated by skills and location. Also land and other natural resources are differentiated by location, so that the general equilibrium model I am going to describe determines also the geographical distribution of productive activities [1].

[14] Also the demand for consumer goods is differentiated by location. In the case of "intermediate" products consumer demand is obviously zero.

[15] This does not necessarily imply that all wages, rents and interests are paid at the end of the period: it may only imply that, as income fluctuates in the course of a period, the consumers prefer to base their consumption plans on the income received over a whole period, the last one. More generally, we could relate consumption to the income of several past periods: as long as consumers' decisions are based on past events, the nature of the model is not altered. Besides, the determination of consumption as a function of income alone rules out substitution between products; thus the consumers' demands should be expressed in terms of broad aggregates such as food, clothing, etc.

$$\mathbf{d}_t = \mathbf{d}(\mathbf{y}_{t-1}) = \begin{bmatrix} d_1(y_{t-1}) \\ \\ \\ \\ \\ \\ d_I(y_{t-1}) \end{bmatrix}$$

where:

$$y_{t-1} = \sum_{n=1}^{N} \left(\mathbf{C}_{t-2}^{(n)}\mathbf{x}_{t-2}^{(n)}\right)' \mathbf{v}_{t-1}^{(n)} + \mathbf{f}(t-1)'\mathbf{w}_{t-1}. \tag{17}$$

The superscript $(n = 1, ..., N)$ identifies the industry to which vectors and matrices refer.

The problem of general equilibrium in the dynamic framework set out above is to determine non-negative values of $\mathbf{x}_t^{(n)}$, $\mathbf{p}_t$, $\mathbf{w}_t$, $\mathbf{v}_t^{(n)}$, $\phi_t^{(n)}$ and $\psi_t^{(n)}$ for each period t, so that

$$\begin{cases} \sum_{n=1}^{N} \mathbf{S}_t^{(n)}\mathbf{x}_t^{(n)} \leqq \mathbf{f}(t) \\ -\sum_{n=1}^{N} \mathbf{Q}_t^{(n)}\mathbf{x}_t^{(n)} \leqq -\mathbf{d}(y_{t-1}) \end{cases} \tag{18}$$

$$\begin{cases} \mathbf{A}_t^{(n)}\mathbf{x}_t^{(n)} \leqq \mathbf{C}_{t-1}^{(n)}\mathbf{x}_{t-1}^{(n)} \\ \mathbf{l}_t^{(n)}\mathbf{x}_t^{(n)} \leqq \mathbf{u}^{(n)}(\mathbf{x}_{t-1}^{(n)}) \\ -\mathbf{I}_t^{(n)}\mathbf{x}_t^{(n)} \leqq -\mathbf{l}^{(n)}(\mathbf{x}_{t-1}^{(n)}) \end{cases} \tag{19}$$

$$\mathbf{S}_t'^{(n)}\mathbf{w}_t - \mathbf{Q}_t'^{(n)}\mathbf{p}_t + \mathbf{A}_t'^{(n)}\mathbf{v}_t^{(n)} + \mathbf{I}_t'^{(n)}[\phi_t^{(n)} - \psi_t^{(n)}] \geqq \mathbf{C}_t'^{(n)}\mathbf{v}_{t-1}^{(n)}. \tag{20}$$

$$\sum_{n=1}^{N} \left[\mathbf{v}_t'^{(n)}\mathbf{C}_t^{(n)}\right]\mathbf{x}_t^{(n)} = \mathbf{f}(t)'\mathbf{w}_t - \mathbf{d}(y_{t-1})'\mathbf{p}_t +$$

$$+ \sum_{n=1}^{N} \left[\mathbf{C}_{t-1}^{(n)}\mathbf{x}_{t-1}^{(n)}\right]'\mathbf{v}_t^{(n)} + \mathbf{u}^{(n)}(\mathbf{x}_{t-1}^{(n)})'\phi_t^{(n)} - \mathbf{l}^{(n)}(\mathbf{x}_{t-1}^{(n)})'\psi_t^{(n)}. \tag{21}$$

Equations (18) are the conditions that the supplies of products and services must be at least equal to demands. Equations (19) are the N industries' capital and flexibility constraints examined in the last paragraph. Equations (20) are the conditions that the price of each product must not exceed the cost of production, which includes the remuneration of capital and of the entrepreneurial function. Equation (21), finally, is the condition that the value of all capital goods and inventories produced in each period must be equal to personal saving—i.e. distributed income minus current consumers' expenditure—plus non-distributed profits.

At this point it is clear that the general equilibrium model hides two linear programming problems: one is the maximisation of investment (the L.H.S. of (21)) subject to the constraints (18) and (19) and the other is the minimisation of saving (the R.H.S. of (21)) subject to the constraints (20), which constitutes the "dual" of the first problem. By the "duality theorem" of Linear Programming [6] the maximum value of the "primal" objective-function is equal to the minimum value of the "dual" objective-function and therefore the values of

$$ x_t^{(n)} \geqq 0, \quad p_t \geqq 0, \quad w_t \geqq 0, \quad v_t^{(n)} \geqq 0, \quad \phi_t^{(n)} \geqq 0, \quad \psi \geqq 0, $$

which solve these dual problems are also the solution of the general equilibrium system[16] (see Table 2).

Thus, the customary Investment = Saving equilibrium condition assumes here the meaning of an optimality condition, whereby the maximum level of Investment (and therefore of future consumption) is achieved with the minimum of Saving (and therefore with the minimum sacrifice of present consumption).

From the duality theorem of Linear Programming [6], we also know that:

(i) If one of the "primal" constraints (18)–(19) is satisfied as an inequality, the price of the corresponding commodity is zero; this eventuality obviously does not occur with storable products.

(ii) If one of the dual constraints (20) is satisfied as an inequality the corresponding process is not activated; this means that a process is not activated if it gives a negative net revenue. The fact that a loss, ψ_j^t, is included in the computation of the net revenue must be interpreted in the sense that the entrepreneurs expect it to be zero and, if this turns out not to be so, the difference between actual and expected costs is charged to the entrepreneur.

We are thus assuming that all prices are perfectly flexible and can even drop to zero. However, in an economy where all the original means of production have been appropriated the assumption clashes

---

[16] This result is perfectly analogous to the one Dorfman, Samuelson and Solow [4] arrived at with Walras' model of general equilibrium without capital formation [10] in the modified form suggested by Zeuthen. What is maximised, there, is the value of the output of consumer goods, and what is minimised is the sum of factor returns.

G

with reality: we often see land not being used because the owner is waiting for a higher price and the phenomenon of "voluntary" unemployment caused by the downward rigidity of the wage rate has long been appreciated. Rigidities in the prices of products also occur because of practices restricting competition or because of the well known mechanisms of monopolistic competition.

If we want the model to reflect the imperfect flexibility of prices, two new sets of "dual" constraints must be introduced setting a *lower limit to the prices of products and services* in each period. Supposing, for simplicity's sake, that this limit is equal to the price levels of the preceding period, we can write:

$$\left.\begin{array}{c} \mathbf{w}_t \geqq \mathbf{w}_{t-1} \\ \mathbf{p}_t \geqq \mathbf{p}_{t-1} \end{array}\right\} \tag{22}$$

Then, two new vectors of "primal" variables, $\mathbf{x}_t^{(N+1)}$ and $\mathbf{x}_t^{(N+2)}$ — that can be interpreted as "voluntary" unemployment of resources

Table 2. Programming Tableau for a General Equilibrium Problem (period t)

Primal Variables →	$\mathbf{x}_t^{(1)}$ .... $\mathbf{x}_t^{(N)}$	Primal Constraints ↓
$\mathbf{w}_t$	$\mathbf{S}_t^{(1)}$.....................................$\mathbf{S}_t^{(N)}$	$\mathbf{f}(t)$
$\mathbf{p}_t$	$-\mathbf{Q}_t^{(1)}$ .... $-\mathbf{Q}_t^{(N)}$	$-\mathbf{d}(\mathbf{y}_{t-1})$
$\mathbf{v}_t^{(1)}$ ⋮ $\mathbf{v}_t^{(N)}$	$\mathbf{A}_t^{(1)}$ ‥‥‥‥‥‥‥‥‥‥‥‥‥‥ $\mathbf{A}_t^{(N)}$	$\mathbf{C}_{t-1}^{(1)} \mathbf{x}_{t-1}^{(1)}$ ⋮ $\mathbf{C}_{t-1}^{(N)} \mathbf{x}_{t-1}^{(N)}$
$\varphi_t^{(1)}$ ⋮ $\varphi_{(N)}^{(N)}$	$\mathbf{I}_t^{(1)}$ ‥‥‥‥‥‥‥‥‥‥ $\mathbf{I}_t^{(N)}$	$\mathbf{u}^{(1)}(\mathbf{x}_{t-1}^{(1)})$ ⋮ $\mathbf{u}^{(N)}(\mathbf{x}_{t-1}^{(N)})$
$\psi_t^{(1)}$ ⋮ ψ_t	$-\mathbf{I}_t^{(1)}$ ‥‥‥‥‥‥‥‥‥ $-\mathbf{I}_t^{(N)}$	$-\mathbf{l}^{(1)}(\mathbf{x}_{t-1}^{(1)})$ ⋮ $-\mathbf{l}^{(N)}(\mathbf{x}_{t-1}^{(N)})$
↑ Dual Variables	$\mathbf{C}_t^{(1)}\mathbf{v}_{t-1}^{(1)}$ .... $\mathbf{C}_t^{(N)}\mathbf{v}_{t-1}^{(N)}$	Dual Constraints ←

and monopolistic restriction of output, respectively—must be introduced in the "primal" constraints. Conditions (18) become:

$$\begin{cases} \sum_{n=1}^{N} S_t^{(n)} x_t^{(n)} + I_t^{(N+1)} x_t^{(N+1)} \leqq f(t) \\[2mm] - \sum_{n=1}^{N} Q_t^{(n)} x_t^{(n)} - I_t^{(N+2)} x_t^{(N+2)} \leqq -d(y_{t-1}) \end{cases} \tag{18'}$$

where $I_t^{(N+1)}$ and $I_t^{(N+2)}$ are an $(H \times H)$ and an $(I \times I)$ identity matrix, respectively (see Table 3). The optimality condition (21) becomes

$$\sum_{n=1}^{N} \left[v_{t-1}^{'(n)} C_t^{(n)} \right] x_t^{(n)} + w_{t-1}' x_t^{(N+1)} + p_{t-1}' x_t^{(N+2)} =$$

$$= f(t)' w_t - d(y_{t-1})' p_t + \sum_{n=1}^{N} \left[C_{t-1}^{(n)} x_{t-1}^{(n)} \right]' v_t^{(n)} +$$

$$+ u^{(n)}(x_{t-1}^{(n)})' \phi_t^{(n)} - l^{(n)}(x_{t-1}^{(n)})' \psi_t^{(n)}. \tag{21'}$$

We have now two alternative formulations of a complete model of economic growth. Given initial information about outputs, prices and capital stocks, equations (18), (19), (20) and (21), or (18'), (19'), (20), (22) and (21')—together with the definitory equation (17)—determine outputs, consumption and prices for all subsequent periods. The only external information needed in each period is the new processes that have to be added to the technology matrices: the flow of innovations that represent the creative moment of technical progress, cannot be "explained" by a mathematical model in any credible way, but the diffusion of innovations is endogenously regulated by the mechanisms of this model. As to the sort of time path that income, outputs and prices are likely to follow, very little can be said without specific assumptions about the form of $f(t)$, $d(y_t)$, $u^{(n)}(x_t^{(n)})$ and $l^{(n)}(x_t^{(n)})$. These dynamic aspects can only be discussed in connection with an empirical application of the model.

The linear programming formulation of this model makes it particularly suited for empirical applications:

(a) *Medium-term forecasts.* For periods of up to five or six years it can be assumed that the list of commodities and techniques available to industry is not subject to substantial alterations. Then, if the technology of a base year is known and the technical coefficients have been estimated statistically, the model can be used to forecast the diffusion or contraction of the existing commodities and techniques, and the effects of such changes on outputs and prices.

(b) *Long-term forecasts.* In the longer run, completely new commodities and techniques will make their appearance. To the extent that one can make reasonable guesses about the technical coefficients and the date of introduction of new processes, the model can be used to make conditional forecasts about the rate of adoption of these new processes and about their impact on outputs and prices.

(c) *Other possible uses* of the model are examined in the next section.

Table 3. *Programming Tableau for a General Equilibrium Problem with Prices Rigid Downwards (period t).*

Primal Variables $\rightarrow$	$x_t^{(1)}\ldots\ldots\ldots\ldots x_t^{(N)}$	$x_t^{(N+1)}$	$x_t^{(N+2)}$	Primal Constraints $\downarrow$
w_t	$S_t^{(1)}\ldots\ldots\ldots\ldots S_t^{(N)}$	$I_t^{(N+1)}$		$f(t)$
p_t	$-Q_t^{(1)}\ldots\ldots\ldots\ldots -Q_t^{(N)}$		$-I_t^{(N+2)}$	$-d(y_{t-1})$
$v_t^{(1)}$ $\vdots$ $v_t^{(N)}$	$A_t^{(1)}$ $\quad A_t^{(N)}$			$C_{t-1}^{(1)} x_{t-1}^{(1)}$ $\vdots$ $C_{t-1}^{(N)} x_{t-1}^{(N)}$
$\varphi_t^{(1)}$ $\vdots$ $\varphi_t^{(N)}$	$I_t^{(1)}$ $\quad I_t^{(N)}$			$u_t^{(1)}(x_{t-1}^{(1)})$ $\vdots$ $u_t^{(N)}(x_{t-1}^{(1)})$
$\psi_t^{(1)}$ $\vdots$ $\psi_t^{(N)}$	$-I_t^{(1)}$ $\quad -I_t^{(N)}$			$-l_t^{(1)}(x_{t-1}^{(1)})$ $\vdots$ $-l_t^{(1)}(x_{t-1}^{(N)})$
$\uparrow$ Dual Variables	$C_t^{(1)}v_{t-1}^{(1)}\ldots\ldots C_t^{(N)}v_{t-1}^{(N)}$	w_{t-1}	p_{t-1}	Dual constraints $\leftarrow$

IV. THE ROLE OF GOVERNMENT AND CONCLUDING REMARKS

So far, the government has been left out of the picture, but its introduction does not alter the basic structure of the model.

If the government confines itself to using the revenue of taxation to provide public services for the community, we only need to subtract the government's demand of factor services from f_t, and to add the government's demand of industrial products to d_t. In this case y_t is redefined as disposable income, and the model can be used to forecast the effects of alternative fiscal policies.

If the government goes to the extent of deciding the level and composition of personal consumption, then d_t becomes a vector of exogenously determined target-variables and equation (17) is eliminated from the model. In this case, assuming that the firms—whether private or public owned—are left to operate on a profit basis, p_t becomes a vector of control-variables: p_t^i are prices that have to be paid, in one way or another, to the firms if the planned levels of consumption are to be fulfilled.

But the most important target-variable, nowadays, seems to be the rate of economic growth. In this model the forces that determine the pace of the economy—given the individuals' attitude towards consumption—appear to be technical progress and the availability of original factors of production. As the most scarce of all original factors of production, in an industrialised economy, is labour—which is not a homogeneous commodity but a collection of personal capacities differentiated by skill—the model could be used to detect future manpower bottlenecks and devise appropriate educational (and maybe also immigration) policies.

As to technical progress, the flow of inventions—which is what provides the raw material for innovations—is not "explained" by the model and could be taken as a control-variable. The government, in fact, finances in every country a large share of the research effort: by directing the allocation of funds among the various research projects, the output of inventions and technical developments can be controlled to a certain extent. The model could then be used to forecast the effects of a major technical development and assess the benefit that would derive from the allocation of funds to that research project.[17]

REFERENCES

[1] CIGNO, A., *Un modello di programmazione territoriale*, Centro di Specializzazione e Ricerche. Portici, 1964.

[2] DAY, R. H., *Recursive Programming and Production Response*. North-Holland Publishing Co., Amsterdam, 1963.

[17] A considerable amount of research on these issues of education and science planning has been carried out by the O.E.C.D. [5] [8].

[3] DAY, R. H., "On aggregating Linear Programming Models of Production", *Journal of Farm Economics*, November 1963.

[4] DORFMAN, R., SAMUELSON, P., and SOLOW, R., *Linear Programming and Economic Analysis*. McGraw-Hill, New York, 1958.

[5] FREEMAN, C., POIGNANT, R., and SVENNILSON, I., *Science, Economic Growth and Government Policy*. O.E.C.D., Paris, 1963.

[6] GALE, D., KUHN, H. W. and TUCKER, A. W., "Linear Programming and the Theory of Games" in T. C. Koopmans (ed.) *Activity Analysis of Production and Allocation*. J. Wiley & Sons, New York, 1951.

[7] HENDERSON, J. M., "The Utilisation of Agricultural Land, a Theoretical and Empirical Inquiry", *Review of Economics and Statistics*, August 1959.

[8] PARNES, H. S., (ed.) *Planning Education for Economic and Social Development*. O.E.C.D., Paris, 1963.

[9] SCHUMPETER, J. A., *The Theory of Economic Development* (transl. by R. Opie). Oxford University Press, New York, 1961.

[10] WALRAS, L., *Elements of Pure Economics* (transl. by W. Jaffe). Allen & Unwin, London, 1954.

SESSION III: DISCUSSION OF MR. CIGNO'S PAPER

Chairman: DR. IAN STEEDMAN (MANCHESTER)

MR. WIGLEY (Cambridge)

I have two points which refer to your paper, page 63. The first is a minor point of notation which, I think, would help our understanding. I suggest the replacement of your equation

$$v_k^{t+1} = v_k^{t-1} \text{ by } v_k^{t+1} = v_l^{t-1}.$$

It is, for example, the value of the eleven-year-old plant at the beginning of the period which is used as the expected value of ten-year-old plant now at the end of the period.

We have already had a suggestion for using a discounting term in this same equation. I would like to argue that that may well be an improvement; not, I think, in the financial sense that £100 next period has the present value of £100/(1 + r) now, but from the rather different point of view that the ten-year-old plant (let us assume for the moment it cannot be modified in any way) is likely to fall in value from the beginning of the period to the end of the period from at least two points of view: the first is that technical progress may increase efficiency of plants of that type and hence its value drops from that point of view (the production function for new plant moving towards the origin) and secondly a new plant may take advantage of changing relative factor prices (a movement round the production function). For one or other of these reasons the value of an existing plant is likely to fall over time. It may be worth saying that there must be some special assumption in this model of lack of perfect competition in that the prices of used machines differ from their imputed valuation—so that you must be thinking of a wide range of situations of firms.

MR. CIGNO (Birmingham)

I do not agree that a discounting term should be introduced to account for obsolescence. The model already has a built-in mechanism which reduces the imputed value of a machine (even to zero) when a more efficient one appears on the market.

As to the last point, competition is compatible—in my model—with the fact that the market values of used machines can differ from their imputed values, because these imputed values—which the entrepreneur uses to plan his firm at the beginning of a period—are not the current ones, yet unknown, but those of the last period, which are the result of market and technological conditions differing from the current ones. However, it is true that I am thinking of a fairly wide range of market situations: I only assume that each "entrepreneur" considers himself as a price-taker—I did not say that there is perfect competition.

MR. WIGLEY

No, I understand that. I just made a suggestion that perhaps might make the model slightly more realistic.

I would like to come to a page, 77 of your paper where you comment on the way in which the diffusion of innovation is endogenously regulated by the mechanisms of the model. To give some concrete basis for this, I suggest, as an example, the use of prefabricated structures in the construction industry. Perhaps members of the audience have some ideas on this possibility. How would you suggest estimating the flexibility constraint associated with either the supply of prefabricated buildings on the one hand, or the unwillingness of constructors to take up the supply of prefabricated buildings on the other? I think this is a question which may well fit into the framework which you have presented, and I know that there is a considerable amount of detailed information available of the kind required for your coefficient matrices. The difficulty I have is in trying to understand just how one could set about estimating your flexibility constraints.

MR. CIGNO

The suggestions made are very useful and pertinent; the only question here is how to estimate these flexibility constraints. I think that there are basically two ways of estimating them. One is to run a sample survey of firms and simply ask the "entrepreneurs" how they would react if a supposedly better technique became available. Or we can estimate the flexibility constraints through time series; this, of course, is problematic because it is very difficult to obtain time series of the diffusion of individual techniques. In the course of an empirical application I could only get time series on the diffusion of commodities but not of techniques, so the flexibility constraints turned out to be less binding than I had intended.

MR. BARKER (Cambridge)

I was very interested in the end of your paper where you say that you are doing some work using the model; I would like to ask you how the solution started, because I know you start with imputed values for capital; these are calculated from these previous years' imputed values—so this is clearly a problem you don't explain. The second question is: once you have forecast outputs and prices using the model, with the assumptions built in, I have no doubt that this will be different from actual prices and actual outputs in a particular industry. Do you attempt to reconcile these?

MR. CIGNO

Would you mind repeating this?

MR. BARKER

Well, using your model to get out outputs and prices in an industry, or outputs anyway, I have no doubt that these would be different from the outputs that actually pertained in the past.

MR. CIGNO

Well, one would of course like the model's results to be as near as possible to the actual results.

MR. BARKER

Well, this is the test of the model, clearly; no doubt there will be differences, and I've no doubt that if you put different assumptions in, there will be differences again, and I wondered if you were relating the actual outputs and the outputs given by the model in any way; and if there was any method that you were using to change your assumptions—to change, for example, the estimates of some of your constraints.

MR. CIGNO

No. I have not got to that stage; I have simply compared the results obtained with the application of this model with the actual results, but I haven't got as far as finding a method of correcting the assumptions to take into consideration the departure from actual results.

But let us go back to the first question, which I think is a very practical question: how do we start the model off? To solve the model in the first place, say for period (t), you must know the solution of period $(t-1)$; that is, we must know the process levels and the imputed values of period $(t-1)$. These can be estimated from a sample survey of firms: you record the process levels for period $(t-1)$ of the firms in the sample and you ask their accountants which values they imputed to the stocks available in period $(t-1)$.

MR. BARKER

I was wondering if anyone from industry would care to comment on that.

MR. CIGNO

I would very much like to have a further comment from industry. I should add that my empirical application was in the field of agriculture and we actually asked farmers how much they evaluated their machines and their livestock, and we used this information to start off the model.

MR. BARKER

In which case I'd like to ask if the computed prices changed very much between the first and second periods.

MR. CIGNO

Not very much, no. Actually, in this particular case, they decreased in each period, and that was due to the fact that the market was falling. But it is very difficult to say *a priori* what is going to happen; it depends on the situation.

QUESTION

Can I ask about a point of fact? I am worried by this assumption where you begin with a stationary state; the assumption is that you only replace machines because of innovation.

MR. CIGNO

No. The assumption is that a machine is disposed of if its imputed value is less than the market value, and a machine is purchased if its market price is less than the imputed value of machines of the same value and age already available (this value can only be guessed at in the case of an innovation). Replacement, therefore, is not necessarily caused by an innovation. There isn't any innovation, by definition, in a stationary state: you just replace the machines that are wearing out (as long as their imputed values exceed the market values).

QUESTION

You do have to replace machines that are wearing out?

MR. CIGNO

Yes, but not because of obsolescence; there is no obsolescence in this case. But if there is no replacement you get contraction instead of a stationary state.

QUESTION

So there is some assumption about the life of a machine?

MR. CIGNO

Yes, the physical life is assumed to be known; what is not known is the economic life of a machine; that is where my model comes in.

DR. STEEDMAN (Manchester)

You did agree, with Mr. Wigley, that you weren't restricting yourself to a perfect competition model, I think. Now it follows from this that unless the number of firms which are playing a leading role is very small relative to the whole of the industry, the question of forecasting the future price becomes rather a difficult concept—this is simply because the future price is going to depend on what these firms themselves are doing, and firms who *are* innovating, making changes, and so on, presumably don't know what each of the other innovating firms is doing, they only know what the non-improving firms are doing, and therefore I would like a rather more precise definition of what forecasting the future price really means.

MR. CIGNO

Yes, I think I should explain this. I am not assuming that in each industry there is one particular firm which acts always as leader, and that this is always the same one. I am assuming that in each period there is (or there might be) one firm which is acting as leader: that there is an entrepreneur lucky or clever enough to forecast, in time, a change in market conditions or to see that a new technology is profitable. In the next period this firm could behave as a "backward" firm, and another firm could act as leader.

DR. STEEDMAN

So the assumption is that the innovator is always small, relative to the industry?

MR. CIGNO

Yes, this is the assumption.

MR. ADELSON (University of Lancaster)

You were asking a few moments ago for an industrialist to comment on the problem of determining imputed values by some survey; and I held back in the hope that some real industrialist would come forward. I can only speak as an ex-industrialist, and in my experience with businessmen I have met, most of them would not know what you meant by the imputed value of a piece of capital equipment; this is not a fact that is normally available to most businessmen; neither is another variable in your model, that is, the current market value of used capital equipment in their possession: in fact the only value you are likely to get is the book value—which, as you know, is pretty arbitrary value.

MR. CIGNO

Well, I agree about the first point—their imputed value is the book value but I don't understand your point about used machines. The assumption I make is that there is some firm in each industry who guesses correctly what the prices of used machines will be in the market. Whenever making a plan everyone makes guesses, some people make correct guesses and some do not make correct guesses or simply (as I assumed) expect the prices to be much the same as they were in the last period. Have I understood your question?

MR. ADELSON

Is there a market for used machines?

MR. CIGNO

In my experience there is, at least for many sorts of machines. If a second-hand machine has no market its price is zero: this does not upset my construction.

QUESTION

Some less specific machines may have a market?

MR. CIGNO

What do you mean by specific machines?

QUESTION

Chemical plant, for example perhaps doesn't have a market, whereas processing machinery definitely does.

MR. CIGNO

Well, there are chemical firms that sell a whole plant, aren't there?

QUESTION

For what?

MR. CIGNO

For a price, equal to the value of the whole plant or even of the whole firm, if this is taken over by another firm.

QUESTION

Even if it's only scrap?

MR. CIGNO

Well, if it's just scrap, then it is sold as scrap, and there is a market for scrap. But if this plant is still operating, then it happens occasionally that a firm buys a whole plant from another firm.

MR. ADELSON

I think I didn't make my point terribly well. As I see it what you are suggesting here is that at the beginning of each period an entrepreneur will examine the current market price of his machinery and will decide whether to sell, or whether to continue to produce with it. Now what I'm suggesting is that this is not the way it works in practice; what will happen in practice? The first decision is "shall I continue to use this?" The only time when you consider selling it is when you have already decided that you are going to innovate (put in some new machinery that will take its place).

MR. CIGNO

You mean the price of used machines doesn't come into it?

MR. ADELSON

You decide to sell it, and then simply get the best price you can; you don't examine it to see whether the market price is such that it would be best to sell it.

MR. CIGNO

So the only reason for getting rid of a machine is that it has become obsolete—not that the market price of this used machine is greater than the internal value of that machine? My assumption is that there is at least one or a few firms in the industry which do this calculation, perhaps only unconsciously, while the others simply repeat what they did in the last period. Is that acceptable or is it completely unrealistic to assume that at least a few take into full account the market prices and the internal values of the machines?

MR. ADELSON

I think you have answered my question.

DR. STEEDMAN

Might it not be, in terms of examining the real world, that it becomes more and more true that there is a firm doing this sort of rational calculation, as, by the same process, it becomes less and less true that this firm is a small part of the whole industry? If this is the case then you are caught in something of a contradiction, I think.

MR. B. C. BROWN (D.E.A.)

I should like, if I may, to take a more general line and ask whether Mr. Cigno has considered some possible implications of his model for the relation between the rate of innovation and the level of profits, and, on the other hand, the rate of adaptation (the speed at which people adapt to new conditions) and the level of profits. On the face of it, it might seem that the higher the general rate of innovation the higher the level of profits, but the faster the rate of adaptation the lower the level of profits. Is this a proper, reasonable consequence to draw from the model?

MR. CIGNO

The faster the diffusion of innovations the quicker the reduction in unit profits; but total profits might increase, because more and more firms are using the new process, and therefore making profits.

MR. LOWE (Birmingham) asked Mr. Cigno to explain the optimality of the solution of his entire model.

MR. CIGNO

I don't want an optimal *industry* solution; I want a solution that is sub-optimal; so to prevent the model from reaching the optimal solution I introduce these flexibility constraints. The solution of the model is obviously "optimal" from a mathematical point of view, but it is different from the solution that the model would have if those flexibility constraints were not there. So the solution of the aggregate model is different from the sum of the optimal solutions of the individual firms. And it should be like that, because it is a mix of optimal solutions of innovating firms and of non-optimal solutions of the other firms—solutions based on conditions that now belong to the past.

DR. STEEDMAN

I am sure you would like me to thank our speaker for presenting a stimulating paper. It has been made clear by the questions raised that while some of us are more sceptical and some more optimistic about the feasibility of applying this model, we all look forward to Mr. Cigno's promised empirical results.

SESSION IV

Production Models and Time Trends of Input–Output Coefficients

by

K. J. WIGLEY

Department of Applied Economics and
Fellow of Corpus Christi College, Cambridge

I. INTRODUCTION

This paper describes two pieces of econometric research forming part of the Cambridge Growth Project.[1] Their common theme is an analysis of the projection of input–output matrices through time. Their common purpose is twofold; firstly to assist in the development of the computable model for the United Kingdom as described in volumes 1 to 7 of *A Programme for Growth* [1], and secondly to develop the model in such a way that it will provide a framework for the discussion of fuel policy questions relevant to this country over the next ten years.

The first part of the paper considers alternative methods of projecting into the future the input–output coefficients for fuels into an aggregate industry group called "Other Industry". This group is one of the principal sectors in the classification of fuel users given in the Ministry of Power Statistical Digest [13]; it represents manufacturing industry apart from iron and steel, petroleum refining, coke and manufactured fuel and includes mining and quarrying (other than coal mining), construction and water. Results for the model finally proposed in this first part of the paper are presented in a nineteen-industry breakdown in volume 8 of the series *A Programme for Growth*, now at the press [4].

The second part of the paper attempts to integrate an input–output table into a vintage theory of production. Again, for brevity, results are presented for an aggregate sector of Manufacturing excluding petroleum refining and the production of coke and manufactured fuel. However, the model appears to be a robust one in that it produces sensible results for other large sectors such as Agriculture,

[1] This project is currently supported by the Social Science Research Council within the Department of Applied Economics, University of Cambridge.

Transport and the combined group Distribution and Services, and for subsectors of manufacturing.

The two models described in this paper have been constructed in such a way that they will form two building blocks in a sequential, long-run dynamic model for the United Kingdom.

II. SECTION 1

1. *Alternative Models for the Projection of Fuel Input Coefficients into Non-fuel Industries*

The usual form for the element of an input–output matrix in row i and column j is the input of commodity i required to produce a unit of output of commodity j, where quantities of both input and output are valued at the prices of a base period. A slightly different form expresses the input of commodity i required to produce a unit of output by industry j, where again the values of a base period are used. The difference arises because industries frequently produce commodities other than their own principal product; these differences are described in [2]. The input coefficients considered in this section are in the form of therms supplied per unit of constant (1960) price industrial output, i.e. the physical consumption of fuels measured in tons or megawatt hours converted into therms using a conversion factor constant for all years and divided by the gross output of the industry revalued at 1960 prices. If these coefficients are multiplied by the price per therm in the base year, the more familiar input–output coefficient is obtained. It is clear that these are average coefficients and the procedure adopted has been to analyse their movements through time in order to project average coefficients for future years. It is worth noting in passing that an interpretation of average coefficients as marginal ones for the investigation of deviations around a long run path necessitates a very strong assuption of proportionality. The conversion into therms merely acts as a scaling factor for purposes of comparison. The emphasis on "therms supplied" implies that no account is taken at the data-preparation stage of the varying efficiencies with which the different fuels are used; this is a problem for the model used to explain fuel substitution.

The fuel consumption data in physical units and the thermal conversion factors are taken from the Ministry of Power Statistical Digest [13]. These fuel inputs exclude use as raw material and include uses for light, heat and power other than for transport. The gross outputs of the component industries making up the sector "Other Industry" have been calculated within the growth project. Individual elements of the Index of Industrial Production have been re-weighted using gross output rather than net output weights and combined together to give a single index which has then been multi-plied by the gross output of the industry in 1960. Fuel prices are not readily available in published form and have been taken from a variety of sources. Tabulations of the data used together with detailed references on sources are given in [4].

The data points in Figure 1 illustrate how the five fuel input coefficients have moved over the period 1951–1964.

Coal, coke and oil supply the bulk fuels to industry. Electricity and gas, in general, provide special needs, although the increasing use of gas to provide bulk fuel needs is a coming possibility as explained later in the section. Gas and electricity are used for heating where particularly clean conditions are required or where control-

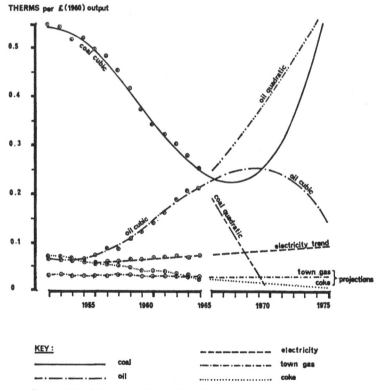

Figure 1. Fuel Input Coefficients into "Other Industry". Trend Analysis

H

lability is of special importance. The increased use of electricity for improved lighting, instrumentation and controls is well known and indicates that the growth of this fuel as an input is likely to follow a law basically separate from that of the bulk fuels.

The principal change observed over the data years in Figure 1 is a substitution of oil for coal and coke, in the sense that in the later years oil is used proportionally more than the other fuels for the general purpose of providing useful energy. The small-scale variation about the trend line may be caused by a number of factors. Errors of measurement in the data certainly exist, less fuel for heating will be required in a relatively hot year, and short period supply difficulties may occur, for instance for oil in 1957, the year in which the effect of Suez was felt. The proportional relationship between inputs and outputs is not strictly valid, so that some variation from the trend will be expected over the trade cycle. Finally the industry is made up of many individual trades having differing fuel input character-istics. Product mix changes, year by year, will add to the scatter of the points. Nevertheless, the broad picture is clear enough.

The solid lines fitted to the coal and oil data points are cubic in time and linear in deviation of average annual temperature from a long-run thirty-year average temperature. It is clear that these time trends fit the data very well. Projections of these time trends up to 1975 (assuming no deviation of average annual temperature from the long-run average) yield highly implausible results as rapid changes in the direction of past movements in the coefficients occur. Quadratic trends fit the data almost as well and, as the dashed lines indicate, provide equally implausible future movements of the coal and oil coefficients in exactly the opposite direction to the cubic projections. Clearly no one would suggest employing time projection methods such as these, but they do illustrate the dangers of using equally arbitrary but perhaps more plausible curves based on logistic or exponential functions of time.

The inevitable conclusion follows that a closer study must be made of the processes leading to fuel substitution if less arbitrary projec-tions of industrial fuel consumption are to be made.

Three important questions arise in connection with Figure 1:

(i) Why is oil chosen as a fuel rather than coal or coke?
(ii) What controls the rate at which the two fuels interchange?
(iii) How can one explain the fact that roughly one therm of oil exchanges for two therms of coal, at the margin?

Over the period considered prices have moved in favour of oil and against coal, apart from brief increases in freight rates in the period of the Korean War and of Suez, and the imposition of the U.K. fuel-oil tax in 1961. Other things being equal a changeover to the cheaper fuel is to be expected. However, such a price movement is not a necessary condition for a movement from one fuel to another.

An increase in boiler or furnace efficiency for oil relative to coal fuels might have been sufficient to cause the switch. The National Industrial Fuel Efficiency Service reported in 1957 [7] that oil-fired boilers were, on the average, 5 per cent more efficient than coal-fired ones. This result was based on a 3-year study covering some 600 boiler plants over the period 1954–1957. Later reports continue to emphasise that large increases in thermal efficiency can be, and are, obtained on existing boilers, but there is no indication of a large efficiency increase in oil-fired relative to coal-fired appliances.

A reduction in the capital cost of oil-fired boilers or a reduction in storage or handling costs (relative to the corresponding costs for coal) might also motivate a move from one fuel to another. No doubt effects other than price movements of the fuels themselves have played their part in inducing fuel substitution and will continue to do so. Lack of data on these "non-price" effects coupled with a desire for as simple an explanation as possible has meant that, in the final model proposed, movements in relative price have been relied upon to explain the relative movement between fuels. It must be emphasised that this is an assumption of the model and not a deduction from it.

It may be asked whether the non-use of coal and the increased use of oil occurs as a direct result of the scrapping of old and the building of new plant or whether it may occur as an independent process. The question is whether the fuel-consumption pattern is embodied permanently in plant as a technical characteristic or whether it may change as a disembodied phenomenon. It is easy to think of individual cases where either process may occur but it is the aggregate process which is important for projection purposes.

It is possible to work through the consequences of making alternative assumptions concerning the processes controlling the rate at which the two fuels interchange.

An extreme assumption associates the non-use of coal with the scrapping of productive plant in the sector and the increase in oil use with new capacity. Unfortunately no information is available on the proportion of output capacity scrapped in any period, only the net increase in output between any two years may be calculated by difference. In order to proceed, further assumptions are required. Suppose that output on new plant brought into use in year t is related to a three year moving average $\bar{I}_t$ of gross investment centred on year $t-1$ by a constant incremental capital-output ratio k, where both output and investment are measured at constant prices. The output of new capacity has to provide the net increase in output between the years t and $(t+1)$, and the capacity scrapped,

$$\frac{\bar{I}_t}{k} = \Delta g_t + R_t \tag{1}$$

where Δ is the forward difference operator, g_t represents the gross output of the industry (at constant prices) in year t, R_t represents the output of capacity in use in year t but not in use in year $t+1$ (in constant prices), $\bar{I}_t = \frac{1}{3}(I_{t-2}+I_{t-1}+I_t)$.

According to our extreme assumptions we shall expect the non-use of coal to be related to scrapping as

$$\Delta(q_1)_t = -\alpha_1 R_t - \eta_1 \Delta\theta_t \tag{2}$$

and the increased use of oil to be related to new plant capacity as

$$\Delta(q_2)_t = \frac{\alpha_2}{k}\bar{I}_t - \eta_2 \Delta\theta_t \tag{3}$$

In equations (2) and (3) the following notation has been used:

q_1 therms of coal consumed by "Other Industry"
q_2 therms of oil consumed by "Other Industry"
$\Delta\theta_t$ the increase in average annual temperature between year t and year $t+1$
$\alpha_1, \alpha_2, \eta_1, \eta_2$ are positive constants.

The temperature coefficient is expected to be negative as an increase in temperature will involve a reduction in fuel requirement.

Equation (1) may be used to substitute for R_t in (2),

$$\Delta(q_1)_t = -\frac{\alpha_1}{k}\bar{I}_t + \alpha_1 \Delta g_t - \eta_1 \Delta\theta_t \tag{4}$$

Equations (3) and (4) may be tested against actual data using least squares regression. The following fits have been obtained over the period 1951–1964:

$$\Delta(q_1)_t = -0\cdot601\bar{I}_t + 0\cdot373\Delta g_t - 87\cdot7\Delta\theta_t \tag{5}$$
$$(4\cdot4) \qquad (3\cdot1) \qquad (1\cdot5)$$
$$R^2 = 0\cdot53$$

$$\Delta(q_2)_t = 0\cdot444\bar{I}_t - 56\cdot4\Delta\theta_t \tag{6}$$
$$(7\cdot3) \qquad (1\cdot5)$$
$$R^2 = 0\cdot50$$

Values of the t statistic are given in brackets for each parameter estimated. Figures for gross fixed capital formation in this industrial sector at 1960 prices extracted from the Blue Book [10] have been used for I_t, and Δg_t is derived from the gross output figures at 1960 prices mentioned earlier.

Equations (5) and (6) represent relationships between observed time series and cannot, of course, prove a causal process. In particular they do not establish the extreme assumptions which prompted their consideration, especially as they leave a large proportion of variability in the changes of fuel consumption unexplained. At best we may say that if the parameters have reasonable estimated values then equations (5) and (6) do not exclude the possibility that the turnover of productive plant may play an important role as a vehicle for producing substitution between fuels. Indeed it would be surprising if the rejection of this proposition were ever contemplated.

The following estimates for α_1, α_2 and k may be calculated from equations (5) and (6):

$\alpha_1 = 0 \cdot 373$ therms supplied per £(1960) output on scrapped plant
$\alpha_2 = 0 \cdot 276$ therms supplied per £(1960) output on new plant
$k = 0 \cdot 621$ £(1960) investment per £(1960) output on new plant.

Thus

$$\frac{1}{\alpha_2} = 1 \cdot 35 \frac{1}{\alpha_1}$$

or a new oil plant is, on average, 35 per cent more efficient than an old coal plant. This of course relates to more than just thermal efficiency; it provides a measure of gross output at 1960 prices relative to therms supplied and is affected by the use of "colder processes", the proportionately higher production of less fuel intensive products and the substitution of other factors of production for fuel by say lagging hot pipes as a method of conserving heat.

The dimensions of α_1 and α_2 have as denominator the output of the plant for which each fuel is an input. As such they are not directly comparable with the thermal input coefficients plotted in Figure 1 which have total output of the sector as denominator.

The value obtained for the incremental capital-output ratio k will be compared with the value obtained by an alternative method in the second section of this paper.

The figures for η_1 and η_2 represent a saving of approximately 1 to 2 per cent in heat supplied per one degree Fahrenheit rise in temperature for years in the middle of the time range considered.

Thus the estimates obtained for the parameters in equations (3) and (4) have sensible magnitudes and the correct signs. They do not force us to reject the original hypothesis.

An alternative, but equally extreme view, supposes that the fuels may substitute for each other purely in response to movements in their relative price and independently of the rate of investment or scrapping. Following the classical theory of production one might suppose a uniform price for each fuel and the existence of a production function illustrating how a given level of output may be achieved with different combinations of inputs of the two fuels as in Figure 2.

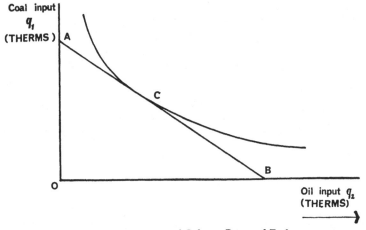

Figure 2. Substitution and Relative Prices of Fuels

The combination of oil and coal for a given relative price is determined at the point at which relative price is equal to the ratio of the marginal physical products of the two fuels. This point is illustrated at C in Figure 2 where the line AB with slope equal to the relative price of coal to oil is tangential to the production function. The existence of a unique point C for each value of relative price is satisfied if the production function is convex to the origin, i.e. on decreasing marginal rates of substitution in both directions.

It is possible to proceed empirically along these lines. The equation for a production function having a constant elasticity of substitution σ between the fuels may be written as

$$g = [\gamma_1(q_1)^{-\beta} + \gamma_2(q_2)^{-\beta}]^{-1/\beta} \tag{7}$$

where γ_1, γ_2 and β are constants. The elasticity of substitution is given as

$$\sigma = \frac{1}{1+\beta} \tag{8}$$

The condition for tangency provides the equation

$$\log\left(\frac{p_1}{p_2}\right)_t = \log\left(\frac{\gamma_1}{\gamma_2}\right) - (1+\beta)\log\left(\frac{q_1}{q_2}\right)_t \tag{9}$$

where p_1 and p_2 are the prices of coal and oil per therm respectively.

Equation (9) has been fitted by least squares regression over the period 1950–1964 as:

$$\log\left(\frac{p_1}{p_2}\right)_t = 0\cdot295 - 0\cdot343\log\left(\frac{q_1}{q_2}\right)_t \tag{10}$$
$$\qquad\quad (4\cdot0)\quad (7\cdot2)$$
$$R^2 = 0\cdot89$$

Values of the t statistic are given in brackets for each parameter estimated.

The constant elasticity of substitution between the two fuels is estimated as $2\cdot9$ yielding a rather flatter curve than the Cobb–Douglas production function. Once again the hypothesis is not rejected by the empirical study.

However, the concept of a highly variable marginal rate of substitution between the two fuels does not correspond with technical reality. The requirement that the production function of Figure 2 be convex to the origin requires that for some installations a small quantity of oil replaces a large amount of coal whereas at other installations the reverse effect holds. Nor too is a uniform price for each fuel known to hold. Fuel oil prices are zoned geographically and vary with size of load. Coal prices are quoted at pit head, transport costs are additional and, in some cases, a coalfield adjustment is included.

An alternative model of fuel substitution for the industrial user may be developed which takes account of these difficulties and to some extent accommodates the need to purchase new equipment when fuel changeover occurs. Asssume, for the sake of simplicity, a rectangular country with the industrial demand for fuel—either oil or coal—spread uniformly over its area. Assume coal to be available at price p_1 along edge AB and oil to be available at price p_2 along edge CD as in Figure 3. Take the dimensions of the country as indicated and assume transport costs of c_1 per unit distance for

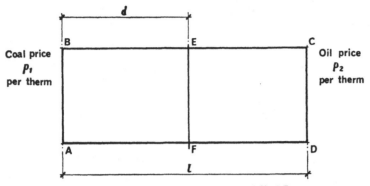

Figure 3. Effect of Location on Delivered Fuel Prices

coal and c_2 for oil. For a range of prices there will exist a boundary such as the line EF at which the delivered price, per therm supplied, of coal and oil are equal, i.e. where

$$p_1 + c_1 d = p_2 + c_2(l - d) \qquad (11)$$

Solving this equation for d

$$d = \frac{p_2 - p_1 + c_2}{c_1 + c_2} \qquad (12)$$

Thus if

$$p_2 + c_2 l \leqq p_1 \qquad (13)$$

oil has the lowest price per therm supplied over the whole area. If

$$p_1 + c_1 l \leqq p_2 \qquad (14)$$

coal will be the cheapest fuel measured in price per therm supplied over the whole area.

Now this picture is a highly idealised one but it does serve to introduce the idea that over a range of relative fuel prices there corresponds an equilibrium level of relative fuel consumption. Of course the dividing line separating coal users from oil users will not be at EF but will be displaced from it taking account of a complex cost preference allowance arising from the total investment calculation. Without specifying the geographical detail it is possible to conceive of boundaries represented by EF in Figure 3, existing in the United Kingdom where coal is available at different pits and oil available at ports or refineries. No doubt the contours would be complicated in practice.

The next step, at least in principle, is to consider the various grades and types of both coal and oil and the multitude of uses to which these fuels are put. Complex as this situation may be to envisage it is still possible to suppose that at specified fuel prices, other things being equal, there will correspond an equilibrium level of relative consumption of fuels. From the point of view of the model, about to be described, other things will not be equal if either the speed of adaptation is variable or if the choice of fuel depends on non-price effects.

The equilibrium level of relative fuel consumption at a given relative fuel price would be achieved in the very long run when all fuel users had been able to adapt to the given level of relative prices. It is likely, however, that changes in relative fuel consumption in the short run will move in the general direction of that equilibrium level. Such a process may be described by the simple adaptive law

$$\Delta\left(\frac{q_1}{q_2}\right)_t = \sigma\left[\left(\frac{q_1}{q_2}\right)^*_{t+1\atop(t)} - \left(\frac{q_1}{q_2}\right)_t\right] \tag{15}$$

Equation (15) states that the increase in relative fuel consumption between year t and year $t+1$ is proportional to an increase between the level existing in year t and a level desired (denoted by the *) in year $t+1$, estimated in year t (denoted by the t in brackets). If we write the desired level of relative consumption in year $t+1$ as a linear function of relative fuel price in year t then

$$\left(\frac{q_1}{q_2}\right)^*_{t+1\atop(t)} = a + b\left(\frac{p_1}{p_2}\right)_t \tag{16}$$

Equation (15) becomes

$$\Delta\left(\frac{q_1}{q_2}\right)_t = \sigma\left[a + b\left(\frac{p_1}{p_2}\right)_t - \left(\frac{q_1}{q_2}\right)_t\right] \tag{17}$$

which may be fitted empirically. Equation (17) may be rewritten as a first order difference equation whose solution expresses the existing level of relative fuel consumption as a function of past prices with geometrically reducing weights. This method has been discussed in the literature by Koyck [6]. A logarithmic version of the adaptive process may be written as

$$\Delta\log\left(\frac{q_1}{q_2}\right)_t = \sigma\left[\log a + b\log\left(\frac{p_1}{p_2}\right)_t - \log\left(\frac{q_1}{q_2}\right)_t\right] \tag{18}$$

The choice between the linear form of equation (17) and the multiplicative form of equation (18) has rested so far on goodness of fit rather than on economic or technical reasoning.

It is possible to combine either equation (17) or equation (18) with a linear substitution schedule which replaces the production function of Figure 2, i.e.

$$g_t = \mu q_{1t} + \lambda q_{2t} \tag{19}$$

where the constant marginal rate of substitution between the two fuels may be written as λ/μ. In practice equation (19) has been extended to include the remaining fuels other than electricity. Some grouping of the time series for the different fuels has been dictated by multicollinearity and by the small number of degrees of freedom available; the particular grouping employed reflects the similarity with which the fuels are used. Accordingly equation (19) may be rewritten as

$$g_t = \mu(q_1 + q_3)_t + \lambda(q_2 + q_4)_t + \eta \theta_t \tag{20}$$

where q_3 refers to the consumption of coke and manufactured solid fuel and q_4 refers to the consumption of gas and creosote pitch mixtures, both inputs measured in therms, θ is the temperature variable introduced earlier and μ, λ and η are positive constants.

Equations (18) and (20) have been fitted by the method of least squares to annual data over the period 1951–1964 for the sector "Other Industry". The time series employed are the result of both long-term and short-term processes. Because the aim has been to capture the long-term process of fuel substitution in the model the identifiable short-term fluctuations have been smoothed by hand. No attempt has so far been made to use more refined methods, for separating out the long and short-term effects in the data. The following equations have been fitted:

$$\Delta \log \left(\frac{q_1}{q_2} \right)_t = \underset{(2 \cdot 1)}{-0 \cdot 051987} \underset{(9 \cdot 7)}{- 0 \cdot 50124} \log \left(\frac{p_1}{p_2} \right)_t \underset{(5 \cdot 5)}{- 0 \cdot 12205} \log \left(\frac{q_1}{q_2} \right)_t$$

$$\tag{21}$$

$$R^2 = 0 \cdot 936$$

$$g_t = \underset{(58 \cdot 8)}{1 \cdot 2258(q_1 + q_3)_t} + \underset{(50 \cdot 5)}{2 \cdot 8125(q_2 + q_4)_t} + \underset{(5 \cdot 3)}{598\theta_t} \tag{22}$$

$$R^2 = 0 \cdot 983$$

Given time series for p_1/p_2, q_3/g, q_4/g, θ and g and an initial value for q_1/q_2 equations (21) and (22) may be used to calculate the values of the input coefficients, q_1/g for coal and q_2/g for oil, year by year. For future years θ is taken as zero, i.e. assuming no deviation from the long run average annual temperature, so that exogenous values for p_1/p_2, q_3/g and q_4/g only are required by this model in order to calculate future values for q_1/g and q_2/g. Thus the model may be used to study the effect on the input coefficients of coal and oil of a change in their relative price as a result, for example, of a variation in the fuel oil tax. Alternatively the effect of different assumptions on the growth in the use of natural gas may be calculated by varying the growth of the input coefficient q_4/g.

The calculated values for the input coefficients of coal and oil derived from the model over the data period are illustrated in Figure 4 and compared with the observed values. Over the earlier period especially the model fits less well than the time trends of Figure 1; however, a degree of rationing was still in force at that time. Two alternative projections are given using the model, one assuming that the input coefficient of gas and creosote pitch mixtures will remain constant and the second assumes that this coefficient will rise in the early 'seventies at roughly the same rate at which the oil coefficient rose in the late 'fifties and early 'sixties. In both projections the relative price of coal to oil has been assumed to rise from 1965 onwards but at a slower rate than in the past.

From equation (22) the marginal rate of substitution of oil and gas for coal and coke may be calculated as 2·3 therms per therm on a delivered basis. This implies that the additional use of oil or gas is 2·3 times as efficient in producing output as the coal or coke displaced. Even allowing for the fact that a new oil furnace is replacing a coal furnace built perhaps thirty or forty years earlier, the difference in efficiency is surprisingly high and much higher than the figure of 35 per cent calculated in the earlier model. However, there are important differences in the specification of the two models; the first assumes that fuel changeover is directly linked with the renewal and scrapping of output capacity, the second assumes no such direct link but has a lagged response between the relative consumption of the two fuels, coal and oil, and their relative price.

The high value of the marginal rate of substitution in equation (22) has important consequences for the last method of projection proposed. The continued substitution of oil for coal is relied upon as the mechanism for projecting the increased efficiency with which total energy is used. A number of attempts have been made to measure separately the rate of substitution of the two fuels and the increasing

efficiency in which total energy is used in producing output. So far
these two factors have been inextricably mixed in the data presently
available.

A further comment refers to the way in which an increase in the
input–output coefficient for town gas affects the coefficients for the
other fuels. An increase in the coefficient q_4/g in equation (22) does
not affect the ratio q_1/q_2 in equation (21). This is a consequence of
the geographical price argument developed earlier. So far, little is
known quantitatively about the differential effects of natural gas on
the use of other fuels, but as more information becomes available it
can be incorporated in the model by amending equation (21).

Separate models for each of thirteen industries (excluding the
fuel-producing industries) based on the arguments of this section

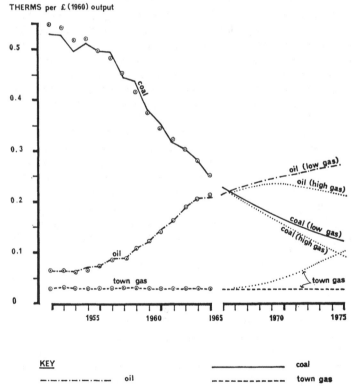

Figure 4. *Fuel Input Coefficients into "Other Industry". Model Analysis*

have been constructed and incorporated into a computable model in which information is exchanged between a main model of the United Kingdom economy and a separate fuel submodel. Details of this work together with the results calculated from the model for the year 1972 are given in [4].

This section has laid stress on alternative models explaining the substitution between coal and oil fuels as commodity inputs into "Other Industry". There is here, a substantial problem of choice in the specification of a preferred model, and one in which goodness of fit to past data plays only a small part. The last model proposed appears to be the most robust of those described, both in interpretation and in its performance over a wide range of industries, but there is still ample room for the construction of new models in this field.

III. SECTION 2

1. *A Production Function for Input–Output Models*

The previous section considered methods for projecting input–output coefficients for the group of fuel commodities. It may be possible to develop similar projection methods for the input–output coefficients of other groups of inputs such as raw materials, prefabricated parts, transport, services or maintenance requirements. No doubt a considerable amount of specialised information would be necessary in the way, for example, in which the data from the Ministry of Power Statistical Digest was used in the first section of the paper. Given that such methods could be devised it is interesting to consider whether some overall constraint should be imposed on the sum of the input–output coefficients for goods and services for each industry (expressed in constant prices) or whether this sum might increase or decrease freely over time.

The implication of having separate projection methods for different groups of input–output coefficients implies that they will generally be projected independently even though the individual models employed may have common variables. From one point of view the different groups of inputs are in competition, for example, in a chemical process more physical output may frequently be obtained from a given consumption of raw material by using greater temperatures and pressures, implying that the fuel coefficient will rise relative to that for raw material.

From another point of view component inputs from one group may be thought of as complementary to components of another group. If the set of average input–output coefficients for the industry is seen as the sum of the set of input–output coefficients for each technique in use weighted by its contribution to gross output then an important component of the variation in average coefficients over time will be the introduction of new techniques and the scrapping of old ones. The complementarity between members of different commodity input groups is represented by their joint presence in the input structures of the techniques at both forward and backward margins. The picture is further complicated, however, to the extent that the coefficient structures of existing techniques may also alter as time goes by.

If full information were available on the input–output coefficients for all techniques available in an industry and the way in which these coefficients changed over time then the average set of input–output coefficients could be calculated using a model which determined the contribution of each technique in producing the gross output of the industry and weighting together their input–output coefficient structures. Linear programming is one example of such a model. However, detailed information for individual techniques is not generally available so that a less ambitious approach has to be adopted.

Consider a single industrial sector producing an output pY at current prices gross of the purchases of intermediate goods and services, some of which may have been produced by establishments within the sector. Here p is a price index ($p_{1960} = 1.00$) obtained by dividing the current price output pY, as given in the Census of Production [12], by the base weighted constant (1960) price output series Y, calculated from the components of the Index of Industrial Production [11] mentioned in the first section of the paper.

The inputs required by this sector have been divided into intermediate goods, labour input and capital goods. The preparation of the data for each of these inputs is described in turn.

The labour input, H, measured in man-hours, represents a mid-year count of insurance cards, prepared by the Ministry of Labour, adjusted for temporarily stopped workers and multiplied by the average number of hours worked during the year. This calculation has been carried out separately for manual and non-manual workers and the results added. An average wage rate w, has been calculated by dividing the total annual wage bill for the sector, including the employer's contributions, given in the Blue Book [10] wH, by the estimate of labour input H described above. For those sectors in which the income of self-employed persons is important the labour input in man-hours of the self-employed has been valued at the average wage rate and the remainder allocated to profits.

The current value of the purchases of intermediate goods and services $\bar{p}M$ has been obtained by subtracting from gross output at current prices the contribution to gross domestic product given in the Blue Book. A price index of intermediate goods for the sector $\bar{p}$ was calculated as a weighted sum of the price indices of each of the individual inputs

$$\bar{p} = \sum_i \frac{a_i}{\Sigma a_i} p_i \tag{23}$$

where a_i is the input–output coefficient and p_i the price index for commodity i. In this calculation separate price indices and input–output coefficients were distinguished for imported and home produced commodities. A constant price series for intermediate inputs was calculated by dividing the current price series $\bar{p}M$ by the price index, thus

$$M = \frac{\bar{p}M}{\bar{p}} = \frac{pY - wH - \pi}{\Sigma_i a_i p_i / (\Sigma_i a_i)} \tag{24}$$

where, in this equation, π denotes total profits. Since

$$\Sigma a_i p_i = pY - wH - \pi \tag{25}$$

$$M = \sum_i a_i \tag{26}$$

Thus the constant price measure of intermediate purchases may be identified as the sum of the input–output coefficients for the sector measured at constant prices. An annual series of input–output matrices does not exist for the United Kingdom so that the constant price series for intermediate inputs M cannot be estimated directly using equation (26). However, within the growth project, matrices have been prepared for 1954 and 1960 on a comparable basis so that a first estimate of a time series of input–output matrices can be constructed for the period 1950–1965 by linear interpolation and extrapolation. This series will be substantially improved when the 1963 matrix becomes available and when a separate study of the movement of the major individual elements over this period has been completed within the Project. Only the proportion of each element to the sum of elements for the industry under consideration has been used in equation (23) to produce the price index $\bar{p}$ for intermediate inputs, which is then used in equation (24) to calculate M for each year.

The treatment of capital goods in this section seeks to avoid the use of a measure of the capital stock. Figures are given in the Blue Book for the stocks of fixed assets at constant prices in each industrial sector and their method of calculation, described in [3, 5, 9], is to sum the investment at constant prices in each asset over an assumed asset life in the immediate past. The net annual change in this measure of gross capital stock is thus the gross investment during the year less the investment in each asset the asset life earlier. Apart from the difficulty of estimating lives for each asset the assumption of a fixed asset life implies that scrapping during a year depends not on current economic circumstances but on the determinants of investment in the distant past. Problems of aggregation arise in the practical measurement of any economic variable but the usual method of construction of the gross capital stock renders it of doubtful value in econometric work.

In the following analysis variables with suffix t and a single prime refer to scrapped techniques used in year t but not in year $t+1$ and variables with a double prime refer to new techniques used in year $t+1$ but not in year t. As specific information is not available on the inputs or outputs of these two types of technique assumptions must be made. Suppose that output per man-hour and output per unit of input of intermediate goods and services (all measured at constant prices) for scrapped and new techniques are proportionally related to the corresponding average values for the industry. In addition, assume a constant capital-output ratio for new techniques. Thus for scrapped techniques

$$Y'/H' = \alpha Y/H \tag{27}$$

$$Y'/M' = \bar{\alpha} Y/M \tag{28}$$

and for new techniques

$$Y''/H'' = \beta Y/H \tag{29}$$

$$Y''/M'' = \bar{\beta} Y/M \tag{30}$$

$$\frac{\bar{I}}{Y''} = k \tag{31}$$

$$\bar{I}_t = \tfrac{1}{3}(I_{t-2}+I_{t-1}+I_t) \tag{32}$$

where α, $\bar{\alpha}$, β, $\bar{\beta}$ and k are constants. As in the first section of this paper a three-year moving average for investment centred on year $t-1$ has been assumed to be related to techniques introduced in year $t+1$. If it is assumed that the only way in which inputs and outputs may change is by the introduction of new and the scrapping of old techniques then

$$\Delta Y_t = Y_t'' - Y_t' \tag{33}$$

$$\Delta H_t = H_t'' - H_t' \tag{34}$$

$$\Delta M_t = M_t'' - M_t' \tag{35}$$

Algebraic substitution yields the equations

$$\frac{\Delta Y}{Y} = \left(1 - \frac{\alpha}{\beta}\right)\frac{1}{k}\frac{\bar{I}}{Y} + \alpha\frac{\Delta H}{H} \tag{36}$$

$$\frac{\Delta Y}{Y} = \left(1 - \frac{\bar{\alpha}}{\bar{\beta}}\right)\frac{1}{k}\frac{\bar{I}}{Y} + \bar{\alpha}\frac{\Delta M}{M} \tag{37}$$

It is tempting to fit equations (36) and (37) to time series data using least squares regression. However, labour hoarding during output troughs discussed, for example, by Neild [8], is likely to occur to some extent on all plants so that the mechanisms underlying equations (27) through (37) cannot be relied upon to explain the short-term variations in output. A method is required for estimating average values for the parameters α, β, $\bar{\alpha}$, $\bar{\beta}$ and k which abstracts from the short-run variation in the time series of the variables but captures the long-run process of the turnover of capital assets.

Suppose that the input and outputs of the technique installed in successive years τ are growing at constant proportional rates with τ and the average life of a technique over the data period is T years. Set constant price output, labour input and intermediate input in year t for technique of age τ as $y_{t-\tau}$, $h_{t-\tau}$ and $m_{t-\tau}$, respectively. The average value of output per manhour in year t may be calculated, by summing over the techniques in use, as

$$\left(\frac{Y}{H}\right)_t = \frac{y_{t-T} + y_{t-T-1} + \ldots + y_t}{h_{t-T} + h_{t-T+1} + \ldots + h_t} \tag{38}$$

$$= \left(\frac{y}{h}\right)_{t-T} \frac{\left[1 + (1+g) + (1+g)^2 + \ldots + (1+g)^T\right]}{\left[1 + (1+n) + (1+n)^2 + \ldots + (1+n)^T\right]} \tag{39}$$

$$= \frac{1}{\alpha}\left(\frac{Y'}{H'}\right)_t \tag{40}$$

where, in expression (39), g is the proportional rate of growth of y and n is the proportional rate of growth of h. In this analysis the output of a plant, once built, is assumed constant until scrapped; however, the output of new plant installed in year $\tau + 1$ is $(1+g)$ times the output of new plant installed in year τ. For fixed values of T, g and n are also the proportional rates of growth of total output Y_t and total labour input H_t respectively. In order to avoid the complica-

I

tion of discussing variations over a year the usual assumption of period analysis will be made that production and consumption in each year are envisaged as taking place at some specified point of time during the year.

Equations (39) and (40) provide an expression for α as

$$\alpha = \frac{(^T[(1+n^{+1}-1]}{[(1+g)^{T+1}-1]} \cdot \frac{g}{n} \tag{41}$$

In equation (29) the new techniques are introduced in year $t+1$, so using equation (27) we have

$$\beta = \frac{(1+g)^{T+1}}{(1+n)^{T+1}} \alpha \tag{42}$$

Similar results may be obtained for $\bar{\alpha}$ and $\bar{\beta}$, i.e.,

$$\bar{\alpha} = \frac{[(1+m)^{T+1}-1]}{[(1+g)^{T+1}-1]} \frac{g}{m} \tag{43}$$

$$\bar{\beta} = \frac{(1+g)^{T+1}}{(1+m)^{T+1}} \bar{\alpha} \tag{44}$$

It is important to show that equations (36), (37) and (41) through (44) are consistent, i.e. that

$$\frac{\bar{I}}{kY} = \frac{g-\alpha n}{1-\alpha/\beta} = \frac{g-\bar{\alpha}m}{1-\bar{\alpha}/\bar{\beta}} \tag{45}$$

Substituting either from (41) and (42) or from (43) and (44) into (45) produces the result that

$$\frac{\bar{I}}{kY} = \frac{g(1+g)^{T+1}}{(1+g)^{T+1}-1} \tag{46}$$

Estimates for g, n and m may be obtained by calculating the average proportional growth rates of the time series for Y, H and M respectively. The time series data are illustrated in Figure 5. Different assumptions about the error structure of the data yield slightly different estimates for these growth rates by fitting in logarithmic, exponential or difference form but the final parameters of the model do not appear to be very sensitive to these alternative estimates.

It remains to provide an estimate for T, the average age of the oldest technique in use over the data period, in order to calculate values for α, β, $\bar{\alpha}$ and $\bar{\beta}$. A further assumption has been introduced, namely that gross profits are zero on scrapped plant, i.e., that

$$pY' = wH' + \bar{p}M' \tag{47}$$

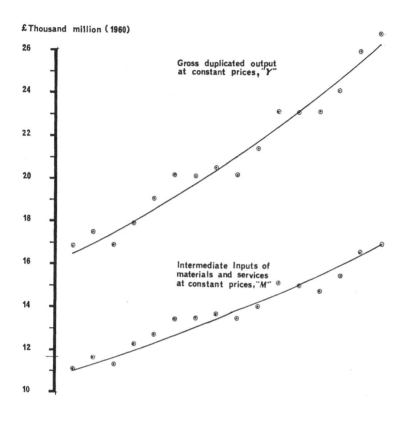

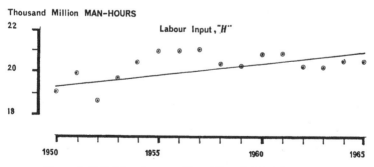

*Figure 5. U.K. Manufacturing (Less Mineral Oil, Coke Ovens
and Manufactured Solid Fuel) Growth of Output and Inputs*

There is the additional assumption in equation (47) that the average prices p, w and $\bar{p}$ apply to the input and output of scrapped plant. This is a strong assumption but insufficient information is available for testing it. Dividing through by pY' in equation (47) and using equations (27) and (28) we obtain

$$1 = \frac{1}{\alpha}\frac{wH}{pY} + \frac{1}{\bar{\alpha}}\frac{\bar{p}M}{pY} \tag{48}$$

Over the data period (1950–1965) the shares of the wage bill and the purchases of intermediate goods in the current value of output have varied but little so that average values have been used in equation

Numerical Ratio

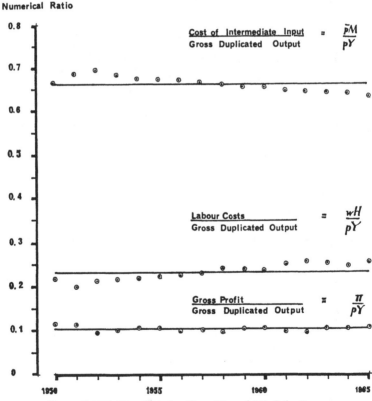

Figure 6. U.K. Manufacturing (Less Mineral Oil, Coke Ovens and Manufactured Solid Fuel) Cost Ratios (current prices)

(48). These ratios are illustrated in Figure 6. Substitution for α and $\bar{\alpha}$ from equations (41) and (43) yield an equation for T as

$$\frac{g}{[(1+g)^{T+1}-1]} = \frac{wH}{pY}\frac{n}{[(1+n)^{T+1}-1]} + \frac{\bar{p}M}{pY}\frac{m}{[(1+m)^{T+1}-1]} \tag{49}$$

This equation may be solved iteratively by computer and a solution located. The value for T may be used in equations (41) through (44) to obtain values of α, β, $\bar{\alpha}$, and $\bar{\beta}$. Employing an average value for $\bar{I}/Y$ in equation (46) yields an average value for k, the capital/output ratio on new plant. The values obtained for the Manufacturing Sector of the United Kingdom (excluding Mineral Oil, Coke and Manufactured Solid Fuel) using annual data over the period 1950–1965 are set out in Table 1.

Table 1. *Estimates of Production Parameters for a Modified Manufacturing Sector*

$g = 3\cdot15\%$ p.a.	$\bar{I}/Y = 0\cdot0394$ £(1960)/£(1960)
$n = 0\cdot542\%$ p.a.	$wH/pY = 0\cdot233$ £(1960)/£(1960)
$m = 2\cdot90\%$ p.a.	$\bar{p}M/pY = 0\cdot662$ £(1960)/£(1960)
$\alpha = 0\cdot729$	$\beta = 1\cdot347$
$\bar{\alpha} = 0\cdot969$	$\bar{\beta} = 1\cdot027$
$k = 0\cdot657$ £(1960)/£(1960)	$T = 23$ years

The interpretation of T as an actual age rests on the assumption that output and inputs for the sector have been growing at constant proportional rates. This is broadly true apart from the interruption of the Second World War. An inspection of the data suggests that eight years should be added to the value of T given in Table 1 to take account of this interruption so that the oldest basket of capital goods in use, on average, over the data period is calculated as 31 years. This figure may be compared with the individual estimates given by Deane [5] set out in Table 2.

Table 2. *Average Lives of Assets, Deane (1964)*

Asset	Average Life, Years
Vehicles	10
Plant and machinery	16, 19, 25, 34, 50
Buildings	80

Apart from the differences in industrial composition of "Other

Industry" and this group of Manufacturing Industry, the figure for the capital–output ratio on new plant k may be compared with that obtained in section 1; the fuel model yields 0·621 and the production model yields 0·657 £(1960) investment/£(1960) output on new plant. Considering the independent nature of the two estimates the agreement between the results may be quite fortuitous. However, the more optimistic reader may well find some encouragement in this result.

The estimates of α, β, $\bar{\alpha}$ and $\bar{\beta}$ indicate that scrapped plant is some 27 per cent less efficient and new plant 35 per cent more efficient than the corresponding average result for the industry in terms of

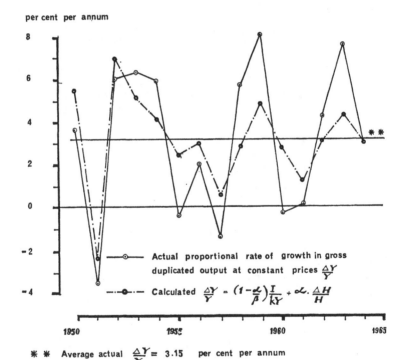

per cent per annum

—○— Actual proportional rate of growth in gross duplicated output at constant prices $\frac{\Delta Y}{Y}$

—·●·— Calculated $\frac{\Delta Y}{Y} = \left(1 - \frac{\alpha}{\beta}\right)\frac{I}{kY} + \alpha . \frac{\Delta H}{H}$

✳ ✳   Average actual $\frac{\Delta Y}{Y} = 3.15$ per cent per annum

Note: This figure does not provide a check on goodness of fit as the variability of $\frac{\Delta Y}{Y}$ about its mean value has not been employed in estimating α, β or k

Figure 7. U.K. Manufacturing (Less Mineral Oil, Cake Ovens and Manufactured Solid Fuel) Proportional Rates of Growth

output per man-hour and that there is only 6 per cent difference in productivity of intermediate inputs between new and scrapped techniques.

The estimates given in Table 1 may be used in equation (36) to calculate the contribution, year by year, to the proportionate increase in output $\dfrac{\Delta Y}{Y}$ resulting from the introduction and scrapping of techniques. The results are compared in Figure 7 with the actual values. Approximately half the variation is accounted for, the remainder may be assumed to arise from the short term variation in output-factor ratios in response to fluctuations in demand relative to supply of both the inputs and the output of the industry. By choosing a suitable value of "normal output" in the earliest year (1950), it is possible to construct a time series of normal output shown as the dashed line in Figure 8 by accumulating the increment in Y calculated from equation (36). When the data point is above this line capacity is operated above the normal level and vice-versa, thus the model yields a measure of capacity utilisation relative to a "normal level". This is plotted in Figure 9. The series for capacity utilisation so calculated is currently being tested in related research.

So far attention has been concentrated on the relationship between

£Thousand million (1960)

Figure 8. U.K. Manufacturing (Less Mineral Oil, Coke Ovens and Manufactured Solid Fuel) Actual and calculated normal Gross duplicated Output

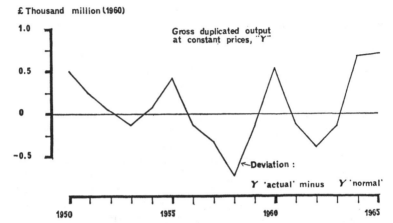

Figure 9. U.K. Manufacturing (Less Mineral Oil, Coke Ovens and Manufactured Solid Fuel) Actual minus normal Gross duplicated Output

scrapped and new techniques and the weighted average of techniques as a whole in use in the industry. It still remains to consider the range of techniques available for introduction and the method of choosing amongst them. Although there is a considerable variety of models which might be used for this purpose the extremely strong assumptions which have been introduced so far suggest that the available data can support only a simple approach. Accordingly a Cobb–Douglas production function has been assumed for new plant of the form

$$Y'' = AH''^\gamma M''^\delta \bar{I}^{1-\gamma-\delta}(1+\varepsilon)^t \tag{50}$$

At some rate of discount r the present value of an investment and its consequential stream of income may be written as

$$Q_0 = \sum_{x-1}^{T^*} \frac{(p_x Y''_x - w_x H''_x - \bar{p}_x M''_x)}{(1+r)^x} - \bar{I}_0 p_{c0} \tag{51}$$

where p_c is the price of investment goods and T^* is the expected life of the project. A further simplification in equation (51) is to take the investment as accumulated in the year before output commences and to calculate the present value at that time. Later work will correct for the assumption that investment is spread over time and the present value will be calculated at an assumed point of decision. The values of variables in the round brackets are expected values and a way is required for expressing the formation of expectations regarding the future movements of inputs, outputs and prices. For the purposes of this paper it is assumed that the inputs and output of the new technique will remain unchanged over its expected life and that the prices of input and output will continue to rise at the proportional rate of growth experienced over the data period so that

$$Y''_x = Y''_0 \qquad p_x = p_0(1+s)^x$$
$$H''_x = H''_0 \qquad w_x = w_0(1+u)^x \qquad (52)$$
$$M''_x = M''_0 \qquad \bar{p}_x = \bar{p}_0(1+v)^x$$

where s, u and v are the proportional rates of growth of p, w and $\bar{p}$ respectively. If the three constants S, U and V are defined as

$$S = \sum_{x=1}^{T^*} \frac{(1+s)^x}{(1+r)^x}, \quad U = \sum_{x=1}^{T^*} \frac{(1+u)^x}{(1+r)^x}, \quad V = \sum_{x=1}^{T^*} \frac{(1+v)^x}{(1+r)^x} \qquad (53)$$

equation (18) becomes

$$Q_0 = p_0 Y''_0 S - w_0 H''_0 U - p_0 M''_0 V - \bar{I}_0 p_{c0} \qquad (54)$$

Maximisation of Q_0 yields the following first order conditions

$$\frac{\partial Q_0}{\partial H''_0} = 0 \quad \frac{w_0 H''_0}{p_0 Y''_0} = \frac{\gamma S}{U} = \frac{1}{\beta} \frac{wH}{pY} \qquad (55)$$

$$\frac{\partial Q_0}{\partial M''_0} = 0 \quad \frac{\bar{p}_0 M''_0}{p_0 Y_0} = \frac{\delta S}{V} = \frac{1}{\beta} \frac{\bar{p}M}{pY} \qquad (56)$$

$$\frac{\partial Q_0}{\partial \bar{I}_0} = 0 \quad \frac{p_c}{p_0} k = S(1-\gamma-\delta) = \frac{p_c \bar{I}}{pY''} = \frac{p_c \bar{I}}{pY} \cdot \frac{Y}{\bar{I}} \cdot k \qquad (57)$$

In this model, plant will last physically for ever but will be taken out of production when its gross profit becomes zero. For this reason $\bar{I}$ is not a function of the expected productive life of the plant T^*.

Differentiation of equation (54) with respect to T^* records the fact that the marginal contribution to Q_0 of running the plant for a further increment of time at T^* is zero.

$$\frac{\partial Q_0}{\partial T^*} = 0; \quad p_0(1+s)^{T^*} Y_0 - w_0(1+u)^{T^*} H_0 - \bar{p}(1+v)^{T^*} M_0 = 0 \quad (58)$$

If these marginal equivalences hold then the present value Q_0 will be zero for any scale of investment $\bar{I}$.

Differencing equation (50) gives, to first order,

$$\Delta Y'' = \frac{\partial Y''}{\partial H''}\Delta H'' + \frac{\partial Y''}{\partial M''}\Delta M'' + \frac{\partial Y''}{\partial \bar{I}}\Delta \bar{I} + \frac{\partial Y''}{\partial t}\Delta t \qquad (59)$$

Setting Δt to one period and obtaining the differential coefficients from equation (50), equation (59) becomes

$$\frac{\Delta Y''}{Y''} = \gamma\frac{\Delta H''}{H''} + \delta\frac{\Delta M''}{M''} + (1-\gamma-\delta)\frac{\Delta \bar{I}}{\bar{I}} + \varepsilon \qquad (60)$$

Estimates for the parameters γ, δ, ε, r and T^* may be obtained by solving the five equations (55) through (58) and (60) if average values are employed for the ratios appearing in those equations. Equation (58) yields a value for T^* by iteration. The equation obtained by substituting for γ and δ from equations (55) and (56) into equation (57) may be solved for r, again involving an iterative procedure. The values obtained for r and T^* may be used in equations (55), (56) and (60) to obtain estimates for γ, μ and ε. The results obtained for the modified Manufacturing Sector are set out in Table 3.

Table 3. *Further Estimates of Production Parameters for U.K. Manufacturing (less Mineral Oil, Coke Ovens and Manufactured Solid Fuel)*

$T^* = 21$ years	$r = 26\cdot4\%$ p.a.
$\gamma = 0\cdot21$	$\delta = 0\cdot64$
$\varepsilon = 0\cdot0046$	$1-\gamma-\delta = 0\cdot15$

The estimate for the internal rate of return expected from a new project given in Table 3 is gross of price inflation and takes no account of company taxation, or capital allowances. Work is in hand to extend the model to accomodate these important details.

The contribution of technical progress ε, or more accurately the residual growth in output not explained by the growth of all inputs, is small at less than one half per cent per annum. The magnitude of this term depends heavily on the specification of the model and can only be interpreted within the framework of the assumptions made.

A theory of production is one of the cornerstones of a model of economic growth and we are giving considerable attention to the construction of an acceptable theory for inclusion in our computable model for the United Kingdom. The argument delivered here is only one of a number of ways in which we are tackling the problem. Again the question of model specification arises. In circumstances in which strong assumptions are needed to overcome the limitations of the data there can clearly be no final solution. A choice between alternative production models will rest, amongst many criteria, on the exact problem the model has to analyse, goodness of fit to past data, properties of the estimation procedures, computability and a subjective view of the acceptability of the framework and assumptions of the model.

IV. CONCLUDING REMARKS

This paper has discussed two topics related to the analysis and projection of input–output matrices. The results of the 1963 Census of Production will serve as a check on the independent data used in the first section of the paper to estimate the time series of fuel input–output coefficients, and, as indicated in the second section, will also serve to improve the estimate of the yearly time series of input–output matrices for the United Kingdom.

In addition this paper has indicated that improved input–output tables, whilst making an important contribution to economic research, are not in themselves enough. They must be supported by improved information on commodity prices, on other inputs into production and on the characteristics of techniques used at the margin of production. This is only a start to the list of additional data requirements if we are fully to exploit the available techniques of economic model building.

REFERENCES

[1] CAMBRIDGE, DEPARTMENT OF APPLIED ECONOMICS, Nos. 1–8 in *A Programme for Growth*. Chapman & Hall, London, 1962 on.

[2] CAMBRIDGE, DEPARTMENT OF APPLIED ECONOMICS, "Input–Output Relationships, 1954–1966". No. 3 in *A Programme for Growth*. Chapman & Hall, London, 1963.

[3] CAMBRIDGE, DEPARTMENT OF APPLIED ECONOMICS. "Capital, Output and Employment, 1948–1960". No. 4 in *A Programme for Growth*. Chapman & Hall, 1964.

[4] CAMBRIDGE, DEPARTMENT OF APPLIED ECONOMICS, "The Demand for Fuel, 1948–1975; A Submodel for the British Fuel Economy". No. 8 in *A Programme for Growth*. Chapman & Hall, London, December 1968.

[5] DEANE, G., "The Stock of Fixed Capital in the United Kingdom in 1961". *J.R.S.S.* Series A (General), Volume 127, Part 3, 1964.

[6] KOYCK, L. M., *Distributed Lags and Investment Analysis*. In the series Contributions to Economic Analysis. North-Holland Publishing Company, Amsterdam, 1954.

[7] NATIONAL INDUSTRIAL FUEL EFFICIENCY SERVICE, Report and Accounts. London, annually.

[8] NEILD, R. R., *Pricing and Employment in the Trade Cycle*. N.I.E.S.R. Occasional Paper No. XXI. Cambridge University Press, 1963.

[9] REDFERN, P., "Net Investment in Fixed Assets in the United Kingdom, 1938–1953". *J.R.S.S.* Series A (General), Volume 118, Part 2, 1955.

[10] U.K., CENTRAL STATISTICAL OFFICE, *National Income and Expenditure*. H.M.S.O., London, annually.

[11] U.K., CENTRAL STATISTICAL OFFICE, The Index of Industrial Production. In the *Annual Abstract of Statistics*. H.M.S.O., London, annually.

[12] U.K., BOARD OF TRADE, *Final Reports on the Census of Production for 1948–1958 and 1963*. H.M.S.O., London.

[13] U.K., MINISTRY OF POWER, *Ministry of Power Statistical Digest*. H.M.S.O., London, annually.

SESSION IV: DISCUSSION OF MR. WIGLEY'S PAPER

Chairman: PROFESSOR M. MCMANUS (BIRMINGHAM)

MR. CIGNO (Birmingham)

There is one small point in the first part of the exposition which is not clear to me. You assume that there is a linear isoquant between q_1 and q_2 and in your problem we take a point on this line. In such a case what we usually say is that, if the price of q_1 is greater than that of q_2, only q_2 is used and vice versa. However, you say that, in a given year, the actual solution is somewhere in between the two extremes ($q_1 = 0$ and $q_2 = 0$) because we cannot depart too radically from the previous year's solution. So you write:

$$\Delta\left(\frac{q_1}{q_2}\right)_t = \alpha\left[\left(\frac{q_1}{q_2}\right)^*_{\substack{t+1 \\ (t)}} - \left(\frac{q_1}{q_2}\right)_t\right]$$

As the "optimal" solution $\left(\dfrac{q_1}{q_2}\right)^*$ can only take the values zero or infinity (because either q_1 or q_2 is zero) we can only get

$$\Delta\left(\frac{q_1}{q_2}\right)_t = -\alpha\left(\frac{q_1}{q_2}\right)_t$$

or

$$\Delta\left(\frac{q_1}{q_2}\right)_t = \infty$$

But you obviously have in mind a different sort of mechanism, because you write

$$\left(\frac{q_1}{q_2}\right)^*_{\substack{t+1 \\ (t)}} = a + b\left(\frac{p_1}{p_2}\right)_t$$

thus implying that the optimal factors' ratio can take all sorts of values and that

$$\left(\frac{q_1}{q_2}\right)^{*}_{\substack{t+1 \\ (t)}} = \infty$$

only when $p_2 = 0$ and *not* when $p_2 > p_1$. Could you explain the economic logic behind this?

MR. WIGLEY (Cambridge)

I think there is an economic explanation. First of all, I am here considering aggregate manufacturing. Let us suppose that I was considering a sector within manufacturing, let us take food, drink and tobacco; clearly there will be a great number of techniques within such a sector and within one technique coal and oil may both be used but for different purposes. Another possibility is that the decision to change technique from one fuel use to another may be a considerable way down the priority ordering in the possible uses of investment funds available to each firm and it may be well below the cut-off point of their available resources.

My principal argument, however, for the coexistence of both coal and oil-burning plant rests on a geographical distribution of fuel price, as explained in the text surrounding figure 3 of my paper. My equations (13) and (14) define the limits, within my assumptions, beyond which plant will be either all coal or all oil burning. Within those limits transport costs enable both coal and oil plant to exist in the country as a whole. Of course, this picture is a highly idealised one but it provides a subjective explanation. This is an answer to your question, is it not? If I allow geographical pricing then I can conceive of situations in which some firms will use coal, and they will be quite happy to do so, because of the distribution of fuel prices.

MR. CIGNO

Then there are two answers to my question: one is that there isn't only one, but several techniques available, and the other is that in this problem prices change according to location. But surely if there are several techniques the isoquant is not a straight line: it is the envelope of several straight lines with different slopes and the resulting "broken isoquant" is convex to the origin, which is the usual situation, and this by itself enables you to say that the solution is somewhere in between the two extremes (except when one of the prices is zero).

MR. WIGLEY

I agree that my assumption of a constant marginal rate of substitution between the two fuels is a simplification; the question is how far you think that the rate will differ between techniques. The types of furnaces that are used clearly do differ; if one considers a coal furnace and an oil furnace producing the same output than I believe, on the average, that an oil furnace is something like 5 per cent more efficient than a coal furnace—in terms of thermal efficiency—that is the efficiency of using fuel to produce heat. Of course, it is rather a different problem to consider the efficiency of using fuel to produce output because there are many additional stages between the heat coming out of the furnace—steam if you like—and the final product. But I am not altogether convinced that there is a very wide discrepancy in marginal rate of substitution of oil for coal—therm for therm—over different types of equipment producing output.

MR. CIGNO

In this case the plant or the economy are using a mix of oil and coal and the problem can only be formulated in terms of "therm requirements".

MR. WIGLEY

You see, coal is available at the pit head, oil is available either at the refineries or ports; transport on coal is additional; oil prices are zoned geographically throughout the country. This geographical price structure is the principal reason for the introduction of my adaptive formula and the fact that both coal and oil are used simultaneously.

DR. SIMPSON (University College, London)

I don't wish to contribute anything about the various alternative techniques of extrapolating coefficients, but I would like just to suggest that all forms of extrapolation are less satisfactory than the alternative, because they cannot take account of technological changes, the kinds of changes which are occurring all the time, such as the development of natural gas, of new synthetic fibres, etc. Therefore the alternative I'd like to propose is that forecasting of coefficients should take place on the basis of incorporating the information that already exists (in the research departments of large companies, with trade associations), concerning the future markets and future technologies of the industry under consideration. So that, for example, if one wishes to forecast the coefficient of fuel into metals one would begin by breaking down the fuel into the component rows for the different types of fuels and one would break down the metals block into component metal industries, and one would go on by asking oneself what are the foreseeable changes in the output composition of metal industries and what are the foreseeable substitutions in fuels. One would get this information by enquiring from the informed people in both industries what they can foresee in their sectors. This is an approach which has already been developed in the U.S.A. and it seems to me that it is likely to be more fruitful on purely logical grounds than the other approach which is based upon extrapolation of past trends and which therefore cannot take account of new technology.

MR. WIGLEY

Yes, I accept the point; we certainly are interested in determining, for example, the type of gas furnaces that might be used in some particular sector and the value of the input–output coefficient for that technique in that sector. But haven't I gone one stage further than that? I am not only asking the question, what would be the thermal input coefficient of a particular sector if they were all to switch to gas, I am also asking the question how many of them are likely to switch to gas. As we use the coefficients at the moment we do not split out the activities within, let's say, the drink industry, as to those which use coal, those which use gas, those which use electricity, because typically that information is not available; we do not know the outputs of those firms which use the different fuels. This is a basic problem. The cement industry is an industry in which I would like to do this work. Here is a relatively homogeneous product, at least to the uninitiated. If I knew the proportion of cement that was produced from coal furnaces and the proportion of cement produced from oil furnaces then I would not be forced to fit equation (22) for example; I could simply work out the input coefficients of the coal-fired cement producers and the oil-fired cement producers separately. Of course, the more information we have, the more satisfactory models we could produce. I am not really solving the problem of what difference there is in coefficient between a technique using a coal-burning furnace and a technique using an oil-burning furnace, I am going a stage further to determine the proportion of output that will be produced from coal and the proportion of output that will be produced from oil as well.

MR. J. M. BARBER (H.M. Treasury)

Can I comment on your figure of 26·4 per cent for the internal rate of return of a new project in manufacturing? Firstly I would like to ask you if you have seen the article in the Board of Trade Journal for 11th February, 1966, which shows the rate of return on capital assets owned by quoted companies to have been fairly steady at around 9 per cent over the period 1949–1963. If the rate of return on new investment in manufacturing was as high as 26·4 per cent then I am sure you would expect to find a rising trend in the Board of Trade's figures.

MR. WIGLEY

May I ask whether this was an attempt to calculate an internal rate of return of a project from its inception, or whether this was an average rate of profit calculated for financial institutions?

MR. BARBER

It is an average rate of profit based on the ratio of gross income at current prices to gross assets at current prices.

MR. WIGLEY

I see. Thank you.

MR. BARBER

I am not saying that it is exactly on all fours with your 26.4 per cent, but if the latter were true then one would expect an upward trend in the Board of Trade figures.

Secondly, I would like to defend my Department over this question of the level of the opportunity cost of capital, i.e. the return on a low risk marginal investment project in industry. It hasn't been possible to get direct estimates of the marginal return on industrial projects which are directly comparable with out test discount rate and hence we have tended to work up to the figure of 8 per cent by considering what alternative uses a firm might find for its funds other than that investing them in new capacity. For example, if a firm could earn more money by investing its funds in the stock maiket than by installing a new machine then the new machine would not in fact be installed. If you look at the figures they suggest that you would get about 7 per cent after tax on a portfolio of stocks and shares. One can argue that firms would require an incentive over and above this figure: say an extra one per cent for luck. Then bearing in mind what we do know about "cut-off rates" in industry we can reasonably say that any investment project which doesn't yield 8 per cent would never be considered in industry. Certainly this enables us to exclude many public sector projects from consideration, but it doesn't solve all the problems; we still have some selection to do.

MR. WIGLEY

On that last part, it seems to me rather a sharp jump from a negative judgement to a positive judgement. In other words, rather a sharp jump to say that an industry, or firm, could earn 7 per cent plus one for luck, 8 per cent at the margin. This may represent the margin, at least on the downward side, but it may still be true that the actual cut-off in private industry is 15 per cent and because of limitations of funds, the lowest project that firms were actually investing in would be substantially higher than 9 per cent and that, in practice, may well represent the opportunity cost of investment funds for a government project.

MR. BARBER

I certainly agree. I agree that this figure of 8 per cent probably looks low but it would not be correct to use 15 per cent just because one or two large firms said that they applied this rate. Perhaps some of the representatives from industry might comment on this.

MR. WIGLEY

In connection with this I would not defend the use of the internal rate of return as used in these discounting calculations as really representing the opportunity cost of capital. Perhaps as a personal view I think it should represent the social rate of time preference for the distribution of income over time, and if you really want to compare an activity with the next best alternative then you should really work out the real flow of net benefits from both the activities and compare the two, having used as rate of discount the social rate of time-preference, which as far as I can see is a value judgement by government. However, perhaps that takes us rather a long way from the topic of the paper.

PROFESSOR MCMANUS (Birmingham)

I would like to thank Mr. Wigley for his very useful paper. We have had quite a good summary of these important and useful new techniques and we can only look forward to seeing the fruition of this type of project in future publications of the Cambridge project.

SESSION V

Input–Output and the Trading Economy

by

J. R. C. LECOMBER

Department of Applied Economics, and
Fellow of Clare College, Cambridge

I. INTRODUCTION

Input–output models are characterised by their wealth of detail
and simplicity of form. It has been the hope that the former makes
up for any deficiencies in the latter. But comparison of the results
with those obtained using regression and other methods (Ghosh
(1964), Barnett (1954), Tilanus (1966)) have not always been very
favourable to input–output.

The assumption that industries purchase inputs in immutable
proportions has some justification in that possibilities of substitution
are limited by technological considerations.[1] But many models
extend the proportionality assumption to the foreign trade sector.[2]
The proposal, in the extreme form originally suggested by Leontief
(1941), allowing the sector to be treated like the productive sectors,
automatically balances the external account and makes for an elegant
and easily computable model. Imports are everywhere proportional
to the outputs of user industries, while the exports required to pay
for these imports are split among commodities in fixed proportions.

This treatment should be contrasted with that generally adopted
in macro-models (see, e.g., Parenti (1965)), whether theoretical or
operational, which emphasise the role of other explanatory variables
and, in particular, prices. Possibilities of substitution between alternative sources of supply are clearly far greater than between different
types of input. Empirical studies confirm that substitution elasticities
between imports and home production of similar products are
generally high. Much the same considerations apply in the export field.

Models incorporating unsatisfactory foreign trade relationships

---

[1] However, Wigley's relationships governing industrial usage of fuels (Wigley
1968, Cambridge DAE fl) cast some doubt on the assumption in this field.

[2] The treatment of foreign trade in a number of recent models is compared in
the annexe.

are totally unsuited to an analysis of the balance of payments, and for countries, like Britain, where foreign trade is a high proportion of total supplies and demands, will not even yield satisfactory projections of domestic magnitudes.

Computer technology has advanced considerably since Leontief's pioneering study, and it is now possible to incorporate increasingly sophisticated relationships into the detailed framework of an input–output model, without running into insuperable computational difficulties.

We, in Cambridge, have, over the last two years, estimated and incorporated foreign trade relationships into our input–output model of the British economy. The model, in its new form, has been used to obtain projections of the U.K. economy, on various assumptions, with particular emphasis on the balance of payments.[3]

This paper is not, however, concerned with the details of our model or the results obtained. The aim is rather to draw from our experience some general methodological conclusions. The context of our model should, however, be borne in mind; it is a medium-term projection model for an industrialised market economy with a relatively high ratio of foreign trade to gross domestic product and highly conscious of a tight balance of payments constraint. These considerations together with data availability to some extent determine the appropriate shape of the model. Generalisations outside this context are not necessarily valid.

The general form of such a model is considered in Section II, its principal components in Sections III–V and its solution in Sections VI and VII. Section VIII concerns the explicit incorporation of policy variables which could be used to correct a payments imbalance. Finally Section IX is devoted to a discussion of a relaxation of the assumption generally made in input–output work that outputs are demand-determined, prices supply-determined. The treatment of foreign trade in other input–output models is shown in tabular form in the annexe.

[3] The Project, under the general direction of Professor Stone, is supported by the Social Science Research Council. The work of the Project is described in a series of volumes under the general heading "A Programme for Growth". Our 1972 projections are to appear next year as Volume 9 (Cambridge DAE fl). Provisional projections were given, together with an account of the method in (Barker and Lecomber 1967).

The author draws gratefully on the experience of the Project, and the paper benefits substantially from discussion with its members, especially Mr. T. S. Barker.

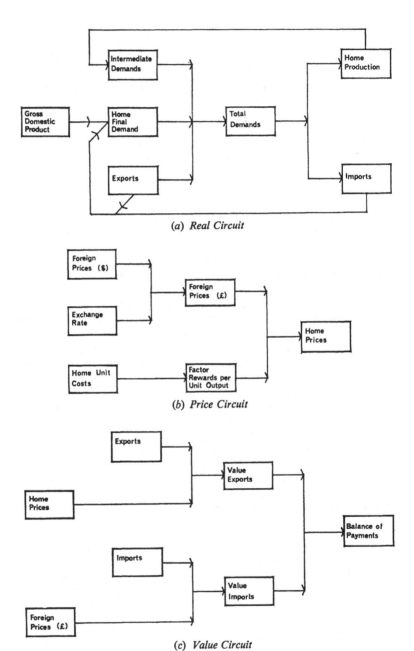

(a) Real Circuit

(b) Price Circuit

(c) Value Circuit

Figure 1. A Model in Schematic Form

II. BUILDING A MULTI-SECTOR MODEL FOR AN OPEN ECONOMY

The shape of a possible model is represented schematically in Figure 1. The model is divided into three parts, a real circuit, a price circuit and a value circuit. This division is associated with an assumption generally made in input–output work that quantities are demand-determined, prices supply-determined (see Stone (1961)). This assumption is adopted for most of this paper, but reconsidered in section IX.

The gross domestic product sets a limit (for given net exports) on total final expenditure. Net exports are not known at the outset, but are obtained with increasing precision as the calculation proceeds. Total final expenditure is broken down, by stages, into home final demands for various commodities.[4] To these are added exports and intermediate demands to give total demands, which are satisfied from either home production or imports. Intermediate demands depend on home production levels using the input–output relationships. Exports and the allocation of demands between home supplies and imports depend, *inter alia*, on prices, which are determined in circuit (b). Other relationships within the real circuit, for example the breakdown of final expenditure, may also be made price-sensitive.

Figure 1 (b) shows how prices are determined. Foreign prices, in, for example, dollars, are converted to sterling using the exchange rate. Factor rewards per unit of output of each commodity are next obtained as a function of home unit costs, and finally home prices derived using the input–output dual which expresses the output price of each commodity in terms of the prices of inputs.

Figure 1 (c) simply shows the calculation of the balance of goods and services. If this is unsatisfactory, appropriate modifications may be made to variables or parameters in one of the other circuits. In particular a modification in the exchange rate or in home unit costs will alter the relative levels of home and foreign prices (Figure 1 (b)) and hence exports and imports.

III. DEMAND FUNCTIONS FOR IMPORTS

Leontief (1941) proposed that imports be proportionately related to the outputs of user industries. Such relationships are reasonably satisfactory only when there is little possibility of substitution from

---

[4] The many complex problems arising in this breakdown are, however, beyond the scope of this paper. The added complication that certain categories of final demand, in particular investment, may depend indirectly on home output levels is ignored in the interests of simplicity.

similar home-produced commodities. Many models distinguish two classes of import, complementary imports, classified by user, and competitive imports, classified by commodity type (see tabulation in the annexe); the former follow Leontief relationships, while the latter are determined exogenously and in some models subsequently crudely modified to satisfy a balance of payments constraint, thus recognising possibilities of substitution. Greater flexibility of treatment may be achieved, however, by classifying all imports by commodity type, at the same time distinguishing special commodity groups to accommodate products not produced in significant quantities at home. This treatment has now been agreed internationally (Stone, 1968).

Arbitrary scaling of competitive imports to satisfy a balance of payments constraint makes little economic sense: at least in a market economy. It is preferable, though it complicates the model, to seek behavioural relationships governing imports. Consider a relationship of the form:

$$\log m_i = a_{0i} + a_{1i} \log (q_i + m_i) + a_{2i} \log (\theta^{-1} p_{fi}{}^{-1} p_i) \qquad (1)$$

where m_i is the import, price p_{fi}

q_i is the output of the home produced substitute, price p_i

and θ is the exchange rate.

This general form of equation covers both competitive and complementary imports. If substitution is impossible, $a_{1i} = 1$ and all other parameters are zero.[5]

Agricultural commodities, however, require special treatment (in a U.K. model) because of the operation of guaranteed prices (Cambridge DAE f1, f2).

Equation (1) is one among several possibilities. For example, a linear relationship has some convenient additive properties and would be easier to incorporate into the model. But it involves the rather implausible assumption that elasticities fall as demand rises, which is particularly unsatisfactory for a medium-term projection model where demand levels are substantially higher than over the period of estimation.

Since exports (x_i) are met entirely from home production,[6] it is argu-

[5] Such imports generally have a few readily identifiable users (e.g. crude oil in oil refining) and import statistics permit the estimation of unusually good relationships for determining the demand for these commodities (Barker and Lecomber, 1967, Cambridge DAE f2).

[6] Re-exports are quantitatively not very important and in any case it is generally convenient to define imports and exports to exclude re-exports.

able that imports should be related to home demands $(q_i + m_i - x_i)$. On the other hand, an increase in export demand may be met by switching goods originally intended for the home market, this deficiency being made up by additional imports. While heterogeneity of product groups often reduces the scope for such a chain of substitutions, the matter cannot be settled *a priori*.

Foreign prices and home prices could be included separately:

$$\log m_i = a_{0i} + a_{1i} \log (q_i + m_i) - a_{2i} \log (\theta p_{fi}) + a_{3i} \log p_i \quad (2)$$

and indeed, in estimating such relationships from annual time-series data for the U.K., we have, in several cases, obtained values of a_{2i} and a_{3i} (the suffix i denoting the i-th commodity) differing significantly from each other.

But equation (2) introduces money illusion which consequently pervades the model. The incorporation of such relationships means for example that the effect of a 5 per cent devaluation is not exactly nullified by a 5 per cent rise in home costs. Money illusion may exist, but it should surely not be introduced accidentally.

In fact m_i may be governed by a more elaborate relationship including the prices of other substitutes:

$$\log m_i = a_{0i} + a_{1i} \log(q_i + m_i) - a_{2i} \log(\theta p_{fi}) + a_{3i} \log p_i + a_{4i} \log p_j \quad (3)$$

The condition that there shall be no money illusion is then $a_{2i} = a_{3i} + a_{4i}$. In such a case $a_{2i} \neq a_{3i}$, and if the p_j term is omitted, perhaps because a_{4i} does not differ significantly from zero, significantly different estimates of a_{2i} and a_{3i} are quite likely to be obtained and yet it would be wrong to infer the existence of money illusion, and wrong to introduce it into this model.[7]

Another consideration is the need to avoid bias in estimating the

---

[7] The question, however, depends partly on the relative movements of p_i and p_j over the period of estimation and the application of the model. Suppose over the period of estimation the movements in p_i and p_j were correlated; then on omission of the p_j term, the p_i term will apparently explain the variation properly attributable to p_j, and the equation will probably be free of money illusion. The relationship obtained would be adequate in an analysis of the effects of devaluation if this led to similar movements in p_i and p_j, but would not be adequate if the effect of a change in p_i for constant p_j' were under consideration. *Per contra*, if, over the period of estimation, movements in p_i and p_j were uncorrelated, then omission of the p_j term will not have much effect on the p_i term, and money illusion will be introduced. The relationship obtained would in this case be adequate for considering the effect of a change in p_i for constant p_j but inadequate for analysing the effect of devaluation.

relationships. This militates against use of q_i or q_i/m_i as the dependent variable; for q_i, much more than m_i, is likely to be correlated with (q_i+m_i) for reasons other than that under investigation: firstly q_i is the larger component of (q_i+m_i) and probably the less accurately measured, so that bias due to errors in measurement will be greater; secondly the supply of home output is much less elastic than that of imports, so that the bias due to a change in supply conditions on dependent and independent variable is also likely to be greater.

This raises the general question as to whether possibilities of bias cannot be eliminated by simultaneous equation methods, and indeed in some cases we have found these useful. Ideally since everything in the model is related to everything else, the whole system should be solved as one vast set of simultaneous equations. Data limitations and computational limitations set bounds to what can be done in practice. In addition there is the difficulty that the reduction in bias is gained only at the expense of considerably increased errors of estimate; such errors can be of such magnitude that the whole system breaks down.

The classification of imports is determined to a considerable extent by the availability of data. The 1963 input–output tables are to include a cross-classification of imports by commodity group and user industry or category of final demand. Were this information available annually it would be possible to estimate relationships of the form (1) for each separate cell, although it is doubtful how far this would repay the time involved.

However, annual data is not classified by user, only by product type. Consequently (1) can only be estimated for total imports of a particular product independent of use. However, two refinements are possible. The first is to disaggregate imports and home outputs into subaggregates of the main commodity groups of the input–output tables (subcommodities). Relationships between subcommodity imports and subcommodity demands, and between the latter and parent commodity demands may then be combined to obtain functions of import-subcommodities in terms of parent commodity demands. This is the course we have adopted at Cambridge.

The second, which will be made possible on publication of the 1963 input–output tables, takes explicit account of the market structure of demand.

$$\log m_i = a_{0i} + a_{1i} \log m_i^* + a_{2i} \log \left(\theta^{-1} p_{fi}^{-1} p_i\right) \qquad (4)$$

is exactly the same as (1) except that (q_i+m_i) has been replaced by

m_i^*, the "expected" level of imports defined by:

$$m_i^* = (m_i + q_i) \frac{\sum_j d_{ij0}\, r_j\, l_{ij0}}{\sum_j d_{ij0}\, r_j} \tag{5}$$

where d_{ij0} is the total demands by user j in the base year (1963),

r_j is an indicator of demands by user j expressed as a ratio to the base year. (In the case of intermediate demands the indicators will generally be industry outputs.)

l_{ij0} is the proportion of demands met by imports in the base year.

In estimation, the greatest difficulties concern the elimination of short-term influences and the separation of price and volume movements. As is well known, even the finest categories distinguished in the Annual Statements of Trade are not homogeneous and there is considerable scope for quality changes, which cannot be detected. The problem is particularly serious for manufacturers. Errors of measurement in the volume series involve equal and opposite errors in the price series and tend to bias the estimates of price elasticity towards unity. Rather similar problems concern the measurement of the prices and outputs of home substitutes. It is very doubtful whether errors of measurement of this kind show much tendency to cancel out when the series are aggregated to provide the price and volume series for broad groups which the authorities are prepared to publish.

The separation of long- and short-term influences is of some importance; for example, if demand for a commodity rises, and productive capacity is already at full stretch, most of the additional demand is likely to be met from imports. In the longer term home capacity will be expanded to meet the new situation and the effect on imports is likely to be much less. There are a number of possible approaches to this problem. Firstly the difference between the short-term and the long-term response may be associated with particular variables (such as capacity utilisation), which may be incorporated in the equation; but often appropriate variables cannot be found or cannot be quantified. A second approach is to make some general algebraic assumption about the relation of the short-term and the long-term response, such as a distributed lag function, or to introduce a concept like the "normal" or the "desired" level of imports, which is then eliminated from two equations. Finally it would be possible to estimate import functions from cross-section data relating to different industrial countries; the problem here is that other factors accounting for intercountry differences in import levels may be difficult to identify; furthermore the number of suitable countries for comparison is rather small, and the data is not fully comparable.

IV. DEMAND FUNCTIONS FOR EXPORTS

A similar function may be written down for exports:

$$\log x_i = a_{3i} + a_{4i} \log d_{fi} + a_{5i} \log (\theta^{-1} p_{fi}^{-1} p_i) \tag{6}$$

where x_i = exports

d_{fi} = foreign demands.

Most of the problems mentioned in connection with imports apply equally to exports. Additional problems are raised by the very heterogeneous nature of foreign demands and difficulties in their measurement.

Since some countries may rely on home sources of supply, it may be appropriate to use total imports by foreign countries rather than total consumption as a measure of foreign demands. Taking this idea one stage further, certain countries derive a higher proportion of their supplies from Britain and, *ceteris paribus*, changes in the demand in such countries will have a disproportionate influence on British exports. This may be allowed for by constructing an index of world demands formed by weighting indices of each country's imports by British exports to the country in some base year. Such an approach, however, involves the assembly of a considerable body of data, and with only a little more work the area pattern of Britain's exports may be treated more explicitly.

Denote the matrix of exports, in year t cross-classified by commodity and destination, by $\mathbf{X}_t$. A separate function may be estimated for each x_{ij}:

$$\text{e.g.} \quad \log x_{ij} = a_{ij} + b_{ij} \log (\theta^{-1} p_{fij}^{-1} p_i) + c_{ij} \log d_{ij} \tag{7}$$

where d_{ij} represents total imports of commodity i in region j. A large number of degrees of freedom may be gained by estimating the whole set of equations together assuming:

$$\left. \begin{array}{ll} (1) \ b_{ij} = b_i & (\text{all } j) \\ (2) \ c_{ij} = c_{1i}c_{2j} & \end{array} \right\} \tag{8}$$

in other words, that the price elasticity of demand for each commodity is independent of region, and that the demand coefficient is composed of a commodity effect and a region effect.

The set of equations becomes, in matrix form:

$$\log \mathbf{X} = \mathbf{A} + \hat{\mathbf{b}} \log (\theta^{-1} \hat{\mathbf{p}}_f^{-1} \mathbf{pi}') + \hat{\mathbf{c}}_1 \log \mathbf{D}\hat{\mathbf{c}}_2 \qquad (9)$$

The above example is illustrative. A variety of alternative hypotheses are feasible, and of course any number of variables can be introduced.

The accuracy of estimation will be increased with the increase in the degrees of freedom, provided the hypotheses are a fair approximation to reality. The deviations should be examined carefully, and particular elements which do not appear to satisfy the hypothesis can be treated separately.

Foreign demands are related to British imports via the foreign trade multiplier, and ideally should not be regarded as exogenous. To introduce these links would convert the model into an inter-regional model with two regions: U.K. and the Rest of the World. However, the foreign trade multiplier is unlikely to be large even for a major trading nation like the U.K., and this refinement is one that can be accorded low priority.

V. SUPPLY PRICES AND INPUT–OUTPUT DUAL

The identity:

VALUE OF OUTPUT = COST OF COMMODITY INPUTS + WAGES + PROFITS   (10)

may be regarded as definitional of profits. Alternatively, it may be used to determine commodity prices, given the prices of commodity inputs and the returns to primary inputs. For this latter purpose, a number of assumptions are necessary.

Define $\mathbf{p}_d$ as the vector of average commodity prices paid by home consumers, so that:

$$\mathbf{p}_d = \mathbf{l}\mathbf{p} + (\mathbf{I} - \mathbf{l})\theta \mathbf{p}_f \qquad (11)$$

where
$$\mathbf{l} = (\hat{\mathbf{q}} + \hat{\mathbf{m}} - \hat{\mathbf{x}})^{-1}(\mathbf{q} - \mathbf{x}) \qquad (12)$$

If it can be assumed that consumers pay these average prices $\mathbf{p}_d$, then the matrix of commodity input costs is simply $\hat{\mathbf{q}}\mathbf{A}'\hat{\mathbf{p}}_d$ where $\mathbf{A}$ is the matrix of average input–output coefficients.

Now, as all prices are indices, the assumption implies not that all purchasers pay the same absolute price but that any differences between the price at which a commodity is sold to different users are proportional to the differences pertaining in the base year. The validity of the assumption will depend partly on the homogeneity of product groups, partly on the success with which other sources of price heterogeneity have been removed. This is one of the reasons why it is customary to value output at producers' prices, deeming the purchasers to make separate payments for distribution and transport which are likely to vary between different classes of consumer. Exactly the same consideration applies to certain tax payments; if the effective tax payments vary according to the consumer of the product, then the taxes should be debited to the consumer, even if they are in fact paid by the producer; the most notable example is tobacco duty, where producers receive a drawback in respect of exports.[8]

Wages per unit of output (g_l) may be expressed as the product of constant price unit labour input ($\mathbf{a}_l$) and wage rates ($\mathbf{r}_l$). Similarly unit profits (g_k) may be expressed as the product of constant price capital per unit of output ($\mathbf{a}_k$) and the rate of return on capital ($\mathbf{r}_k$):

$$g_l = \hat{\mathbf{a}}_l \mathbf{r}_l \tag{13}$$

$$g_k = \hat{\mathbf{a}}_k \mathbf{r}_k \tag{14}$$

In the long run, competitive forces maintain a certain stability in the relative ratio of return on capital in different industries.[9] $\mathbf{r}_l$ and $\mathbf{r}_k$ may in turn be expressed in terms of a general measure of unit factor rewards (ω).[10]

$$\mathbf{r}_l = \mathbf{b}_l \omega \tag{15}$$

$$\mathbf{r}_k = \mathbf{b}_k \omega \tag{16}$$

Collecting the expressions for costs together and substituting in (10):

$$\hat{\mathbf{q}}\mathbf{p} = \hat{\mathbf{q}}\mathbf{A}'[\hat{\mathbf{l}}\mathbf{p} + (\mathbf{I}-\hat{\mathbf{l}})\theta\mathbf{p}_f] + \hat{\mathbf{q}}\hat{\mathbf{a}}_l\mathbf{b}_l\omega + \hat{\mathbf{q}}\hat{\mathbf{a}}_k\mathbf{b}_k\omega \tag{17}$$

$$\mathbf{p} = \mathbf{A}'[\hat{\mathbf{l}}\mathbf{p} + (\mathbf{I}-\hat{\mathbf{l}})\theta\mathbf{p}_f] + [\hat{\mathbf{a}}_l\mathbf{b}_l + \hat{\mathbf{a}}_k\mathbf{b}_k]\omega \tag{18}$$

$$\mathbf{p} = [\mathbf{I}-\mathbf{A}'\hat{\mathbf{l}}]^{-1}[\mathbf{A}'(\mathbf{I}-\hat{\mathbf{l}})\theta\mathbf{p}_f + (\hat{\mathbf{a}}_l\mathbf{b}_l + \hat{\mathbf{a}}_k\mathbf{b}_k)\omega] \tag{19}$$

VI. SOLVING THE MODEL FOR FIXED PRICES

Let us now fit these relationships into a complete model.

$$\mathbf{q} + \mathbf{m} = \mathbf{Wi} + \mathbf{h} + \mathbf{x} \tag{20}$$

is simply an accounting identity equating demands for exports, home final consumption (**h**) and industrial use (**Wi**) with supplies. Industrial demands are for simplicity here represented by a proportional relationship:

$$\mathbf{W} = \mathbf{A}\hat{\mathbf{q}} \tag{21}$$

---

[8] It is to be regretted that the official U.K. input–output tables [UK 1961 and f2] debit these taxes to producers making for price heterogeneity and instability of the corresponding columns of the input–output matrix.

[9] This point is developed further in Section IX.

[10] The Blue Book item "Home unit costs" is appropriate.

Home final demands are, in total, constrained by resource availability:

$$\mathbf{h'i} + \mathbf{x'i} = \eta + \mathbf{m'i} \tag{22}$$

where η is the gross domestic product. This equality is in practice maintained either by government action to regulate demand or, if this is not forthcoming, by the operation of inflationary or deflationary pressures. The possibility of substantial unemployment is ruled out by the assumptions of a medium-term model. In any operational model such influences must be made explicit, and the various constituents of home final demands (public and private consumption *and* investment) must be distinguished and their determinants examined. But, as this paper is primarily concerned with foreign trade relationships, these influences have been condensed into a single linear relationship giving $\mathbf{h}$ in terms of total resources available:

$$\mathbf{h} = \mathbf{a}_5 + \mathbf{a}_6 \mathbf{h'i} = \mathbf{a}_5 + \mathbf{a}_6(\eta + \mathbf{m'i} - \mathbf{x'i}) \tag{23}$$

where:

$$\mathbf{i'a}_5 = 0, \quad \mathbf{i'a}_6 = 1 \tag{24}$$

How the parameters in $\mathbf{a}_5$ and $\mathbf{a}_6$ depend on government policy will be considered briefly in Section VIII.

Rewriting the foreign trade functions (1) and (6) in vector notation:

$$\log \mathbf{m} = \mathbf{a}_0 + \hat{\mathbf{a}}_1 \log (\mathbf{q}+\mathbf{m}) + \hat{\mathbf{a}}_2 \log (\theta^{-1} \hat{\mathbf{p}}_f^{-1} \mathbf{p}) \tag{25}$$

$$\log \mathbf{x} = \mathbf{a}_3 + \hat{\mathbf{a}}_4 \log (\theta^{-1} \hat{\mathbf{p}}_f^{-1} \mathbf{p}) \tag{26}$$

Foreign demands may be taken as exogenous *and* included in the *constant* term. For given prices, these reduce further to:

$$\log \mathbf{m} = \mathbf{b}_0 + \hat{\mathbf{b}}_1 \log (\mathbf{q}+\mathbf{m}) \tag{27}$$

$$\mathbf{x} = \mathbf{b}_2 \tag{28}$$

The non-linearity of the import function is inconvenient, but presents no insuperable problem. It may be replaced by the linear approximation:

$$\mathbf{m} = \mathbf{b}_3 + \hat{\mathbf{b}}_4 \mathbf{q} \tag{29}$$

valid in the region of an initially assumed demand vector. Substitution in equation (20) gives:

$$\mathbf{q} + (\mathbf{b}_3 + \hat{\mathbf{b}}_4\mathbf{q}) = \mathbf{Aq} + \mathbf{a}_5 + \mathbf{a}_6(\eta + \mathbf{b}_3'\mathbf{i} + \mathbf{b}_4'\mathbf{q} - \mathbf{b}_2'\mathbf{i}) + \mathbf{b}_2 \tag{30}$$

where:

$$\mathbf{q} = [\mathbf{I} - \mathbf{A} + \hat{\mathbf{b}}_4 - \mathbf{a}_6\mathbf{b}_4']^{-1}[\mathbf{a}_5 + \mathbf{b}_2 - \mathbf{b}_3 + \mathbf{a}_6(\eta - \mathbf{b}_2'\mathbf{i} + \mathbf{b}_3'\mathbf{i})] \tag{31}$$

Imports and hence new estimates of demands are immediately obtained and used to reapproximate the import function. The calculation proceeds until the differences between the assumed and calculated values of demands are considered sufficiently small. The (dollar) balance may then be calculated, using:

$$\beta = \theta p'x - p_f'm \tag{32}$$

Convergence is in practice extremely rapid.

VII. A GENERAL BALANCE OF PAYMENTS ADJUSTMENT MECHANISM

So far the model has been solved for fixed prices; the balance of payments implications of given price trends is of some interest but the matter can hardly end there. Balance of payments disequilibria, particularly deficits, cannot be maintained for long; any medium term projection implying an imbalance is in a sense a false projection since the imbalance must somehow or other be removed. It is useful if the model can by simulating the government's corrective measures also provide a projection with the external account in balance.

One method of correction is to change relative prices, devaluing the currency for example. Imports and exports and hence the dollar balance $(\theta\, p'x - p_f'm)$ are functions of $\theta^{-1}\, \hat{p}_f^{-1}\, p$ and from equation (19):

$$\theta^{-1}\, \hat{p}_f^{-1}\, p = \hat{p}_f^{-1}\, [I - A'l]^{-1}[A'(I - l)p_f + (\hat{a}_1\, b_l + \hat{a}_k\, b_k)\theta^{-1}\omega] \tag{33}$$

l is endogenous but is also expressible in terms of $\theta^{-1}\omega$. Hence a reduction of the home price level and devaluation have the same effect. This satisfactory feature depends on using import and export functions which are free from money illusion (see Section III).

The balance of goods and services may be plotted against $\theta^{-1}\omega$ (Figure 2). The shape of this function will depend on the values of the parameters, and in particular the price elasticities for imports and exports, a_2 and a_4. In practice, for Britain, as for other advanced nations, the elasticities are sufficiently large for a fall in home prices relative to those abroad, represented in the model as a fall in $\theta^{-1}\omega$, to improve the balance of goods and services.

The point, P, where the balance of goods and services is equal to some target magnitude (β^*)[11] may be found by successively varying $\theta^{-1}\omega$ according to some systematic iterative scheme such as

$$\frac{(\theta^{-1}\omega)_n - (\theta^{-1}\omega)_{n-1}}{(\theta^{-1}\omega)_{n-1} - (\theta^{-1}\omega)_{n-2}} = \frac{\beta^* - \beta_{n-1}}{\beta_{n-1} - \beta_{n-2}} \tag{34}$$

[11] The appropriate value of β^* depends to some extent on the capital and transfer items which also contribute to the overall balance of payments. The determinants of these are not considered in this paper.

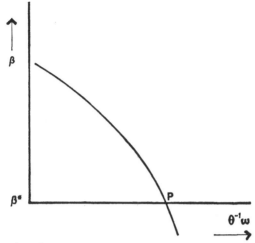

Figure 2. Relative Prices and the Balance of Goods and Services

where β^* is the desired balance of goods and services and the suffix n numbers iterations. $(\theta^{-1}\omega)_0$ and $(\theta^{-1}\omega)_1$ may, within limits, depending on the shape of the function, be chosen arbitrarily.

VIII. OTHER ADJUSTMENT MECHANISMS AND THE ROLE OF THE GOVERNMENT

In recent years the most commonly used method of correcting British balance of payments disequilibria has been to cut back home demand; in the short run the capacity to supply is unaffected and the impact is strong; imports are reduced while exports are unaffected or may even be increased as the home market becomes less attractive. Control of demand also has two long-term effects, on home unit costs (ω) and on productive capacity (η). The effect of changes in ω has already been discussed.

According to the model, as so far described, a fall in η improves the balance of payments. For the import function includes a demand term, while the export function does not include a supply term. This raises the whole question as to whether a higher level of productive capacity involves higher exports ceteris paribus, and what ceteris paribus assumption it is appropriate to make.

International comparisons reveal a striking association between growth in exports and G.D.P. [O.E.C.D., 1966]. Part of this may be attributable to the favourable impact of growth on inflation, in which case an equation should be introduced into the model relating ω and η. But the association between exports and growth persists even after allowance has been made for this factor—although it may be questioned whether price indices ever take adequate account of quality changes, which are likely to be systematically associated with growth. Unfortunately hypotheses must be formed in terms of available data, model-building being rather more exacting than theorising in this respect. Various writers (Beckerman (1962), Emery (1967)) favour the idea of export-led growth, caused by multiplier effects, dissemination of knowledge and easing of the balance of payments constraint. Others (Linnemann (1966), Waelbroeck (1967)) maintain a converse causal relationship. Waelbroeck considers that, in the face of considerable ignorance as to the possible sources of supply, export demand depends to a great extent on the efforts of exporters to sell their wares, which will depend in turn on their capacity to supply. As none of the protagonists produce convincing empirical evidence to distinguish between the rival theories the question remains wide open—and it is one of vital importance to model building and policy formation alike.

Other methods of balance of payments adjustment appropriate to a western mixed economy will be briefly considered. Tariffs may quite easily be incorporated by modifying equation (25). $\mathbf{p}_f$ is replaced by $\mathbf{p}_{ft}$ where

$$\mathbf{p}_{ft} = \hat{\mathbf{p}}_f(\mathbf{i}+\mathbf{t}_v)+\mathbf{t}_s \tag{35}$$

where $\mathbf{t}_v$ is a vector of ad valorem duty rates, $\mathbf{t}_s$ a vector of specific duties. For most commodity groups either $\mathbf{t}_v$ or $\mathbf{t}_s$ will be zero.

Similarly export rebates or subsidies ($\mathbf{s}_v$, $\mathbf{s}_s$) involve the replacement of $\mathbf{p}$ by

$$\mathbf{p}_t = \hat{\mathbf{p}}(\mathbf{i}-\mathbf{s}_v)-\mathbf{s}_s \tag{36}$$

Import quotas present a greater difficulty. If the quota levels ($\overline{m}_i$) are given then imports can be represented by

$$\begin{cases} \log m_i = + \log (q_i+m_i) + \log (\theta^{-1}\, \hat{p}_{fi}^{-1}\, p_i) \text{ provided } m_i<\overline{m}_i \\ \quad m_1 = \overline{m}_1 \text{ otherwise} \end{cases} \tag{37}$$

the equations being written in suffix notation to avoid ambiguity.

The model may still be solved using a linear approximation appropriate to the level of demand (q_i+m_i) obtained in the previous iteration. Convergence problems may however be aggravated by the kink.

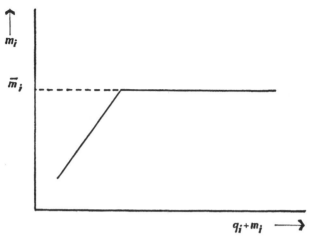

Figure 3. The Operation of Import Quotas

But it may well be asked whether it makes much sense to set quota levels independently of (expected) levels of demand. A function of the form:

$$\log \mathbf{m} = \mathbf{z} + [\mathbf{a}_0 + \hat{\mathbf{a}}_1 \log (\mathbf{q} + \mathbf{m}) + \hat{\mathbf{a}}_2 \log (\theta^{-1} \hat{\mathbf{p}}_f^{-1} \mathbf{p})] \quad (38)$$

might be preferable. The vector $\mathbf{e}^z$ represents the proportions in which categories of import would be cut back if quotas were brought into operation.

Another problem is that foreign prices might be affected by the imposition of quotas.

The introduction of all these policy variables raises the problem as to how they should be determined. Considerations of space prohibit more than a brief indication of alternative approaches; in order of sophistication:

(1) variable exogenous,
(2) exploration of various alternative combinations of these variables,
(3) variables expressed as a function of an overall policy variable, which may be adjusted in response to payments imbalance, thus performing a role analogous to $(\theta^{-1}\omega)$,
(4) a programming approach.

Finally it should be noted that certain government measures to improve the balance of payments, ranging from exhortation to the

L

provision of easier credit terms to exporters, even if difficult to quantify should not be ignored altogether.

IX. THE INTERACTION OF SUPPLY AND DEMAND

The model has so far been developed on the assumption of perfectly elastic supply (diagrams (*a*) and (*b*)). The shape of the demand curves is then immaterial, since prices can be found at the outset, using the input–output dual, and the price terms in the demand

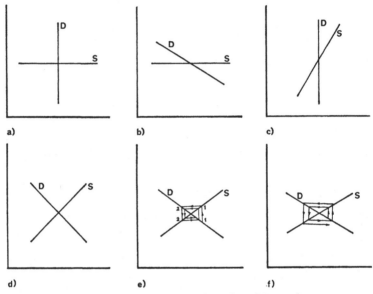

Figure 4. The Interaction of Supply and Demand

functions evaluated. Conversely if demand is everywhere inelastic (*c*) the real side of the model may be solved first, and the price circuit then solved for the values of output obtained. But, if neither perfectly inelastic demand nor perfectly elastic supply can be assumed, solution of the model becomes considerably more complicated. Various iterative schemes can be devised, the most obvious being to alternate between the primal and the dual calculation using the prices and output levels (respectively) obtained in the previous iteration (*e*). There is, however, no guarantee that the cobweb will converge (*f*). The computational problems associated with estimating and solving simultaneous sets of supply and demand equations in a multi-sector model are hardly insuperable but they are sufficiently great to be avoided as far as possible.

The perfect elasticity of the supply curve rests on two assumptions. The first is that primary and secondary inputs are everywhere proportional to outputs. Unit capital costs are likely to vary substantially with output both in the short term and the long. In the short term changes in output will be associated with changes in capacity utilisation, while in the long term there will be economies of scale in many sectors. In the uncomfortable medium-term of the planners there is the added complication of the legacy of old plant; the higher the level of output, the greater the proportion that will be produced using new plant, embodying more efficient techniques, probably also involving different combinations of other inputs. Wigley (1968) describes a production model of the kind required to elucidate this kind of problem.

The second assumption is that the rate of return on capital is independent of output. In what might be called the theoretical long term, mobility of factors ensures that entrepreneurs in all sectors earn normal profits, though there may be some intersectoral variation in what is normal, depending on for example, risk. However, the forces of competition work slowly, and indeed entrepreneurs may, by restricting entry, be able to earn supernormal profits indefinitely. In the medium term it cannot be assumed that changes in input costs will simply be passed on leaving unit profits unchanged if this would involve a substantial change in sales.

Let us consider the effects of the recent British devaluation. Supply prices of British goods rise by amounts varying from about 3 to 15 per cent. This variation is reduced by any additional inflation at home. Where the relative supply prices of close substitutes change markedly (e.g. coal and oil), it is probable that, in the short and medium term, competition on the demand side will moderate the actual movement in relative prices. But by and large the movement in relative supply prices of close-substitutes produced and sold at home is not great, so that, as our industrial contacts confirm, devaluation will have little effect on their competitive position vis-à-vis other home-produced commodities.

But the position of home-produced goods vis-à-vis their foreign-produced counterparts is rather different. In each market, the price will tend to be set by the predominant group and other suppliers will tend to move their prices into line. In most British markets, British suppliers predominate, and foreigners may lower their dollar prices following devaluation in an attempt to maintain their share of the

British market. But often they may prefer to switch their supplies to some non-devaluing country. There may be some tendency for British producers of goods closely competing with imports to raise their profit margins.

In foreign markets, foreign suppliers generally predominate, and their prices are unlikely to drop much following devaluation. Consequently British exporters will be able to raise their profit margins and still secure a substantial increase in sales. As a result, export prices are likely to rise by more than the prices of similar goods sold on the home market (cf. N.I.E.R. (1967)). It might be thought that supplies could quite easily be shifted from one market to another, especially when the same firm supplies both markets, and that firms will allocate their supplies between markets to maintain price differentials which reflect differences in selling costs, risk, etc. However, in practice, it would seem that price differentials, which cannot be explained in this way, can persist for a long time, possibly because firms consider other objectives than profits. Whether or not these differentials would vanish eventually in the absence of further external stimuli, it would be unilluminating to fall back on a theoretical analysis to discount effects that can persist for so long.

A further complication is that the rise in exporters' profits following devaluation is likely to increase firms' efforts to capture export markets. Marketing will be intensified, after-sales services improved and greater priority given to exports when supplies are scarce. The demand curve for exports will be raised by these efforts (which we shall refer to as "sales effort").

The following is an attempt to express these ideas algebraically.[12] The demand function must include a vector of terms representing sales effort (s), e.g.:

$$\log \mathbf{x}_D = \mathbf{a}_3 + \hat{\mathbf{a}}_4 \log \mathbf{d}_f + \hat{\mathbf{a}}_5 \log (\theta^{-1} \hat{\mathbf{p}}_f^{-1} \mathbf{p}_x) + \hat{\mathbf{a}}_6 \log \mathbf{s} \quad (39)$$

The problems of measuring s are very great, but this may be avoided by writing down another equation determining s, which may then be eliminated by substitution. The main effect which we wish to include in this context is that sales effort, etc., will be stimulated by higher prices and profits relative to those pertaining in the home market. Hence:

$$\mathbf{s} = \hat{\mathbf{a}}_7 \hat{\mathbf{p}}_h^{-1} \mathbf{p}_x \quad (40)$$

---

[12] A more satisfying but at the same time much more complicated theory could be developed making firms' objective functions and the costs of extra sales effort, etc., explicit. Assumptions about the structure of an industry would also be necessary in passing from the individual firm to the industrial aggregate.

might be a reasonable first shot. Then, by substitution:

$$\log x_D = a_3 + \hat{a}_4 \log d_f + \hat{a}_5 \log (\theta^{-1} \hat{p}_f^{-1} p_x) + \hat{a}_6 \log (\hat{a}_7 \hat{p}^{-1} p_x) \tag{41}$$

The supply of exports (x_s) may also be made to depend on the relative prices of exports and home sales:

$$\log x_s = a_8 + \hat{a}_9 \log (\hat{p}_h^{-1} p_x) \tag{42}$$

For given values of p_h, x and p_x may be found by simultaneous solution of equations (41) and (42). In fact the position is a little more complicated, since p_h cannot be found independently of p_x; they are connected by the identity:

$$\hat{h}p_h + \hat{x}p_x = \hat{q}p \tag{43}$$

and the export equations must be solved simultaneously with the complete price circuit.

The ideas introduced in this section raise problems of measurement and estimation which may prove somewhat intractible, at least until considerably improved price indices are available. Meanwhile we have incorporated these relationships into our model even though the parameter values used are pure guesses. We have done this because the simpler model presented in the earlier sections involves the assumption that the supply elasticities of exports (a_9) are infinite, which is not only equally arbitrary but demonstrably biased.

X. CONCLUDING REMARKS

The publication of the 1963 input–output tables will mark an important landmark in British statistics. The new information provided, immensely valuable in its own right, should provide a much needed fillip to input–output work in this country.

But two points should be borne constantly in mind. The first is that the 1963 tables provide a frozen picture of intersectoral relations, frozen at a point of time already five years back and receding rapidly into the distance in a period of rapid changes. If full value is to be derived from these tables, changes and the reasons for them must be carefully examined in an intersectoral framework. To this end it is vital that time series data be closely integrated with the 1963 input–output tables. In Cambridge we are setting up a computerised data bank with this end very much in view.

The second point is closely related. We must not be so impressed with the structural detail of an input–output table, that we accept uncritically the proportionality assumptions which its form suggests. I have tried in this paper to indicate how, in the field of foreign trade, realistic assumptions, formal regression methods and sectoral detail may be combined within the general framework of an input–output model.

ANNEXE*

Of the seventeen models, ten closely resemble the original Leontief (1951) pattern. Exports are either exogenous or (5) proportionally related to total imports. Nine of these models classify imports by user and industrial imports are proportional to output levels. The external account is either left unbalanced (2, 7, 8, 11, 14, 15), or balanced by *ad hoc* methods (1, 4) or by scaling exports (5). Model 12 divides imports into competitive and complementary; competitive imports, classified by commodity type are linearly related to total competitive imports allowed by the balance of payments constraint. Some of these were early models, and many were prevented from lack of adequate data or computing facilities for attempting anything more elaborate.

Four are programming models (3, 6, 9, 10). The computational demands of this approach dictate a fairly simple structure, and in all cases the treatment of foreign trade is unsatisfactory. It may also be questioned whether, in a free market economy, the government is in a position to control the variables of the linear programme, and whether the programme ought not instead to be set up in terms of tax variables and other instruments more directly under government control. Finally the maximand of all the models is a very simple expression, such as total consumption. Simpson (model 6) derives shadow prices for a past year and compares them with actual prices, it being concluded from the divergence that resources are being misallocated; but the shadow prices depend on the maximand, and the only conclusion that can validly be drawn is that, implicitly, the government was, as it surely should have been, maximising something other than total consumption. Until more realistic assumptions can be built into these models, they will remain interesting rather than useful.[13]

Models 13 and 17 aim instead at spelling out the behavioural relationships of the economy as accurately as possible. Presentation of a number of alternatives accurately described is arguably a better

---

* Numbers in round brackets refer to the numbered models in Table 1 below.

[13] Model 9 incorporates an unusual feature. The price of services is one of the variables of the programme and appears in particular in the equation for imports. This is an interesting attempt to introduce behavioural as well as technical relationships into a linear programme.

Table 1. Treatment of Foreign Trade in Selected Input–Output Models used for Medium-term Projection and Planning in Market Economies

Country	Reference	No. of prod. sectors	Special features and remarks	Balance of payments	Treatment of exports	Division of imports into compel/compl	Treatment of competitive imports	Role of prices	Determination of prices
1. Belgium	Paelinck, J. (1965) Le modèle econometrique d'exploration utilisé par le Bureau de Programmations Economique Belge in (ed.) Parenti, *Modelli Econometrie per la Programmazione.* Florence.	14		Balanced by *ad hoc* adjustment	Exogenous (targets)	Yes	Proportional to demands	1. Construction of current price matrix. 2. Explanatory variables in consumption function	Primary input prices exogenous $p_x = p_m = p$
2. Egypt	Eleish, G. (1963) The input–output model in a developing economy: Egypt in (ed.) Barna, *Structural interdependence and economic development.* Macmillan, London.	33		Not balanced	Exogenous	No	All industrial imports proportional to user outputs	None	—
3. France	Nataf, A. (1965) Variante marginale d'un plan; problèmes d'adjustment. In (ed.) Parenti, *Modelli econometrie per la Programmazione.* Florence.	12	Programming	Yes	Exogenous	Yes	Exogenous	—	Shadow prices derived
4. India	Manne, A. S. (1964) *Studies in the structure of the Indian economy.* Report No. 1. A consistency model of India's 4th plan. M.I.T. Center for International Studies.	30		Ad hoc adjustment to import coefficients	Exogenous	No	Some exogenous. All other industrial imports proportional to user outputs	None	—
5. Ireland (1)	Geary, R. C. (1965) Towards an input–output decision model for Ireland. *Proceedings of the Statistical and Social Inquiry Society for Ireland,* XXI 2.	16		Balanced	Fixed proportions of total	No	All industrial inputs proportional to user outputs	None	—
6. Ireland (2)	Simpson, D. (1968) *A medium-term planning model for Ireland.* Economic and Social Research Institute. Paper No. 41. Dublin.	16	Programming	Balanced	Free to vary between exogenous bounds	Yes	Exogenous	—	Shadow prices derived

Table 1. Treatment of Foreign Trade in Selected Input-Output Models used for Medium-term Projection and Planning in Market Economies—continued

Country	Reference	No. of prod. sectors	Special features and remarks	Balance of payments	Treatment of exports	Division of imports into compet/compl	Treatment of competitive imports	Role of prices	Determination of prices
7. Israel	Bruno, M. (1963) Some applications of input-output techniques. In (ed.) Barna; Structural interdependence and economic development. Macmillan, London.	20		Not balanced	Exogenous	No	All industrial imports proportional to user outputs	None	—
8. Italy	Chenery, H. B., P. Clark and V. Cao Pinna (1953) The structure and growth of the Italian economy. USA Mutual Security Agency.	56 (200 prods.)		Not balanced	Exogenous	No	Linear relationships between imports and demands by product group capacity constraints introduced	None	—
9. Netherlands	Sandee J. (1965) An experimental phased sector model for the Netherlands. In (ed.) Parenti, Modelli econometrie per la programmazione. Florence.	71	Programming. Multi-year.	Balanced	Free to vary	No	All imports proportional to industry outputs or final demand total imports adjusted with price of services	Only one price introduced (services). Included in equations. Free to vary to achieve optimum.	—
10. New Zealand	Blyth, C. A. and G. A. Crothall (1965) A pilot programming model of the New Zealand economic development. Econometrica.	7*	Programming	Balanced	Fixed proportions of total	No	All industrial imports proportional to user outputs	—	Shadow prices derived
11. Norway	Per Sevaldsen (1964) An inter-industry model of production and consumption for economic planning in Norway. In (ed.) Clarke and Stuvel, Income redistribution and the statistical foundations of economy policy. International Association for Research in Income and Wealth, Series X.	129		Not balanced	Exogenous	No	All industrial imports proportional to user outputs	1. Conversion between current and constant prices 2. Explanatory variables for consumers' expenditure	Exogenous?

* Of the seven sectors distinguished, three (oil, agriculture, sea and air transport) are treated as exogenous.

Table 1. Treatment of Foreign Trade in Selected Input-Output Models used for Medium-term Projection and Planning in Market Economies—continued

Country	Reference	No. of prod. sectors	Special features and remarks	Balance of payments	Treatment of exports	Division of imports into compet/compl	Treatment of competitive imports	Role of prices	Determination of prices
12. U.K. (1)	Cambridge, Department of Applied Economics (1965) Exploring 1970. Some numerical results. Vol. 6 in *A Programme for Growth*, Chapman & Hall.	31	Earlier version of present model. Used for national plan	Balanced (at constant prices)	Exogenous	Yes	Linear function of total compet. imports (set by balance of payments constraint)	Determinants of consumers' expenditure	Exogenous
13. U.K. (2)	Cambridge, Department of Applied Economics (forthcoming) Exploring 1972, with special emphasis on the balance of payments. Vol. 10 in *A Programme for Growth*, Chapman & Hall.	35		Balanced	Functions of prices	No	All imports functions of demand and prices	1. Foreign trade functions 2. Consumers' expenditure functions 3. Valuation of balance of payments	Input-output dual
14. U.S. (1)	Leontief, W. W. and M. Hoffenberg (1961) The economic effects of disarmament. *Scientific American*. Reprinted in W. W. Leontief, *Input–output Economics*. O.U.P., New York, 1965.	20		Not balanced	Exogenous	No	All industrial imports proportional to user outputs	None	—
15. U.S. (2)	Almon, C. (jr.) (1966) *The American economy to 1975. An inter-industry forecast.* Harper & Row, New York.	90	Dynamic	Not balanced	Exogenous	Yes	Exogenous	None	—
16. U.S. (3)	Isard, W. (1951) Inter-regional and regional input-output. A model of a spare economy. *Review of Economics and Statistics.*	20 in each of 3 regions		Not balanced	Endogenous via foreign trade multiplier	No	All industrial imports proportional to user outputs	None	—
17. World	Group d'Etudes Prospectives sur les Echanges Internationaux (1967) Equations of GEPEI model (mimeo).	13 in each of 18 zones		Not balanced	Trade flows calculated on assumption of fixed import-output coefficients, adjusted in response to (1) relative prices in exporting and importing country, (2) proxy for sales effort, (3) size of exporting industry relative to world			Determinants of trade flows	Exogenous

basis for decision-making than an optimum derived from a mis-specified linear programme.

Model 16 is an early example of a multi-regional model. From the viewpoint of one region, foreign demand is no longer an independent variable, account being taken of the foreign trade multiplier. In this model trade flows are simple proportional functions of user industries in the importing region. Finally, model 17, a multi-regional model of the world, incorporates quite sophisticated trading relationships, although as yet prices are entirely exogenous and no attempt is made at balance of payments adjustment.

REFERENCES

BARKER, T. S. and J. R. C. LECOMBER (1967), "British Imports 1972". Report to the National Ports Council.

BARNETT, H. J. (1954), "Specific industry output projections long-range economic projection," *Studies in Income and Wealth*, Vol. XVI. Princeton University Press.

BECKERMAN, W. (1962), "Projecting Europe's growth", *Economic Journal*, December.

CAMBRIDGE, D.A.E. (f1), "Exploring 1972, with special reference to the balance of payments", No. 9 in *A Programme for Growth*. Cambridge, Department of Applied Economics. Chapman & Hall, London. Forthcoming.

CAMBRIDGE, D.A.E. (f2), "The demand for British imports 1949–66". No. 10 in *A Programme for Growth*. Cambridge, Department of Applied Economics. Chapman & Hall, London. Forthcoming.

EMERY, R. F. (1967), "The relation of exports and economic growth". Kyklos.

GHOSH, A. (1964), *Experiments with input–output models. An application to the economy of the United Kingdom 1948–55*. Cambridge University Press.

LEONTIEF, W. W. (1941), *The Structure of the American Economy 1919–39*. Second edition. Oxford University Press. New York.

LINNEMANN, H. (1966), *An econometric study of international trade flows*. North-Holland Publishing Company. Amsterdam.

N.I.E.R. (1967), "The economic situation", *National Institute Economic Review*, November 1967.

O.E.C.D. (1966). *Economic growth 1960–1970. A mid-decade review of prospects*. Organisation for Economic Co-operation and Development, Paris.

PARENTI (1965) (ed.), *Modelli econometrie per la programmazione*. Florence.

STONE, RICHARD (1961). *Input–output and National Accounts*. Organisation for Economic Co-operation and Development, Paris.

STONE, RICHARD (1968), "The revision of the SNA: an outline of the new structure", Paper presented at the symposium on National Accounts and Balances, Warsaw 1968. To be published.

WIGLEY, K. J. (1968), "Production models and time trends of input–output coefficients", Paper presented to the 1968 University of Manchester Conference on Input–Output.

WAELBROECK, J. (1967), "On the structure of international trade interdependence". Cahiers Economiques de Bruxelles.

TILANUS, C. B. (1966), *Input–Output experiments. The Netherlands 1948–61.* Rotterdam University Press.

U.K. (1961), Input–output tables for the United Kingdom 1954. *Studies in Official Statistics*, No. 8. U.K. Board of Trade and Central Statistical Office, H.M.S.O. London.

U.K. (f). Input–output tables for the United Kingdom 1963. U.K. Board of Trade and Central Statistical Office, H.M.S.O. London, forthcoming.

SESSION V: DISCUSSION OF
MR. J. R. C. LECOMBER'S PAPER

Chairman: PROFESSOR E. T. NEVIN (U.C. WALES)

PROFESSOR NEVIN

A reduction in the level of income or demand is a very different matter indeed from a reduction in the foreign exchange rate. Am I right in assuming that the statement which you made there is a purely mathematical statement and does not qualify the operation of the input–output model?

MR. LECOMBER (Cambridge)

Well, what I was really against doing was introducing money illusion, as it were, accidentally, into some of the import equations. In fact, there will be, I quite agree, all sorts of differential reactions; for example, following the British devaluation, a lot of other countries have devalued; this is one obvious thing, and it's doubtful whether they would have devalued if, instead, Britain had succeeded in curbing inflation rather more. In fact, in practical operation of the model, with the recent British devaluation, we did a special analysis where we took into account these effects of the pattern of foreign devaluations; we did this by assuming that devaluation affected p_x (or $\theta.p_x$ if you like), according to the source of the imports. Here, in fact, we introduced money illusion in a quite deliberate way in analysing a particular case.

The other example that I think you mentioned was whether a reduction in the price level would affect incomes.

PROFESSOR NEVIN

That was really the point I was trying to make. That is to say, there are two issues here: there is the relative price question—and this sentence could be interpreted to mean that a rise of 10 per cent in our home prices is the same as a fall of 10 per cent in foreign prices, as far as our exports are concerned—but that does not mean, does it, that the consequences of a fall in home costs or a "holding" of home costs, to put it more realistically, on the level of final demand within the home economy are neglected?

MR. LECOMBER

Well, we are thinking in terms of a medium-run context, so that one is presumed to be operating at full capacity either way; one isn't thinking of, say, a short-run credit squeeze: I think that's probably the answer.

Of course, there is, on the other hand, one built-in institutional money illusion: in the tax structure, in that these are fixed in money terms, and ignoring money illusion completely one assumes that the government will adjust its tax rates to cater for that.

DR. GOSSLING (Manchester)

I wish to ask the speaker about this relationship that he has found between the rate of growth of G.D.P. and the rate of growth of exports in an intercountry study: that is, comparing countries, what is the relationship between the rate of growth of exports and the rate of growth of G.D.P.? We have indications from a model for the United States, based on 1939 data, that—you could put it in this way—the higher the demand for a particular product, the more 'favourable are "your" terms of trade, if either "you" are the industry within the American economy or the exporting country within the world economy. The higher your market price, the lower, relative to other industries, or countries, are your dollar-per-dollar input–output coefficients, and therefore the easier it is for you to grow.

MR. LECOMBER

Well, on the relationship, we have tried various cross-section studies and there are various others by people like Linnemann,[1] for instance; the results vary a bit but, if one uses a log relationship, the elasticity is not far from unity. The difficulty is, though, the causality; they produce various arguments such as: that the exporters are offering a greater range of products; because their capacity to supply has increased; or they make more efforts to sell them. There is also the argument which is difficult quite to know how to cater for in an

[1] See References to Lecomber's paper.

econometric sense: that the faster you grow, the faster the quality of your product is increasing—you are producing more technologically advanced things—and this, as we know, should appear as a falling price, but the statistics probably don't pick it up in that way. For instance, computers are measured in terms of weight in the export statistics; this puts the quality change in the wrong variable, and then the econometrician is rather in a cleft stick: he knows, theoretically, how he ought to explain it, but the statistics, because of difficulties in measurement, are telling a different story. But this is one reason for increase in growth causing or appearing to cause increase in volume of exports.

MR. BERMAN (C.S.O.)

I'm not sure whether what I'm going to say is a lot of nonsense; if it is I'll strike it off the record; you can tell me if it is. I'm not quite sure how one handles all this; we are looking at input–output in a trading economy. I can understand that when one works with an input–output model one wants to arrive at reasonable projections of imports, and this is a difficult thing to do, and Mr. Lecomber has suggested a way of doing it. What worries me is: why does he bring in exports? What have exports to do with imports—except in so far as one has to balance the payments. I mean, imports are determined not only by exports; they are determined by consumption, public authorities' expenditure, fixed investment, all of which are forms of final demand. So why does he bring exports into this picture here? I would have thought exports were something quite separate; one should forecast exports independently based on what happens in other countries, growth of world trade, and so forth, and just feed them into the system; the forecast of imports just comes out in the wash. One could forecast final demand, put in projections for final demand, see what imports are, get an export requirement in order to reach a balance of payments target, but I'm not really sure why one has to bring exports and imports into the calculation at this stage. I'm not sure whether I've made myself clear.

MR. LECOMBER

It depends a bit on what one's trying to do, first of all. If one's trying to forecast imports as, for instance, we basically were for the National Ports Council, then exports are, if you like, only 25 per cent (or whatever it is) of final demand, and needn't be given very much attention. Mr. Berman did point out, however, in passing, that there was the difference that they are a component of the balance of payments, and if the initial projections, on given price assumptions, involve any imbalance, then this must be corrected and this will affect exports as well as imports; if you leave exports where they are, then imports are going to adjust too much. I think that's part of the answer.

Secondly, the purpose of our model isn't simply to project imports; it partly is to find out the balance of payments, and partly to estimate demands on sectors, and so on and so forth, and exports are an important contributory factor; so, it is true, are consumers' expenditures in our model and so on, but although these are points in our model that we devote a certain amount of time to, I just concerned myself with exports and imports today. Perhaps another reason for taking the two together is that they do raise quite a lot of similar problems; the statistical sources are the same; on a more theoretical level they both respond to changes in the exchange rate in a rather similar way.

Finally, on the question of targets; of course this is a method that has been used in plans: that you start off by estimating import requirements and then you derive export targets. One could do the opposite: one could start off by estimating export demands and then determine what imports would have to be; and, in fact, we did this at one time at Cambridge. We squeezed competitive imports to satisfy the balance of payments constraint. And both these seem to me rather arbitrarily asymmetric ways of doing it; it seems to me that one should look at both at the same time and try to adjust both exports and imports: and, moreover, in some explicit, rather than some arbitrary way in response to some variable that the government might manipulate.

MR. BAYLISS (Birmingham)

I haven't heard of the particular model in your article; we do know of another multi-sector model which Professor Coucier is doing in Paris (the Bureau of External Studies); what Heesterman and I at Birmingham are trying to do ultimately is a model of world trade where you have approximately fifteen interrelated regions which are, at the moment, rather geographically grouped, so we have as examples the U.S.A. and Canada, South America, the E.E.C. as groupings. We are trying to do a forecast for aggregate world trade and exports and imports for each region (if we are going to take these as the flows of world trade). You have a block diagonal structure for each of the fifteen regions which will be bound by the joining export equations. We work on the assumption that the exports of one region are some function of the imports of the other regions, which seems reasonable; the equations are starting to work out reasonably well anyway. If you are given this structure where you have got your vector of your forecasting variables; you then have the endogenous variables of the current period in terms of the lagged endogenous variables. If you invert this in the normal way and multiply through we should theoretically at least be able to forecast for the next period. We particularly want to try to find out the effects of the levels of liquidity and the effect it has on the other regions' trade. So given the United Kingdom, if you increase or decrease the level of liquidity of this country, what effect is it going to have on the other regions: will it increase or decrease their balance of payments or their level of investment or their rate of consumption? At the moment we have just finished a seven-region sub-model of seven developed regions, results of which ought to be out by Christmas 1968.

MR. LECOMBER

What data are you using?

MR. BAYLISS

A miscellany. Essentially the three sources are the U.N. Year Book of National Accounts Statistics, the I.M.F. International Financial Statistics, and the Directory of Trade (the latter for the export equations).

MR. LECOMBER

So you have got annual data out of all of these?

MR. BAYLISS

Of the majority of them, yes; I think 84 of the 100 U.N. countries are listed in the book, or else we have other data available.

MR. BROWN (D.E.A.)

There is one factor which you mention, in effect, when you put in a factor for sales effort, towards the end of your paper. There is a general feeling that maybe relating changes in actual export prices (compared with foreign prices) and changes in the level of exports may result in an underestimation of the elasticity—which really applies to a considerable extent not to the prices charged but to the costs. Now this would apply to a certain extent to imports too. Foreign exporters might be prepared to lower their prices in this country by the full amount of our devaluation; but it may well be that under these circumstances they are not prepared to devote quite as much money to sales promotion as in the past. There is a passage which I have glanced at, but not fully understood, at the end of Mr. Lecomber's paper which suggests one way of making some allowance for sales effort (which is taken to increase when export profits increase relative to home prices). I would be grateful if he could say something by way of explanation on this.

MR. LECOMBER

I think the *idea* is fairly clear: Mr. Brown has expanded a bit on what I was saying, that the higher prices or profits are, the more sales effort will be put in; and in fact responses to devaluation, putting in this sort of formula does get you a combination of effects: the price movement is moderated, but on the other hand there is this sales effort effect. The precise form of the equation (40) I wouldn't care to defend at all, really: this is just a suggestion; we haven't started estimating it; so I really can't say whether it is a plausible one or whether one should put an expression for profits there, or for prices, or whether one should put in the two price terms separately there, with separate coefficients. I'm not quite sure what one should do; that remains to be seen. I did just suggest at the bottom of page 142 in footnote 12 that this is a very abbreviated account and really doesn't get to the bottom of the explanation, it just tries to express it in terms of variables of the model; it is clear what one would like to do, in terms of expressing the firm's objective function, what they are trying to do, and what this implies for their pricing; but the practical difficulties in the way of doing anything explicit like that seem to be very formidable. Does that answer what you were saying?

MR. BROWN

I think it does; what I really hadn't appreciated, on a quick glance through, is that equation (40) looks reasonable, but the question is how you get the prices of exports. You have got something which I myself had not followed through.

MR. LECOMBER

How you get at them in terms of some statistics or in terms of a model?

MR. BROWN

In terms of a model.

MR. LECOMBER

Well, equation (41), which is simply obtained from eliminating the unmeasurable from equations (39) and (40), is a demand relationship for exports, and (42) is a supply relationship. Now if we assume for the moment that p_h is given (in fact, we can't assume that), then from (41) and (42) we can find at the same time x and p_x, thereby solving the supply and demand relationship. In fact p_h is not known at this stage, because p_h and p_x are prices of home sales and export sales, and they are related to the prices of total sales which was obtained from the input–output dual; these are connected, and it means solving that set of equations simultaneously with the export demand and supply equations.

MR. LUKER (I.C.I.)

I have a simple question for Mr. Lecomber, and then one on which I think the C.S.O. will wish to make a comment.

As I understand it, the model at the moment is concerned with visible trade and I wondered if Mr. Lecomber would care to comment on how invisibles and capital movements might be incorporated.

The second question is one of nomenclature: it is far easier to get good data on imports than it is on home activity, because of the greater detailed split in import and export statistics. I believe there is a move to put imports and exports and the import classification for tariff purposes on the same basis as B.T.N.; I wonder whether Mr. Berman would care to comment as to whether there is any hope of putting the S.I.C. on the same basis as the B.T.N. so that we might have one consolidated system.

MR. LECOMBER

Well, if I might take my bit of the question, this model in principle does deal with invisibles as well as visibles; it deals with imports and exports of goods *and services*; in practice the data for services is not what the data for visibles is, and the problems that I mentioned of

M

separating prices and quantity movements are virtually insuperable and one is very much plugging gaps with guesses.

The capital side we don't really attempt to do anything with at all; this is a separate and complicated story in itself. All we have done in making projections is to make rough projections of what we think the capital items might be, and these have affected our estimates of β^* the target balance of goods and services. But, of course, there is the conceptual problem that in the balance of payments adjustment mechanism one of the government's possible policies is to act on the capital and transfer side instead of on the real side; so that really something of this sort ought to be incorporated in the adjustment mechanism.

MR. BERMAN

Well, in the 1963 input–output tables which we are preparing, exports, imports and home production will be classified by seventy commodity groups; so one will be able to compare production, imports, and exports, for each commodity group. How far we do this for other years depends on how much updating we do, and how detailed the division of commodity groups will depend on how detailed the tables that we produce will be.

On the general question of classification: over the next two or three years there will be about 150 little working groups looking at each of the 150 manufacturing industries to see what sort of statistics ought to be collected from industry to serve the needs of industry and also the government. In doing this a lot of attention will be devoted to making sure that the output headings are congruent with the import headings and the export headings as far as possible. We have got a standard industrial classification; eventually we will have a standard commodity classification; I suppose for the manufacturing industries this will include something over 5,000 headings, perhaps 6,000 or 7,000, I don't know yet; this has to be worked out. The National Computing Centre have done some work on this too; they have worked out a very detailed commodity classification, but this goes into hundred of thousands I believe, which is not much use to us but it may be of use to industry. To get the export headings and the import headings into alignment is a bit difficult; there are lots of things which are imported that we don't export, but I think that pretty well everything we export we also import! But on the import side there is the statutory problem that a lot of detail is needed to meet the Customs duty and tariffs; one needs an awful lot of detail to work out what the Customs duty is. Anyway, the short answer is that these matters are under consideration and over the next few years we hope we will have a better set of statistics than we have at the moment.

PROFESSOR NEVIN

May I very briefly thank Mr. Lecomber, on your behalf and my own, for presenting his paper? I am not surprised that some of the comment was perhaps a little difficult and oblique; I read the paper twice and my feeling was that this was an exceedingly technical and advanced piece of work on which only a specialist as expert as Mr. Lecomber himself could really comment—and I don't think there are many of us in that category here.

SPECIAL SESSION

Input–Output Studies of the Construction Industry

by

A. J. SLUCE

Building Research Station, Garston, Herts.

I feel I am going to introduce a few trees after everyone else has been talking about the woods; this will be quite a change of scale in comparison with what the previous speakers have been saying.

As part of the work on an econometric analysis of the construction industry at the Building Research Station, it was decided to investigate the building of an input–output model, disaggregated for construction into eight sectors and some other sectors supplying construction, and to examine the particular value of the model to potential users, considering the level of accuracy obtained, and also considering future possible levels of accuracy. The input–output formulation was chosen as it provided a rigorous framework into which to fit the information which we found was available and in which inter-industry comparisons could be made as well.

The basis of the table was the 1963 provisional input–output table of the C.S.O. (which Mr. Upton prepared), and the disaggregated transactions were built up "from underneath" in that technical coefficients were constructed and then multiplied by total outputs to form transactions. This was felt to be possible using the expertise available in the station (where we have a large number of people who know a lot about little bits of construction). This expertise has been embodied in a report called *Design Series'58* (which is on material usage in new buildings); it lists sufficient information to be able to construct technical coefficients and to approximate a transaction. The approach has a number of difficulties in that you have to establish prices for volumes and lengths of material; we hadn't made any allowance for wastage (except as "5 per cent on the total") and also we had nothing about labour inputs, really. We are trying to improve all this at the moment on the Station (which will be a two- or three-year job) and work which is current at the Building Research Station and could be used in a future table is:

(i) an examination of the basic parameters of the building types, for example by splitting up houses and bungalows into detached, semi-detached and terrace houses (or bungalows); much more significant window, wall, and roof areas can be established, and so average areas, and areas and qualities of material can be established;

(ii) the methodology of determining the material usage is being examined; one method being a sampling of drawings submitted to the planning commission.

These two stages are necessary to be able to establish the total transactions; from the first one we can find total areas of certain elements in the building; we can establish what the total roof area is in Great Britain in semi-detached houses; we can then apportion this between the different materials from our material usages which we have established.

Then the third thing which we are doing which will be useful is the labour input by trade into different types of building and civil engineering. This is being done actually on building sites, so that it will include all the men which official statistics tend to miss, like labour of the subcontractors, or specialists engaged on a temporary basis (who are rather prevalent in the construction industry). We could also use this approach for establishing the values of materials purchased for a particular job; perhaps by looking at the contractors' invoices we could see how much he had spent on materials for a particular job number; and given the resources this would be a very good method to adopt, and this is the method we are using to establish the labour figures.

The results of our work on the 1963 provisional table has been to explain 30 per cent of the purchases ascribed to construction in the table. Some of the industries we have not attempted to tackle at all; taking only those industries that we have considered, in that we have disaggregated them and split up their sales (to construction) between building types, we have explained 45 per cent of these, so that we have only got about half the total materials we have tried to consider. So the method has failed in testing the provisional table transactions as a whole, except for the cases of other mining and quarrying and metal manufacture, where we get an 80–90 per cent coverage. The main failure has been in obtaining details of inputs into civil engineering, which is rather an institutional factor in that the Building Research Station has tended to look at building rather than civil engineering, and from the sales of the construction side the lack of information about the Service, Engineering, Other manufacturing, and Other chemical and allied industries (all of which supply over £100 million) has made rather a large hole.

The model which we have finished up with is peculiar to construction in having almost all the disaggregated sectors dependent on final demand. This occurs in two ways: by definition, construction, except for repair and maintenance appropriate to industries, is assumed to go to final demand; secondly, industries that were disaggregated were often found to supply exclusively to construction, and so become directly dependent on final demand. Thus for the bulk of the industries defined, the model does not generate any indirect demand: one of the most interesting aspects of the model. As a measure of this, the amount of indirect demand relative to direct demand can be calculated. If the industries are grouped, by the indirect input to construction expressed as a direct input (these values being taken from the coefficient and inverted matrices which we have established), out of the nineteen industries which had the largest share of indirect inputs, seven of them have been apportioned *pro rata* from building types as we have no information about them.

This is not, however, the only way of viewing the table; another field of considerable interest is the effect of changes in the price levels. As you know, these are usually generated by the exogenous items of labour, imports, taxes, and profits. The disaggregation then distinguishes many different mixes of these items; some industries depending heavily on imports, others labour intensive. Changes in these items will generate different price changes through the model for each industry. A better model would be one in which sales of construction to capital investment could be shown in fact, if we had a capital matrix, this would then be of considerable interest to construction.

This is a brief survey of what we have done; the work is now in abeyance while the other work is being carried out: the basic studies into material-usage, labour inputs, and the parameters of building types. When these have been worked on again, and when more information is available from the C.S.O. we shall have another go at establishing a model.

DISCUSSION OF MR. SLUCE'S PAPER

Chairman: DR. W. F. GOSSLING (Manchester)

PROFESSOR BLAKE (Dundee)

This is a very small point, but it interests me partly because we have a research student working on just this question, and that is, how did you estimate the input coefficients for maintenance and repair work?

MR. SLUCE (Building Research Station)

We just took the figure from the C.S.O.; we have not attempted to do anything on repair and maintenance; a very knotty problem.

MR. WIGLEY (Cambridge)

May I just ask if you have continued these studies into the field of final demand? Have you any suggestions on ways in which one might estimate the demand for houses as opposed to bungalows, and high flats as opposed to low flats and so on?

MR. SLUCE

We did have a group working on the demand for dwellings in particular; they were not able to relate them to final demand in any way. Unfortunately in the dwellings sector, demand seems to be decoupled from supply in some sense: Building societies have a large fund, and they have to go on buying more houses just to keep their funds turning over, so that the demand and supply position is very confused in dwellings. In fact, we have not really done anything on final demand projections.

DR. SIMPSON (University College, London)

I'd just like to say how much I appreciate this type of work; I can see the benefits for other users, for national forecasts, is enormous, and I wonder whether Mr. Sluce could tell us whether he found any benefits for construction industry users in this, because I think if we can encourage other representatives of other industries to do the same thing: to disaggregate their rows and columns, this would be of enormous benefit to everyone; and yet we have got to be able to show them that there is something in it for them.

MR. SLUCE

The only aspect we really were able to identify was for really big construction firms tendering for contracts which were going to go on for three or four years into the future, and if the model was more accurate, they might be able to use it for establishing price changes in the future. We thought this might be useful, if you were having to tender for such a long time-span, as there are hundreds of variables to consider, all lumped into one big entity, and all this will just eliminate one of the variables. But until you improve the demand projections (as Mr. Wigley was asking) the predictions would not be very accurate. The demand projections would be the main interest to construction, which doesn't really involve having an input–output matrix.

MR. HEELEY (Turner and Newall)

I feel I must congratulate the Building Research Station on doing this type of work; however, particularly from the point of view of the building-material suppliers, I am a little concerned about the future direction of their work being concentrated on housing.

MR. SLUCE

But they are looking at all types——

MR. HEELEY

Well, that takes some of the weight from the point I was going to make because we have had meetings with the B.R.S. and demonstrated in fact that there is a lot of data available on housing; it is the other categories of building types where we would like the B.R.S. to concentrate their resources in the future.

MR. SLUCE

Yes, people have always selected housing because it is nicely easily identified; the house "unit" is quite clear.

DR. GOSSLING

I think that the construction industry is a very interesting one in that it brings out some problems which we seldom encounter with output from manufacturing; for example the period of gestation of the output is often well over a year: it may take three years to put something up. The construction industry also provides a whole row of capital-stock to capacity-output coefficients in what is called a "fixed-capital-to-capacity" coefficient table. This is a second input–output matrix: up to the present we have been discussing the current-flow input–output matrix. I should mention in passing that there is a third one: the inventory-to-output coefficient matrix which was used, of course, in *A Programme for Growth, Vol. III*, as a diagonal matrix. On top of that we can split all those matrices by domestic and imported components. So we can see that construction has given us a sidelight on to a whole set of further subjects for research.

It remains for me to thank the speaker, Mr. Sluce, for coming up to Manchester and speaking briefly on his illuminating paper; it takes us inside the industry. We have had a look into the chemical industry earlier, and now we have had a look into something a little bit less liquid and more solid.

SESSION VI

The Use of Input–Output Methods in DEA

by

B. C. BROWN

D.E.A.

I. INTRODUCTION

The principal use to which input–output methods are put in D.E.A. is the projection of the industrial pattern of output and employment in the medium-term on given assumptions about the level of gross domestic product and the main categories of expenditure in it. Input–output is also used from time to time for estimating the effect on costs and prices of changes in taxes, subsidies, wages and so on; it was used for instance to estimate the effect of devaluation on the sterling costs of various industries.

This paper deals with the main D.E.A. use of input–output methods. The next section describes the model we use, and discusses some of the difficulties we have met, and the deficiencies in the model which have become apparent. In the final section I set out my own view of priorities for future work as a basis for discussion.

II. THE MODEL

Our model is fairly heavily based on work done in the Department of Applied Economics in Cambridge. We use their 1960 inter-commodity tables, with some minor adjustments, projected forward, at constant 1960 prices, to 1964 and 1970. The 1970 tables were compiled by Mr. Lecomber as part of the work of preparing the 1965 national plan. They are based on the projection of coefficients so far as trends in these can be discerned and on the estimates of demand and output which were obtained from various industrial sources in the course of the preparation of the plan. The 1964 tables were compiled subsequently, starting with an assumption of inter-commodity coefficients interpolated between the 1960 and 1970 estimates. The processes of reconciliation involved are described in a paper prepared for a meeting organised by the Economic Commission for Europe in Geneva in 1966, recently published in *Macro-economic models for planning and policy making, U.N. Geneva, 1967.*

The model based on these tables is essentially simple. It is characterised by working within constraints rather than following through the consequences of one or two assumptions, for instance about the level of personal consumption. It works from given estimates of the level of gross domestic product, of each of the main elements of expenditure on it and of total imports. Some estimates of output of certain products and of imports and exports of them which are made independently, usually in other Departments, act as further constraints. Among these I would particularly mention estimates for the energy industries and for agriculture. The model recognises no connection between output and investment or between total imports and the pattern of output. As mentioned above it works on a commodity and not an industry basis. It is completely computerised and one programme moves from the input of the major categories of expenditure and of total employment to the production of estimates of output indices for individual industries and their employment requirements.

There are four main stages in the model:

(1) estimating the commodity composition of final demand;
(2) estimating demands on industries and imports;
(3) converting the results to industry production indices;
(4) applying projected estimates of output per head to given demand for labour in each industry and scaling these estimates up or down to match the given estimate of total demand for labour.

Strictly speaking only the second stage might be regarded as an input–output operation. The first stage could be regarded as ancillary to it and the third and fourth stages as the process of interpreting the results of the input–output work. However, there is no doubt that the first stage is absolutely essential to any input–output projections and that errors at that stage are at least as important as errors in the input–output work. Indeed the estimation of intermediate demand is essentially secondary to the estimation of final demand.

For this reason we have been content to adopt the inter-commodity coefficients in the 1970 plan-based tables though we realise that they are not necessarily the best estimates that could be made; some of the output estimates which they had to accomodate did not merit the weight they were in fact given. They have been amended only to take account of specific factors such as the introduction of North Sea gas and changes in the expected composition of fuel consumption in power stations. We have in fact assumed that the plan target level of g.d.p. will not be reached by 1970 and assumed that the coefficients in the 1970 plan input–output tables are appropriate to 1972. For intervening years we interpolated between 1964 and 1972.

The estimation of the composition of final demand presents a series of major problems. In general the form of the model is to have, for a given future year, a set of trend estimates for the components of a category of final expenditure, such as personal consumption, and allocate the difference between the sum of these estimates and the given total for the category by a vector of coefficients adding to unity. This is simple and convenient both for the algebra and for the computer; and provided that the amount to be allocated is not too large, is broadly consistent with an assumption of constant total expenditure elasticity for individual items. In some cases the whole procedure is carried through in terms of commodities. In others the allocation is initially in terms of different categories, for instance the categories of consumers' expenditure used in the National Income Blue Book. A classification converter is then used to move to a commodity analysis. The former method provides a short cut but it also leads to considerable awkwardness when modifications are made, because the classification converters are not reversible.

The real difficulty is in the substance. A great deal of work is being done on the analysis of consumer demand for particular commodities but comparatively little on the composition of total personal consumption. Work is in hand in Cambridge on the development of the Stone–Brown–Rowe 8 Sector Model "Demand analysis and projections 1900–1970: A study in method" in *Europe's Future Consumption* (North-Holland Publishing Company, Amsterdam, 1963.) We look forward to seeing the results. Even so we do not expect to be able to swallow them whole and hold them down. For instance, we should not expect that they would give the best possible estimates of expenditure on cars. This for example is a special field of study, and we should expect to modify the results of any overall analysis to take account of intensive work in particular fields. Meanwhile, the trend estimates and marginal coefficients we are using are an amalgam of real projections of past trends, allowances made for special factors of one sort or another, cross-section and time series analyses of demand for particular products, and judgement, both our own judgement and that of production Departments, and generally through them, of people in the industries concerned. I should note that no specific allowance is made for the effect of changes in relative prices. The effect of past changes will be reflected in trends and their projection assumes that prices move as in the past. This seems not unreasonable. It is perhaps most questionable where price changes have been due mainly to increases in indirect taxes.

The other categories of final expenditure are dealt with in much the same way. At present capital expenditure gives us little difficulty because we make no distinction between the products of the large group of engineering and electrical goods industries, so that the great majority of capital expenditure on plant and machinery is allocated to one heading. The problem will clearly increase substantially when we break this heading down. On public consumption we get help from the spending departments; there is a substantial problem of making the fullest possible use of it with the resources we have; at the same time there are some fairly substantial fields where we get very little help.

With both exports and competitive imports we use extremely crude assumptions and put the results to the Board of Trade and Production Departments for their comments. We should like to take in the results of Lecomber and Barker's work and get rid of the awkward distinction between complementary and competitive imports; but we should still expect to make adjustments to take account of independent estimates. The algebra of the input–output work proper is set out in the Appendix. This shows how imports are allocated.

The second stage of the model gives us estimates of gross output for each industry. Corresponding figures of gross output are, however, not available for all previous years. Strictly corresponding figures, in our case, are available only for 1960 and 1964. Gross output figures can be obtained for other years in which censuses of production were taken, at least for industries within the field of that census, but they are available only at current prices and reliable deflators are not compiled. (The Board of Trade indices for output of individual industries refer to the industries' unduplicated sales, excluding sales by one firm in the industry to another.) The only available continuous series which represent the output of individual industries are the components of the index of industrial production and the real product index of g.d.p. It is to these that we relate employment series and it is therefore necessary, if we are to project and use these relations to estimate labour needs, that we should have projections of production indices for the industries concerned.

In a simple industry the change in gross output will be much the same as the change in the index of production for the industry, which purports to measure the change in net output (all at constant prices). Our model however recognises only thirty-one or thirty-two industries and naturally few of these approach this degree of simplicity. It is not simply a matter of producing a technically homogeneous output, but also of selling it to different classes of customers at roughly the same prices. For instance, the output of the electricity supply industry is measured, for the purposes of the index of production, in terms of kilowatt hours. But the average price charged to major industrial consumers is different from the price charged to householders or commercial users. Consequently the increase in gross output at constant prices as shown by the input–output projections is by no means the same thing as the increase in total production or sales in terms of kWh. There are further complications arising from the nature of the index of production for the industry. Although this purports to measure changes in net output at constant prices, in fact it takes no account of changes in the proportion of the electricity generated by burning coal or oil or at atomic or hydro power stations. The effect of such changes is reflected in the model estimate of net output at constant prices, because the input coefficients are adjusted to take account of them. To this extent it might be regarded as a better indicator; but not better for the estimation of labour requirements from a productivity projection based on the index of production. (In practice we tend to use estimates of employment requirements which are prepared in the industry and based on detailed forecasts of plant likely to be in operation. But the principle applies to other industries.)

In general we use a crude method of estimation. The 1970 plan incorporated projections of production indices for each of the industries distinguished in the input–output model, and indeed many more, and these were carefully related to the projected input–output tables for 1970. As a first approximation we assume that the relation between the increase in the index between 1964 and 1970 and the increase in gross output is applicable to new projections to the early 1970s.

One further point should be mentioned about our methods. Since we work within the constraints of given national totals for output and employment and the projections for individual industries naturally do not add precisely to these totals, it is necessary to introduce a scaling stage. In the case of output the discrepancy is spread pro rata over all industries except those for which we have specific estimates which we wish to hold firm. In the case of employment we have chosen to assume that the productivity estimates which show the greatest increase on 1964 are the ones which are most subject to error and amenable to adjustment. The overall adjustment to the productivity increase on 1964 is taken as a constant proportion of that increase—except for those industries where a firm estimate of productivity or employment in the forecast year has been brought in from outside. This method has the advantage that the estimates for industries where output per head has shown very little change, possibly because of the way in which the index of production is calculated, are not required to show a sudden change.

In general the model has the merit of a fair degree of simplicity. It is possible to introduce corrections or hold certain figures at a given level and make corresponding adjustments to others and the results can be displayed in a way in which they can be reviewed by people knowledgeable about particular industries or particular areas of expenditure. The value is, however, limited by the relatively high degree of aggregation which means that the industries distinguished are very often too large to be considered as single industries by people with specialist knowledge.

This description has already shown up some of the deficiencies in our present methods, and some of the difficulties we have come up against. The next sections sets out my view of priorities.

III. NEEDS AND PRIORITIES

First my view on what needs to be done to improve our model. (I take it for granted that further disaggregation is needed; no doubt there is an optimum, but it is not in sight.) Secondly, I suggest research work necessary for the immediate needs to be met, and to enhance the value of work with the model.

A. *Improvements to the Model*

First priority must go to the better estimation of the commodity composition of final demand at home, and within that to consumers' expenditure and public consumption. As I mentioned, we are still hoping to be able to use Cambridge D.A.E. work on consumers' expenditure, but that will not be sufficient in itself. Their answers will be in functional terms, and a classification converter to the 1963 tables' commodity classification will be needed. We hope to be able to make use of work done in the compilation of the tables, using the Family Expenditure Survey.

On public consumption, there is scope for a great deal of analysis of accounts. This is under way, partly as a contribution to the 1963 tables, and there is already more information available in official records than we have been able to incorporate in our present model.

At the same time there are important fields, particularly in local government expenditure, which are still virtually unexplored.

Capital expenditure has given us little trouble so far, because we recognise so few industries making capital goods—the engineering and electrical goods complex of industries is treated as a single unit. The disaggregation of this complex will mean that, in order to estimate demand on its components, we shall have to have an industrial analysis of the (given) estimate of total investment in plant and machinery.

Secondly, we must incorporate the Lecomber method of estimating the composition of exports and imports, or something very like it. The present split of imports between complementary and competitive is positively embarrassing and the allocation of marginal coefficients for both exports and competitive imports is extremely crude. This did not matter so much in the past, when our projections were not very far from trend, but it has become obtrusive since devaluation.

Thirdly, we must devise a method of projecting the 1963 intercommodity coefficients into the 1970s. We shall use crude methods to start with, but hope to have the results of deeper studies before very long.

Fourthly, we must improve our methods of converting the results of the input–output part of the model into production indices. This might be done by making use of projected sales to various classes of customer, net output and even purchases and output of other commodities, as well as total gross output. It should be eased to some extent by the 1963 disaggregation.

Some of these developments might be classed as research in themselves, but they will be mainly crude and provisional. They will need to be backed up by thorough research.

B. *Research work*

(i) *Direct needs.* The best basis for work on changes in input–output coefficients might be the reconstruction of the 1954 tables on the same basis as those for 1963, but in addition there is scope for analysis of the very incomplete short period information available, and, possibly, for detailed analysis of records of the activities of individual establishments and firms, starting with the Census office records. My own hunch is, however, that since we are operating the model at a high level of aggregation, useful analysis will be done mainly at a level of aggregation not much below this.

An important point to consider is whether coefficients tend to change with time or with the level of output. Some Dutch work has suggested that the latter is frequently the case.

Research work in the field of estimating the composition of final demand has already been mentioned above; the main need is for consumer demand analysis. In addition, however, changes in the commodity composition of functional categories of demand (for example, "food", or "meat and bacon" or "radio and electrical and other durable goods") need analysis. We have so far assumed no change in the classification converters, but this is doubtfully realistic.

There is clearly also plenty of room for further work on the composition of exports and competitive imports and its relation to changes in home costs per unit of output (relative to overseas) in total and for individual industries.

(ii) *Longer term needs.* Looking more widely about us, and looking further ahead, the value of our model would be enhanced by successful research in a number of fields. These I do not propose to describe in any detail, but merely to list.

First, stability and sensitivity; not only stability of coefficients or rates of change in them as mentioned earlier, but also stability of inverses with moderate or random variations in transactions coefficients. Studies in this field would help us to locate key factors for closer analysis.

Secondly, connected with this, analyses of short term movements in coefficients, or, in errors of estimates of industry outputs, using constant, or constantly changing coefficients.

Thirdly, the introduction of labour and capital into the model. Methods of doing this have, of course, been suggested and worked out; what is missing is convincing estimates of the parameters, suitable for short or medium term work.

Fourthly, in relation to the use of input–output for estimating the effect of changes in input prices (tax rates, etc.) on output prices, research into the immediate reaction of businesses to increases in their costs, and the somewhat longer-term reaction, reflecting the real effect in the market for their products as well as their first estimate of it, would be most valuable. The effect on prices of, for instance, a change in S.E.T., might be very different if firms absorbed 25 per cent of all increases in the costs of labour and materials instead of simply passing them on (or maintaining their percentage margins for overheads and profits).

IV. SUMMARY AND CONCLUSIONS

I have described briefly what we in D.E.A. now do as a regular exercise, namely the operation of a simple model centred on an input–output pattern of output and employment corresponding to a set of medium-term projections of the main aggregates of national expenditure and of total employment.

I have outlined some respects in which I feel this work ought to be improved as soon as possible, and expressed the view that the most urgent need is in the first stage, the disaggregation commoditywise of the main expenditure aggregates, and of imports, and the third stage, the conversion of the input–output results into industrial production indices, rather than for the improvement of the input–output stage, though the 1963 tables will be no good to us until we can somehow project the coefficients. I did not mention the need to improve the projections of labour requirements per unit of output, only because it is rather outside the field of this conference.

Nor did I mention the need to get out of the constraints at present imposed, and use the model to forecast the total of imports and not just the pattern, and to estimate industrial investment requirements and total labour needs instead of taking these from a macro-economic projection. This will follow almost automatically when the improvements I have outlined have been accomplished.

Finally, I set out briefly what seem to be our main research needs. I shall not be surprised to learn of work already in hand to meet them. This conference has been an excellent vehicle for the exchange of information as well as ideas, and so far as we are concerned I hope and believe that links formed and reformed here will be strengthened by more frequent contact in the future.

APPENDIX

The Algebra of the D.E.A. Model

All vectors (small letters) are $[31 \times 1]$ column vectors, e.g. $\mathbf{q}$. A dash ($'$) denotes a transposed vector; a circumflex (e.g. $\hat{\mathbf{p}}$) denotes a diagonal matrix, with the elements of $\mathbf{p}$ in the leading diagonal, and zeros elsewhere. $\mathbf{i}$ is the unit (summation) vector, and $\mathbf{I}$ the unit matrix.

The model

$$\mathbf{q} = \mathbf{Aq} + \mathbf{f} - \hat{\mathbf{i}}\mathbf{m} \tag{1}$$

$$\begin{aligned}\mathbf{m} &= \mathbf{m}_o + \mathbf{a}_2(\gamma - \mathbf{i}'\mathbf{n} - \mathbf{i}'\mathbf{m}_o) \\ &= \mathbf{m}_o + \mathbf{a}_2(\gamma - \phi - \mathbf{i}'\hat{\mathbf{a}}_3\mathbf{q} - \mathbf{i}'\mathbf{m}_o)\end{aligned} \tag{2}$$

Substituting equation (2) into equation (1)

$$\mathbf{q} = \mathbf{Aq} + \mathbf{f} - \hat{\mathbf{t}}\mathbf{m}_o - \hat{\mathbf{t}}\mathbf{a}_2\gamma + \hat{\mathbf{t}}\mathbf{a}_2\phi + \hat{\mathbf{t}}\mathbf{a}_2\mathbf{i}'\hat{\mathbf{a}}_3\mathbf{q} + \hat{\mathbf{t}}\mathbf{a}_2\mathbf{i}'\mathbf{m}_o$$
$$[\mathbf{I} - \hat{\mathbf{t}}\mathbf{a}_2\mathbf{i}'\hat{\mathbf{a}}_3 - \mathbf{A}]\mathbf{q} = \mathbf{f} - \hat{\mathbf{t}}(\mathbf{I} - \mathbf{a}_2\mathbf{i}')\mathbf{m}_o - \hat{\mathbf{t}}\mathbf{a}_2\gamma + \hat{\mathbf{t}}\mathbf{a}_2\phi$$
$$\mathbf{q} = [\mathbf{I} - \hat{\mathbf{t}}\mathbf{a}_2\mathbf{i}'\hat{\mathbf{a}}_3 - \mathbf{A}]^{-1}[\mathbf{f} - \hat{\mathbf{t}}(\mathbf{I} - \mathbf{a}_2\mathbf{i}')\mathbf{m}_o - \hat{\mathbf{t}}\mathbf{a}_2\gamma + \hat{\mathbf{t}}\mathbf{a}_2\phi]$$

$\mathbf{q}$ = gross output, 197x, of commodities
$\mathbf{f}$ = final demand, 197x, equal to the sum of consumers' expenditure, public consumption, investment, exports and stockbuilding
$\mathbf{A}$ = [31 × 31] matrix of technical coefficients, 197x
$\mathbf{t}$ = tax vector for adjusting competitive imports
$\mathbf{i}'\mathbf{m}$ = total competitive imports
$\mathbf{i}'\mathbf{n}$ = total complementary imports = complementary imports to final demand, ϕ, plus complementary imports to intermediate demand, $\mathbf{i}'\hat{\mathbf{a}}_3\mathbf{q}$
γ = Total imports = $\mathbf{i}'(\mathbf{m}+\mathbf{n})$, all before tax
$\mathbf{m}_o$ = Competitive imports, trend values
$\mathbf{a}_2$ = Column of coefficients, adding to unity, for allocating marginal competitive imports over commodities.

SESSION VI: DISCUSSION OF MR. B. C. BROWN'S PAPER

Chairman: MR. L. S. BERMAN (C.S.O.)

MR. WIGLEY (Cambridge)

May I raise the problems I have had in relation to the gross output figures which were based on the input–output calculations given the available series we have for the index of industrial production figures. Perhaps I might make a plea for the reweighting of the individual series which go to make up the index of industrial production using gross output rather than net output weights in order to produce series indicators of gross output by sectors.

MR. B. C. BROWN (D.E.A.)

This would not be difficult, provided that an appropriate and clear definition of gross output were available. I suppose Census of Production gross output would serve, but not all input–output tables use this definition; some eliminate within-industry sales. But if gross and net output in input–output industries do not move tolerably closely together (at constant prices) one important use may be ruled out; for labour requirements in such a case are more likely to be determined by net output than by gross, while an input–output model provides estimates of gross output.

MR. LECOMBER (Cambridge)

As Bernard Brown explained, I was myself involved in the input–output work in the D.E.A., and I would like to amplify some of his remarks, before adding some comments as an outsider.

The typical input–output exercise is to estimate industry outputs and primary inputs given final demands and input–output coefficients. The D.E.A. exercise was very different, in that for many industries the data most readily available to us related to industry outputs. This information came from the Industrial Inquiry. Wherever possible we pressed industries to break down their estimates by user industry or type of final demand. But most industries found it very difficult to provide the kind of breakdown required. This meant that the industrial information could not readily be interpreted in terms of the *variables* and *parameters* of the model. It was difficult even to be sure that the assumptions underlying their estimates were fully consistent. We were faced with the difficult choice of either ignoring this mass of information or of making arbitrary adjustments to final demands or to input–output coefficients, or both, to bring the model into line. We tended to do the latter except where the industrial estimates were demonstrably absurd. As this has met with some criticism, I would like to offer the following defence: first it is necessary to consider the purpose of the input–output work; this was partly to provide a framework for discussion of estimates from industries, and partly to provide a model to be used in examining variations in policies or assumptions without reference back to industry; erroneous estimates of industry output are detrimental in both contexts; if an exogenous estimate of the output of, say, the chemical industry is inserted, then the model will cease to provide any checks on the chemical industry's submission, but (assuming the industry's estimate to be sufficiently accurate) the amended model provides a better check on the submission of any industry selling to the chemical industry, and a better basis for the exploration of alternatives. But there are two important provisos: first the industry figure must be a demand-based estimate, second it must be better that the pure input–output estimate.

What worries me much more is the scaling of imports to satisfy a balance of payments constraint, and of employment to fit a manpower constraint. These are not alternative estimates of the same thing, they are economic constraints. Discrepancies indicate a real rather than a purely statistical problem and should on no account be "swept under the carpet". Bernard Brown rightly stresses the importance of incorporating more satisfactory import functions that are sensitive to demand and perhaps to relative prices such as we have estimated at Cambridge. But such functions cannot satisfactorily be introduced into the D.E.A. model if total imports are arbitrarily constrained.

Bernard Brown has very openly laid bare the deficiencies of the present model, and the magnitude of the area for further research is daunting. But Whitehall appears to be unwilling to provide the necessary resources. The D.E.A. has never had more than one man working full-time on input–output, nor have they had access to an adequate high speed computer. The Department has attempted to overcome this by drawing on the work of others, particularly the Cambridge Growth Project. And let me say at once that we at Cambridge welcome this. Indeed my point is that there is an urgent need to bring the D.E.A. and the Cambridge model closer together. Unfortunately problems of confidentiality and differing needs probably rule out a joint model, but there would seem to be scope for linking the models in a more formal way than at present. This will need to be carefully thought out. So too will the best manner of bringing in the expertise of industry. Even the intelligent utilisation of other people's work cannot be done on too fine a shoe-string. If more than lip-service is to be paid to the value of input–output models in making projections, more resources must be made available.

MR. BROWN

There is very little I want to add to what Mr. Lecomber has said. We still depend to a very large extent on the work he did when he was in the D.E.A. and, as I have made clear, his work on the basis of the next major improvement I should like to see. I should, however, like to say that, much as we should like to be able to maintain that estimates of total labour requirements or of total imports derived from the model are better than direct estimates of these aggregates, we cannot yet do so, and until then there is sometimes advantage in constraining to such direct estimates though not losing sight of the unconstrained estimates.

MR. HILTON (Southampton)

I too would be interested to see the reweighting of the index of industrial production on a gross output basis but the crude analysis we have made suggests that the use of gross output rather than net output weights makes little difference to the index.

The point I was particularly concerned with in Mr. Brown's paper (I think Mr. Brown was concerned with this as well) is the possibility of getting co-operation from academics. This is important if the best use is to be made of resources. In this respect I would like to make the point that it is not very pleasant for academics to be associated with an exercise if some of the decisions as to what coefficients are put into the system are determined by Whitehall's, or Westminster's decisions. One example that he gave was the Customs and Excise didn't like the D.E.A. assuming a trend for tobacco duty, and therefore he had to adjust the results even though their objections were purely political ones. Academics are likely to be discouraged if their analyses are to be overthrown by an arbitrary Whitehall decision.

The other point which interests me was that Mr. Brown spoke frequently about the lack of resources in government departments. Is this lack of resources a lack of finance or is it a lack of staff? If it is not finance then why haven't the government gone out and hired outside academics to do some specific pieces of work for them? I ask this as a disinterested observer, because I am not seeking such employment myself!

MR. BROWN

Well, first of all the question of gross output again. There are great difficulties in handling gross output figures. Gross output figures for an individual industry are very often not comparable from one census to another because the amount of duplication is different. This is the really great difficulty—one reason for attempting to use net output for a lot of purposes. If one is, for instance, going to update a set of input–output tables, it is one reason for using, even for prefering to use, a set of output indicators rather than using actual figures collected from firms of the total value of their output at current prices. It may be more important to have comparable figures, and figures collected with exactly the same definitions for gross output in two separate years may, in this sense, not be comparable; this is a nasty little problem which I've never seen discussed very much, but it's always at the back of my mind. Secondly, Customs and Excise really do make for their own purposes very careful forward estimates of tobacco consumption, for instance, and on the whole I believe they are good estimates, but, of course, they make them on the assumption that the present level of duty remains unchanged.

Our first estimates were based on the projection of past trends, modified to take account of deviations of income from trend. But over this period taxes were rising, and, by implication, our estimates assumed a continuation of this trend; this was not among our intended, explicit assumptions. That is why we accepted the Customs estimates.

MR. ROE (Cambridge)

Mr. Brown's paper is entitled "The use of input–output methods in D.E.A." I wonder if you might ask him to depart from his terms of reference very briefly to talk a little bit about the use of input–output results in D.E.A. I ask this question because I think he may have left the impression with some people that the major use of these methods involves industries' opportunities to get a look along the row to see to whom they are selling and what the prospects are for increasing these sales in the future. I think this is a wrong impression and one which Mr. Brown might want to correct, and specifically (since Professor Nevin has left) perhaps I might ask him how he sees D.E.A.'s role in co-ordinating input–output work in relation to regional planning. Regional planning is one of the responsibilities of D.E.A. as I understand it, and it seems it might be one of those areas where the use of some resources—I'm not suggesting D.E.A.'s resources—perhaps academic resources, might bear some useful fruits. I wonder if he has any comments or personal view about that possibility.

MR. BROWN

Perhaps I could deal with the second part of that question first, because my answer is really rather negative. There is no work going on in regional input–output within D.E.A. I believe that some people feel that this regional input–output work could be useful, but I personally am by no means convinced that full-scale input–output tables (much less, in some ways, national-income type of information for regions) is of positive use. But I don't claim to be particularly knowledgeable about regional work and this is only my own personal opinion; it is not the considered opinion of D.E.A. This doesn't help very much: in effect you have come to the wrong man. To turn to the use of the results of input–output work on a national scale: the main use is for looking ahead and estimating the demands on industries to see whether bottle-necks of one sort or another are likely to appear; in particular bottle-necks on the labour side. This is the day-to-day use or, at any rate, month-to-month use of this sort of work; maybe Mr. Roe feels that there is something else that it ought to be used for. The other use, which I think is very important is to provide a perspective within which people dealing with individual industries and individual subjects can work; an idea of the rest of the economy.

Now I envisage that just as the best estimate for any particular industry will not come out of the sort of input–output model that we are using or are likely to use, or indeed perhaps out of any national general input–output model, nevertheless the maintenance of the model and its modification within a consistent framework does seem to me to be a very valuable way of bringing together detailed work on individual subjects and on individual industries, comparing estimates, and setting out the consequences of work done on one subject or in respect of one industry, for other industries. This, I think, is important; it is not of such immediate use as a quick look forward to see what the prospects are for individual industries; but it provides a better basis for this. It can scarcely be done continuously, but the intention is to do it periodically, perhaps once every two years or so, more thoroughly than has been possible so far, bringing in as many people as possible.

MR. BERMAN (C.S.O.)

I should just like to say one or two words about consumers' expenditure and the Family Expenditure Survey. Consumers' expenditure is, of course, the largest component of final demand and for input–output purposes it is essential to reclassify this according to commodity group; but this is not as easy as it may seem. For the year for which you have a census of production one can do this by using the commodity-flow approach, but for *other* years all one has got are figures of retail sales. We get figures of retail sales of hardware shops. What do they sell? They sell products of the chemical industry, caustic soda, paraffin, as well as tin baths. They sell a whole range of commodities coming from a whole range of industry groups and how does one check on the product-mix of figures of retail sales by type of shop? And this is all one can get, except when one has a Census of Distribution which is taken every five years. But under the new system of production statistics we will be getting details of manufacturers' sales each year or each quarter, which will add up to quite a lot of detailed information and then it should be possible to provide this information using this commodity-flow approach and it could be that the whole method of getting at consumers' expenditure would change. Some people have said we should make more use of the Family Expenditure Survey; this is a very tiny survey; I think it covers five thousand households. It is going up to twenty thousand. There are sixteen million households in the country. I don't really know how good the results will be, but it is used for little bits and pieces of consumers' expenditure, like expenditure on water rates and local rates, building materials and repairs to houses and a few other things like that, and this, of course, is the approach we adopt for getting at consumers' expenditure. We just estimate the little bits and pieces, add them up and to get at the total. It is all explained in the *Sources and Methods* publication which came out two weeks ago, you may have noticed it, it hasn't been very widely publicised.

The other thing people spoke about which I find very interesting is the Index of Industrial Production. The total index is calculated correctly; the right way of getting at it is to add up the net output weights of each industry group to get at the total for all industries. But if you are looking at an individual industry, I agree that it would be more appropriate to have a gross-output indicator and not a net-output indicator, but I think this is a bit difficult to compile with present statistics. One uses gross-output indicators and net-output weights, one really wants to use gross-output weights as well. Perhaps this will be done in the future. When we have the new system of production statistics, we'll have output classified by industry as well as commodity. We'll have all the "carried ins" and "carried outs", if you know what they are, sorted out, and life will be much better. There is also a lot of confusion about gross output, as Bernard Brown said; the gross output is returned in a census of production. In his view and in mine it is a meaningless concept because it depends on the way in which companies make their returns. They may make one combined return in respect of three establishments, it depends on their accounting procedure. There may be mergers, take-overs and all sorts of things between one census and the next, but of course, when one goes over to an annual census, the differences between one census and the next should be very much less, but I don't know. We will have to see. Gross output free from duplication is a much better concept. It's something which means very much more.

Would anyone else like to say something, non-Cambridge; non-Scotland; Ireland, Wales? Everyone seems to be satisfied then with what D.E.A. does.—Well, the last speaker, as we are getting near closing time in both respects!

MR. BARKER (Cambridge)

The first point or question is that on the first page of your paper, Mr. Brown, in the paragraph beginning, "The model based on these tables", you say that some estimates of output of certain products (and of imports and outputs which are made independently), usually in other departments, act as further constraints. Now surely the whole point of input–output analysis is to find out whether there are constraints or not. You mentioned that you are using input–output to find bottle-necks in labour supply; but clearly you want to find out, if in an industry, you are going to project from the use of your input–output tables, an output which is inconsistent with the supplies available to come forward. Now if you make as a constraint on the model the output of the industry, then you are defeating the point of the exercise. That's the first point.

The second one is, this is a government model and I'm rather surprised to find that it doesn't really have very many policy variables in it. Surely you want to use this model to find out what's going to happen, what the implications of various government policies are: taxes, purchase taxes, income taxes on the future of the economy. In other words the long-term implications of the short-term policies which are put into action by the Treasury.

MR. BERMAN

Perhaps you had better stop there as time marches on. . . .

MR. BROWN

Right. Well, briefly on that, yes, there is a constraint, there is reason to believe, for instance, that the level of employment in agriculture is not dependent on the level of output, or indeed, probably, on anything else; a time-trend is almost as good as anything, although the level of unemployment in the rest of the economy is important. Now, using this sort of information, these sorts of estimates, the Minister of Agriculture will provide us with a good estimate of employment in Agriculture. It doesn't depend really on the rest of the model. It does, once provided, amend the constraint for employment in all other industries. Some of the output estimates are of the same type. It is sensible to put them in if they are better estimates. Now the question of policy. I suppose that the effect of policy will come up in two or three ways. First, it will affect final demand, in terms of either affecting the level or composition of consumers' expenditure, affecting investment, and so on. We can take this into account, feed it in to the model, and see what the effect is on the demand on particular industries and so on. These are the main links with policy. The model is used to see what the consequences of given measures may be, but the measures are not usually fed into the model direct; normally their primary effects have to be separately estimated.

MR. BERMAN

I am sure you would all like me to thank Bernard Brown for his very full and frank account of the activities of the D.E.A.'s "input–outputtery".

SESSION VII

Future Input–Output Research

Chairman: PROFESSOR I. G. STEWART (EDINBURGH)

PROFESSOR STEWART

Ladies and gentlemen, we have, I think, all too little time for what is a very important aspect of the conferences. We have come together as producers and users of statistics in a particular way, under the heading of input–output tables and analysis, and we have had opportunities of hearing about what the C.S.O., and the Board of Trade's Census production office, are doing and plan to do, and we've heard what is happening at Cambridge and to some extent in some of the other universities.

It would be I think, very helpful indeed if we can observe this morning a general order of presentation of ideas on current work, and plans for future work, such that those members of the conference who are here from industry could tell us something of their views on the present work they are doing, what they are about to do and, of course, adding suggestions about the general nature of input-output work throughout the country. There are all sorts of ways one might slice this, but it will be almost impossible to reach an optimal solution in fifty-seven minutes; I think perhaps if we can all observe the rules that we might be fairly succinct, be fairly brief, this would help to give everyone a fair opportunity to put his or her point of view.

We should really begin by asking those who have indicated that they were interested to say a word, if they would come up and give us the benefit of their ideas and experience on their particular aspects of input–output data, input–output analysis, and work that they are planning to do. Could Mr. Gielnik start us off on behalf of industry?

MR. GIELNIK (Unilever)

We started working with input–output techniques some three or four years ago when Professor Stone visited us, and Owen Hooker was working with him as a liaison-with-industry man; he suggested that perhaps we could create a Unilever (U.K.) input–output matrix. We began to prepare such a matrix, the purpose of which was really to help to ensure the mutual consistency of all long-term plans put

forward by the various operating companies in the U.K.; to assess
the combined future demands of Unilever companies for factors of
production in the light of their projected supply, for example,
labour, wage rates, and similar things; and finally, to assess the
impact on Unilever of the growth of the U.K. economy at various
annual rates. We've built a model, and it is a very complicated one:
the matrix is about forty-eight by forty-eight. But when the model
was nearly ready, Unilever promptly changed its organisation from
a national type of management to international product groupings!
Therefore although there is still some use for this U.K. model, we
had to begin to look really at the product-group areas. And therefore
we started working with the Battelle Research Institute who developed
three types of model.

The first stage was a consumer demand type of model where you
have a matrix projecting the population structure, by age, sex,
education, income, occupation, with forecasts for 1975, broken down
by consumer expenditure by something like fifty sectors, so that you
can project the consumer demand for 1975 by head of household,
occupation or by income-group for the six European countries,
including the U.K. "Year two" of this work was the supply side
which was a typical input–output type of analysis for the six European countries and we are still using this; finally "year three" was a
marriage of the first two years' work imposing upon it also government influences, such as taxation, economic policies, and so on.
This work has now been completed. It's being adjusted, the rates of
growth are agreed, various industrial firms are using it, and we are
now proceeding to put it to use, namely by trying to disaggregate
various sectors of interest to us both in consumer markets (we've
just, for example, completed a major work on toilet preparations in
Europe) and in industrial markets.

On the industrial input–output side I've got here with me a paper
where we've just completed work on the disaggregation of the French
packaging industry sectors. There were originally two sectors, types
of packing paper and packages. We've disaggregated types of packing paper into nine subsectors and packages into six subsectors, and
again we are using here input–output to forecast industrial demand;
we have eighty using-industries and we are trying to forecast what
type of packaging they would be demanding by 1975. There are
various complications, of course, and various forecasting methods
have been used, but all within the framework of the work which
we've done with Battelle.

On quite another plane, we have begun to build micro-economic types of models; we began, again, with one of our paper mills, Thames Board Mills, and built—and are still building—a company model which takes into account the raw materials, primary production, intermediate production, final production and end-users. The purpose of this model is to have a sort of dynamic accounting system. It is basically going to be used for accounts, but you will be able to simulate a variety of alternatives from the end-use point of view; if the demand changes you will load your machines differently or you will use different raw materials—this type of thing.

Then, finally, we've built a world model for oils and fats, where, as you know, Unilever is using a very substantial proportion of the world's supply (there are supplying countries and there are consuming countries) and we use it really basically for price forecasting. It is a type of balance-sheet method, if you like, where you take into account the forecasts of sowing, crops, acreages and so on. You establish what will be available. You forecast demand separately. You take account of stock changes and any American surpluses which might be coming to the market. It's again quite a large complex model. The significance of this model is that it is linked to very large linear programming systems which calculate allocations of oils and fats to products, to factories and to countries. This particular forecasting model is used in conjunction with linear programming to see what will happen, let's say in 1972, when certain prices are rocketing down or there will be a surplus of certain oils, and so on, to check whether we have enough technical resources, say, hydrogenation capacity, or whether we ought to do any specific research in substitution improvement of the mixes. So again we are using input–output in this way. This is the work which has been done so far. Furthermore, we are now just beginning to build up information systems for our chemical raw materials where we shall again try to develop an input–output analysis for the chemical raw materials as opposed to the natural raw materials. For the future we feel that some form of model similar to that which we've designed for the U.K. will have to be built for Europe (that will take a little time), and the type of model which we are building for Thames Board could perhaps be extended to other companies; we'll see how it will work. I think perhaps we have another two year's work to do there.

MR. HEYWOOD (I.C.I.)

These are just some thoughts I'd scribbled down last night after Mr. Berman had finished speaking. I've been corresponding with him for a couple of years on this problem. Our Central O.R. Group certainly could use a large matrix and I'm a bit doubtful, even more doubtful after this week, of the data that has already been supplied for earlier U.K. input–output tables. I wonder if it is possible to build up technical coefficients from standard or estimated costs on a budgeted basis as an option to the proposed quarterly records of past operations. Any firms with reasonable accountancy systems (this must include the ones who produce most of the output of the country) have to create budgets just before the end of the year for the following year's operations. I can't see that these are going to be any more inaccurate than four quarterly lots of figures when people are trying to make predictions forward in any case. Normally, the following year's production is produced at the prices estimated as at 1st January, but there is nothing to stop you putting last year's production through (and this is easy if you have a cost model) at next 1st January's prices. This is likely to be the most up-to-date position and will certainly have in it all the latest products and processes. A further suggestion which I have already made to Mr. Berman would be to give each firm a registered number for the S.I.C.s which it is to produce and to request that these numbers are printed on the sales invoices. This means that it would be a relatively simple job for the receiving firms, even shops and very small businesses, to analyse the purchases over S.I.C.s of input. In that case a shop or a very small business would have one S.I.C. output number, and even in the very large ones you only have a minimal number; I.C.I. wouldn't have a thousand S.I.C.s of output in any one area, obviously. I would think that by a clever piece of data-processing and a determined teaching job (one has to fill in the forms properly), possibly using auditors and tax men to help (because these are the men who usually get the job of helping the small businesses) something could be done. I would like to see some research on simulating the problem of obtaining data. I can't see that this is an impossible task at all. You could put in a big multi-product firm, a small shop, a distributor, a power producer (and even perhaps a Whitehall office!). I am not at all clear just what the objectives are in producing this data. I've not had a clear picture of what is wanted all through from anybody. I would have thought it would be feasible to simulate data-raising by a model.

May I now say something about our work, or shall I leave that till later?

PROFESSOR STEWART

I think there is just time if you could mention it very quickly.

MR. HEYWOOD

The internal cost processors and cost models in existence number eight. Three or four are substituted for manual calculations, four being attached to linear programming models of divisions or subsidiaries of the company. Three of the eight are production and cost models which have demands and capacities linked to the production processes. One is a Leontief-type package of a thousand nodes, one a three thousand node model using an iterative solution to balance the flows. We then have a $13,000^2$ model of two divisions linked together and this uses a semi-iterative method of cost ascertainment and covers batch production, continuous production, joint productions, and packing operations. Obviously, several of the models have to deal with loops (recycles) in our type of business. The model with the Leontief-type package has in it a three-hundred-step loop. The achieved results on these models are that we have found them to be the quickest way of introducing standard costing with its attendant advantages. The standard cost can be continuously updated, which is virtually impossible manually. In the case of the largest model it used to take eight months from start to finish to complete the next year's standard costs for one selected pattern and one selected volume of output for each product.

The "break-back-break-forward" table (the input–output table) is available, in the case of the largest model, on overnight call, and all the models produce validated data for linear programming and many kinds of data processing operations. I would say that for four years the three big models have been the vertebrae of the information systems. There have been four pay-offs in money. The most dramatic, I suppose, was that in the case of the largest model, we'd one man working full time on the job of collecting rebates of import duty where we were re-exporting material. The first time the break-back table was used we collected several thousand pounds extra each month. Technical time has been saved. For example, if you have a capital project which could involve a thousand sales products, the number of nodes which are going to be affected could be considerable, say, affecting half a Division. The work involved in assessing new costs and eliminating old ones, preparing the before-and-after picture, is tedious. As a small example, it could take three weeks for a man in a technical department to ascertain which nodes are likely to be affected by a large project. Now, he can submit the names and codes of the sales products likely to be affected to the computer department at night, and next morning has a break-back of all the production nodes and all the raw materials needed for the sales products concerned. Updated nets are used to simulate the revenue costs from new capital projects by taking out old cost centres and putting in new processes. By rerunning the model "before and after" pictures for discounted cash flow calculations are obtainable. A further advantage is that in cases of sudden emergencies like devaluation, and Suez crises, it would not have been practicable to adjust and recalculate all the costs of our products and find out which sales products were likely to be affected by the changes. In one case it took three days to recalculate eight thousand costs, because, of course, since it is an updating system we do not renew all the data. The changes involved in devaluation and Suez only consisted of a handful of punched cards. In the future there should be extensions of these methods in other divisions. Interdivisional models should arrive also, giving better guides to long-term bottle-neck elimination and pricing decisions.

MR. LUKER (I.C.I.)

I'd like to talk about three things. First of all the situation as it exists today in one Division of I.C.I.: I think I can best deal with this in terms of a brief sketch, which I'll have to put up pretty rapidly. The Division we are involved in is called Mond, and we could represent that by a box labelled chemicals. We are backward-integrated into various minerals and forward-integrated into engineering. Now the bulk of the chemical sector is covered by an L.P. optimisation model, and our first task is to extend this L.P. model which is concentrated in this area because of the circular flows of particular chemicals inside the Division which are extremely complicated. Now at the moment all the external demands from the rest of the economy are put in from marketing estimates. These are prepared variously, on "the backs of envelopes," or by trends, or by correlations, depending on how the marketing people feel like doing it at the time. It seems to me that it's in this area, the transposition of demand from being exogenous to endogenous, that we ought to aim at bringing in input–output. This also brings a link with what Mr. Heywood has been saying, because we receive a contribution on the raw material side from another division and a growing chunk of output is dependent upon the demand from another division. I think that input–output techniques could bring demand in endogenously and help with the supplying end as well. So we've got a very large problem of interdivisional company co-operation—where Mr. Heywood's going to do a selling job, I hope.

I'd like, now, to go on to the question of input–output as a market

o

research tool. Obviously this is a related question, but I personally think this is where input–output will find its most immediate impact in industry. Here, I'm afraid, I must come back once again to the point I made yesterday about disaggregation. Unless the input–output material is disaggregated it is virtually useless as a market research tool, and furthermore, I submit that unless definitions are standardised it is also virtually useless as a market research tool, both as to the input and the output side. Furthermore, with all respect to the electronics people here, one of the fastest growing bits of British industry is in the plastics sector, and I think it's essential that the Board of Trade and/or C.S.O. people drawing up the definitions should be made aware of these fast-growing new industries (which, at the moment, are relegated to bits of engineering and something called "all other trades" or something way down at the end: I think it's M.L.H. number 496). They should recognise the importance of these growing products. Now I know it's difficult for them because the plastics industry hasn't been as forthcoming as it might have been, but more and more people are saying "plastics are going to grow at 15 per cent per year". You can't get anything very much faster than that nor more potentially important.

My last point is that the job of looking at the economy as a whole is one for head office in I.C.I. and here I would imagine, in time, macro-economic input–output will be used.

MR. BERMAN (C.S.O.)

As I understand it, what Mr. Heywood proposes is that each establishment, when it sends out its invoice, should include on the invoice a code number which would say what the establishment S.I.C. or minimum-list heading number is. Is that right? Yes. Well, there are a number of difficulties here as I see it, looking at it very quickly. First of all, who is sending out the invoice? I mean, will it be the establishment or will it be a financial unit which will include a number of establishments straddling across different S.I.Cs? The idea is that the firm which buys the commodity will be able to see from the invoice the S.I.C. heading or the commodity code of the commodity that it buys. Well, this is O.K. in so far as the invoice received relates to a fairly uniform commodity group; if it straddles several S.I.Cs, then it would not work. That is one snag.

A more important snag is that in many cases an establishment does not sell direct to another manufacturing establishment, it sells to a distributor. In this case the distributor would know who he buys from but then the distributor sells to the next chap but the next chap will not know who he originally buys from. I.C.I. might sell paint to a wholesaler, and then the wholesaler might sell paint to the builder or somebody in the timber industry, or the shipbuilding industry, but it wouldn't be possible for the person in these using industries to know from the invoice where the commodity originally came from. Of course, he knows it's paint, and paint is made by the paint industry, but we know this anyway. If one just went to the purchasing establishment and asked them to give a list of all the goods and services they buy, which is what the Census of Production does, then we are back to the old fashioned "steam system". The idea here really is to get all the invoices and sort them by number and that will also provide you with the detailed input–output table straight away.

A third difficulty is what happens in the case of imports? I suppose the importer could classify his sales by commodity group and put a code on the invoice, but this sort of thing goes against the whole system, instead of the importer having one number, he'd have to go through the S.I.C. and do all the work and I'm not so sure whether he would be happy to do this.

There are 130,000 establishments in manufacturing industry and some $2\frac{1}{2}$ million non-farm business establishments in the country, and to make this system work (I don't think it would work anyway theoretically) but to make this system work, you have got to get the co-operation of all these $2\frac{1}{2}$ million establishments. I think this would be a very difficult thing to sell to the business community. Well, these are my thoughts. I think eventually, each establishment in this country will have a unique reference number. We will have to have this in order to be able to classify each establishment in exactly the same way in different departmental statistics, that is, if we are going to have a common register. This is basically a list of names and addresses of firms and establishments classified in the same way in all enquiries. This is the way statistics are compiled in many other countries, like in France, in Canada, where one reference number is used by all reporting units. This is the only way to get a unified statistical system going, I think. So maybe we would go some way towards Mr. Heywood's ideas but I doubt very much whether we would go the whole way, it seems a bit difficult. On the question of the detail (I'm afraid I missed part of the talk on this) I had an idea that they were talking about the degree of detail in the input–output table, but from the point of view of the government, I don't think the government is particularly interested in very great detail tables; up to seventy is probably detailed enough for the government's own use. If industry wants very detailed tables then it really depends who wants it. I.C.I. wants it and Unilever want it, that's all right; but what about the other firms, do they want it as well? We have got no idea at all whether other firms are interested in very detailed tables.

PROFESSOR STEWART

Perhaps we shall get an answer to that in a moment.

MR. BERMAN

Well, it's a very important question, you know, whether industry is really interested in very detailed tables. In America, as I understand it, industry actually compiles detailed tables themselves. They give money to the market research agencies and tell them to expand the government's table, so that it is not done at the government's expense. Maybe this is what should be done here, I don't know.

MR. PELLING (Dunlop)

I would like to confirm the interest in further details for market research purposes, and particularly for forecasting. Our interest in input–output at the moment is very exploratory; I think it will develop in the future, and the more detail we can get the better it be for us, certainly.

MR. YATES (English China Clays)

I, again, would like very much more detail, but the classifications which we're interested in are so small, even down to coated paper, I accept this proposition that it's not really the government's job to do this. The cost of getting them in such great detail is outside the scope and the interest of the government.

PROFESSOR STEWART

You wouldn't like to amplify that just a little and say what degree of disaggregation you have in mind? I think we would all be interested in the extent to which you want to disaggregate only a part but still rely on, for example, the C.S.O. census-of-production type of table as a frame. I mean, do your operations fit in with this view of input–output analysis or are they really on a separate set of considerations?

MR. YATES

Well, at the moment our output comes under mining and quarry-ing; we are a very small part of this, so that this part is of no use whatsoever to us; but to split this section into every category would involve a great deal of effort. I don't think this is a proposition that the government could consider. In the classification of the paper industry for forecasting purposes (which is our main use of input–output) we would need to split the paper industry into more cate-gories than they do attempt to do, and I don't think they could ever get down to the required details of coated paper and coated board, e.g. blade-coated printing paper.

MR. UPTON (C.S.O.)

Could I please make a brief comment on that last point. Coated paper is, for example, one item in the American disaggregation of the paper industry. Here they have taken the paper line and column of the American government's input–output table, which is eighty by eighty I think, and they have disaggregated it into forty or fifty sub-items and one of these sub-items would be coated paper. We seem to be getting down to the level which the last speaker wanted.

MR. WOLFRAM (Economic Consultants)

It is rather difficult for me to deal in detail with what we are doing because our work is on a commissioned basis and this, in a way, affects private confidentiality. But just to give an illustration of the use input–output methods and tables: one of our main activities is regional planning (in co-operation, for example, with local authori-ties) and the use of input–output methods and tables in this field is fairly extensive. For new towns or new industrial areas, we forecast, first, the impact effects on population and migration, and then try to work out—through known industrial interaction—what would be the ideal pattern of new industries which would generate the most efficient growth, absorbing the increased working population in that area.

Regarding the industrial field, I am at the moment working on an assignment which might be described as something where "angels fear to tread". That is, we are extending the official 1954 input–output tables to 1966 and bringing it up even to 1972—using information from various academic and other sources. The main objective is to assist the firm in its diversification effort. Strangely enough, we find that even the 46×46 table is a useful tool; not because we disaggregate it but because we use it in an even more aggregated form. Through aggregation we form a limited number of sectors, the total of these sectors representing the economy as a whole. The industry, however, to which our firm belongs is not included in the total. Then, we form a series of 3×3 matrices, consisting of: the particular industry in question (i), a given sector (ii), and the rest of the economy (iii). In each case an inverse matrix is worked out and what we are trying to measure are the dynamic effects on our selected industry and the rest of the economy caused by the expansion of a given sector's final demand. For these calculations we assume that each sector would expand at the same, uniform rate. The end result, when tabulated, will show how each sector's growth will affect the particular industry in question and from this information one can work out the ranking of the sectors according to their growth-effects on our industry. The ranking we express in standardised values, i.e., in terms of plus or minus standard deviations. The next stage is to superimpose this optimum (from the point of view of our industry) pattern over the actual growth pattern of the same sectors observed over a longer period, say between 1954 and 1966. The problem then becomes that of defining the areas where actual and ideal growth effects tend to coincide and to use such definitions as a basis for further market research. Although the particular exercise I am mentioning here deals with certain aspects of a specialised objective (i.e. diversification), my view is that even with the presently available input–output tables useful work can be done, even for industry. What is needed is imagination and inventiveness to extract the most from the available information. Our approach is a pedestrian, common-sense method but it illustrates the point that, however aggregated, practically useful information can still be squeezed out from the published input–output tables. Afterwards, one naturally has to combine the results with those obtained through market research.

MISS MASON (Morgan Grenfell)

As far as I know, no real use has been made of input–output methods in the financial industries. I think there is some potential for doing this. A lot of forecasting work is done on particular industries and particular companies, and I think that one could possibly use input–output techniques to bring these together and relate them both to the macro-economic forecasting that is done; but I think if one is going to try to do this there are two things one must have. One is the closer co-operation that everybody has been talking about, and I think one would have to have this to get the information more closely related to the sort of groupings that one's wanting to forecast. Another is bringing the existing tables up to the present day and having methods of forecasting changes, for the future, in the various coefficients. That is on the sort of input–output that we've been talking about.

The other area, of course, that we are even more interested in is developing the parallel flow-of-funds matrix; this, I know, has had a lot of work done on it, and it's been done at Cambridge, but I think anything further that can be done to disaggregate sectors and get more industry information there, would be very valuable.

MR. ARMSTRONG (Cambridge)

I'll keep this as short as I can, because you've heard quite a lot already this last day or two from Cambridge. If I can just say briefly how I, and the group of us, see the use of input–output. Firstly as a tool for medium-term economic planning; this seems to be the prime use which has been made so far and probably will be in the future. A second use which has been touched on is integrating the input–output tables into the national accounts using constant-price input–output tables to get better measures of changes in real domestic product. The third use which we see for this is in building up a year-by-year planning model, to take us year by year from the present date to the ultimate target date.

What have we done with these three headings so far, and what are we doing? We explored 1970 at about the same time as the national plan did so. We have explored 1972 and this is in the pipeline to the printers at the moment. We have plans to look further ahead to 1975 and 1980. On the question of constant-price tables and double deflating for indices of gross national product we've been very limited in that respect—using our own tables for 1954 and 1960. The results are quite interesting and I think it's a line which is worth pursuing. The year-by-year process is at the moment still in its infancy, but is progressing. Our plans for research and for development here are these; we would like to build up a time series of input output tables taking as our bench marks the tables for 1954 and 1963 and by various processes of updating, filling the intervening years, and carrying on to 1967, if possible 1968. The updating process is a mixture of exogenous information where we can get hold of it and where we can't, and if we have no ideas, we use purely mechanical mathematical means for filling in the cells in the table.

In order to handle all this data we are proposing to establish an input–output data bank, or rather more than an input–output data bank, holding on the computer not only the input–output tables for each year, but all the associated matrices which go to build up the whole S.A.M. framework: the flow of commodities into consumer categories, the flow of commodities into government, the taxes analysed by different types paid by different classes of purchaser. We shall store all this data and as much related data as possible (data on employment by skill, and by sex, and also, capital-stock data)—any data, in fact, which has any bearing on the use of input-output and its uses as a planning and projection model. This work is beginning at the moment and I think any suggestions, any ideas any other people would have on this, we'd gladly welcome.

On the size of tables we, as you know, began working with a table 31×31 largely, I think, as a matter of convenience and based on the amount of data that was originally available. The original C.S.O. table had forty-six commodities; we had to get over the problem of a change in S.I.C., and this often dictated coming down to a thirty-one-table. Since then we have gradually expanded and we are now working with a forty-five-commodity breakdown with possible plans for extending to fifty or slightly more. I think from our point of view for using input–output seventy or eighty is certainly probably as large as we would like to handle. If you take all the different views expressed by industry one can see that a table as aggregated as eighty is of little use to people in particular industries. To accomodate every industry's view would mean a table of at least one thousand sectors, I would think; possibly even more. It seems to me that the way of doing this is to work something on the lines outlined by the Building Research Station, which is to take industrial sectors in which an industry is particularly concerned and to do a lot of disaggregation on those particular sectors and possibly even to aggregate the other sectors in which you are not really interested. The question as to who does this work is the vital one. I can't see—and following what Mr. Berman says—I am more convinced of this, that the government has any particular interest in anything more than above an 80-square table. I don't think we have. I can certainly see the great value for this in industry. One is inclined to feel that this is where some sort of co-operation between the parties concerned is looked for with industrial expertise coming in to do the disaggregation but ensuring that this is linked in and co-ordinated with the overall table. This is obviously something which has got to be thought about because if we only keep to an 80-table then I don't see industry being particularly interested in this technique. I think this would be a great shame.

PROFESSOR STEWART

Thank you. May I change the course of the discussion slightly, now, and ask Professor McManus to speak about input–output research at the University of Birmingham.

PROFESSOR MCMANUS

We have already heard the paper by Mr. Cigno of my department at this conference. He next plans to make some empirical investigations into his model, but this will be mainly in the nature of field work at the level of the firm rather than from public statistics at an industrial or sector level. Another man in my department, Mr. Lowe, is making a survey of input–output studies. Mr. Heesterman of the Department of Econometrics and Social Statistics is working on a book on Linear Forecasting Models.

The brief comment by Mr. Bayliss, a student on the National Economic Planning (N.E.P.) course, indicated that at Birmingham they (Mr. Heesterman and Mr. Bayliss) are developing a world input–output interregional model. This is an ambitious project; some of it is actually already working but it will take a long time before it is fully developed. There are also two N.E.P. students working on input–output models for different countries: one for Iraq and one for Iran. Incidentally, the emphasis of this group, as the name N.E.P. implies, is mainly on the planning and control aspects of input–output and programming-type systems.

I would also like to mention that at the Graduate Centre for Management Studies Mr. Tzoannos has under way a regional input–output project, which will examine interactions between the West Midlands and the rest of the country and world.

PROFESSOR BLAKE (Dundee)

I think that it is only right that a very small "plug" be put in for regional input–output work. I don't know that I am the best person to do it. If Professor Nevin had been here I think it ought to have been very much his job to say this. I think one ought to admit that, compared with other applications of input–output technique, applications to regional economic problems probably can show a rather badly defined, not very clearly estimated return for the effort that

P

would have to be put in. The pay-off is not high as far as one can see; nevertheless, I think the job certainly should be looked at and it has already been attempted in the case of Wales, and I know there are several others who would like to try it in the case of Scotland. The problems are these: first of all I think we would have to have, by courtesy of the Census office, regional intercommodity and inter-industry coefficients. Now this quite clearly would represent an enormous additional load on top of the extraction of these coefficients nationally from census returns. We would also have (and this is really where the problem becomes almost unimaginably large), we would have to have considerable co-operation even to do the job for one region; co-operation from industry in that region on source and destination analysis of flows. Now there are two practical problems here: one which Mr. Berman already mentioned, that in so many cases the invoice address is not necessarily the address of the supplier or the consumer. The other difficulty is that from the point of view of individual companies the sales areas in which they conventionally analyse their disposition of output don't coincide with standard regions. This is a lesser difficulty but very often if you are going to elicit the co-operation of individual firms in preparing regional tables, you have to get what they can provide easily and very often sales statistics are quite easily extracted but as I say very often they are analysed geographically in a way which is not a great deal of help.

All I've really done, Mr. Chairman, is to spell out the problems and paint a rather gloomy picture of what I think the pay-off is, but I still think we should look seriously at this, and I think particularly if the Census could see their way to provide regional tables of coefficients eventually, then this should be tried.

MR. BROADBENT (C.E.R.)

Can I just say something in reply? I've worked in the Ministry of Transport and in fact they have got a considerable amount of commodity-flow data already on tape, and on a number of outputs; they have compiled data recently on regions, with a rail and road survey. They have got 78×78 interregional flow for thirteen commodity groups so this may be the starting-point of something.

PROFESSOR STEWART

I think one of the problems about that is that these are volumes, not values.

MR. BROADBENT

Yes.

MR. DWORKIN (Board of Trade)

I'm probably speaking with a lone voice here as a collector of basic industrial statistics. It has been very interesting listening to the discussion over the last few days. You are, however, facing a great problem of just collecting the necessary data. If I can speak specifically for a moment on Professor Blake's point on input–output tables for the regions: the problem that we face in trying to estimate within-regional flows between supplying and purchasing industries is that although we collect census returns basically from establishments, in the 1963 census we received quite a number of combined returns because some businesses are not organised on an establishment basis. Very approximately about one-third of the total employment in manufacturing was recorded on combined returns. It is a little difficult to say how many of these combined returns cross regions, but inevitably a large proportion do. This is an indication of the magnitude of the problem to be faced in attempting to break down the detailed sales and detailed purchases on combined returns between the establishments which go to make up the combined returns. More generally it seems to me that, on the way we have designed the census forms, we can within the government produce input–output tables of the order of 130×130 (subject to a resource limitation). To disaggregate this for industry needs, even assuming that there is sufficient demand for such disaggregation, to say a matrix of 400×400 means a very substantial increase in the assumptions which have to be made in spreading the purchases between the supplying industries. Mr. Heywood suggests a possible method of overcoming this problem. I would contend, that, in fact, it is just not of practical application. I.C.I. might be in a position to do the sort of analysis which he suggested: I'm not even too sure about that on an *establishment* basis. I.C.I. probably can do the analysis on a financial basis, but, generally, business units in this country are not organised accounting-wise to give us the information needed for the adoption of the system that Mr. Heywood suggested.

MR. BERMAN

Just a comment on the regional input–output tables. As I understand it, in America, Leontief and somebody else whose name I can't remember, has developed what is known as a "gravity trade

Table 1. Summary

Company or Institution	Recent and Current Research	Proposed Research, or Research Interests
Unilever (U.K. *et al.*)	Unilever (U.K.) input–output matrix. European consumer-demand model. European input–output type of analysis. French packaging industry's sub-sectors. World model for oils and fats.	Micro-economic dynamic-accounting model for Thames Board Mills. Input–output analysis for chemical raw materials.
Management Services I.C.I. (U.K.)	Eight processors including input–output, production and cost, and other models adaptable to linear-programming systems.	Extension of model-methodology to other I.C.I. divisions; also inter-divisional models.
Mond I.C.I. (U.K.)	Linear-programming optimisation model.	Input–output linkage with other I.C.I. divisions and with the U.K. economy.
The Dunlop Co., Ltd.	—	Interest in input–output for market-research and forecasting purposes.
Economic Consultants Ltd.	Input–output and regional planning. Specially aggregated input-output tables to relate particular firms and industries to the whole economy.	—
Morgan Grenfell	—	Flow-of-funds matrix with additional industry-level breakdown.
Cambridge Growth Project	Exploring 1970 and 1972. Constant-price input–output tables.	Exploring 1975 (+). Time series of input–output tables. Data bank for input–output and other S.A.M. matrices.
University of Birmingham	Linear forecasting models. Optimal aggregation. World input–output inter-regional model. Input–output models for Iraq and Iran.	Empirical work using the Cigno model. World input–output inter-regional model. Regional input–output model for the West Midlands.

model"[1] on the basis of which, given national details of input–output and just regional aggregate totals, it's possible to produce regional input–output tables on the basis of very limited assumptions which show two-way flows between regions and not just net flows between regions. It is possible to do this kind of thing without collecting special data in the census of production.

PROFESSOR STEWART

Thank you very much indeed. I think it is abundantly clear this morning that there is need for a more extended series of opportunities at which these kinds of problems could be examined without being quite so pressed for time; this does seem to flow very naturally, from the way in which this most interesting and stimulating conference has developed, to the suggestion that clearly more work might be done in some form of organised or informally organised grouping.

It remains to me to thank all those who have spoken both at this session and at earlier sessions, for giving us the benefit of their ideas and their experience.

---

[1] See List of General and Recent References, Section D, No. 20.

Index of Authors and Discussants

(N.B. Roman numerals refer to the paper and session; S to the special session.)

List of General and Recent References

A. BIBLIOGRAPHIES

1. *Interindustry Economic Studies* (B.R.S. 4), ed. V. Riley and R. L. Allen. Johns Hopkins University Operations Research Office, Baltimore, May 1958.
2. *Linear Programming and Associated Techniques* (B.R.S. 5), ed. V. Riley and R. L. Allen. Johns Hopkins University Operations Research Office, Baltimore, May 1958.
3. *Input–output Bibliography 1955–60*, ed. Charlotte M. Taskier. (United Nations ST/STAT/7), United Nations, New York, N.Y., 1961.
4. *Input–output Bibliography 1960–63*, ed. Charlotte M. Taskier. (United Nations Series M No. 39), United Nations, New York, N.Y., 1964.
5. *Input–output Bibliography 1963–66*, ed. Charlotte M. Taskier. (United Nations Series M No. 46), United Nations, New York, N.Y., 1967.

B. SELECTED STANDARD WORKS

1. *The American Economy to 1975*, by Clopper Almon, Jr. Harper and Row, New York, N.Y., 1966.
2 *Matrix Methods in Economics*, by Clopper Almon, Jr. Addison-Wesley, Reading, Massachusetts, 1966.
3. *The Structure of American Economy, 1919–1939*, by Wassily W. Leontief. Oxford University Press, New York, N.Y., 3rd edition, 1960.
4. *Studies in the Structure of the American Economy*, by Wassily W. Leontief and others. Oxford University Press, New York, N.Y., 1953.
5. *Input–output Economics*, by Wassily W. Leontief. Oxford University Press, New York, N.Y., 1966.
6. *Essays in Economics, Theories and Theorising*, by Wassily W. Leontief. Oxford University Press, New York, N.Y., 1966.
7. *Social Accounting and Economic Models*, by J. R. N. Stone and G. Stone. Bowes & Bowes, London, 1959.

C. SELECTED PAPERS MOSTLY AFTER 1966

1. Agarwala and Goodson, *An analysis of Consumer Goods Prices*

in an Input–output Framework. London Business School E.F.U. Discussion Paper No. 4.

2. Alterman, J., "Framework for Analysis of the Industrial Origin of Income, Product, Costs and Prices", in *Studies in Income and Wealth*, Vol. 32, ed. J. W. Kendrick, N.B.E.R., New York, N.Y., 1968.

3. Armstrong, A. G., "The Motor Industry in the British Economy", *District Bank Review*, September 1967.

4. Armstrong, A. G., and D. C. Upton, *Input–output Applications: A Review* (forthcoming).

5. Bacharach, M., *Biproportional Matrices and Input–output Change* (forthcoming).

6. Barker, T. S., "Devaluation and the Rise in U.K. Prices", *Bulletin of the Oxford Institute of Economics and Statistics*, May 1968.

7. Barna, T., "The Interdependence of the British Economy", *Journal of the Royal Statistical Society*, Series A, 1952.

8. Berman, L. S., "Flow of Funds in the United Kingdom", *Journal of the Royal Statistical Society*, Series A, 1965.

9. Cambridge, Department of Applied Economics, *A Programme for Growth*, Volumes 1–8, and 9–11 (forthcoming).

10. Carter, Anne P., "Changes in the Structure of the American Economy, 1947 to 1958 and 1962", *Review of Economics and Statistics*, 1967.

11. Central Statistical Office and Board of Trade, *Input–output Tables for the United Kingdom, 1954*, H.M.S.O., London, 1961.

12. Central Statistical Office, *Input–output Tables for the United Kingdom, 1963* (forthcoming).

13. Deming, W. E., and F. F. Stephan, "On a Least-squares Adjustment of a Sampled Frequency Table when the Expected Marginal Totals are Known", *Annals of Mathematical Statistics*, 1940.

14. Dominion Bureau of Statistics, Ottawa, *Input–output Tables for Canada*, 1961.

15. Fisher, W. D., "Criteria for Aggregation in Input–output Analysis", *The Review of Economics and Statistics*, XL, (1958) pp. 250–260.

16. Friedlander, "A Technique for Estimating a Contingency Table, given Marginal Totals and some Supplementary Data", *Journal of the Royal Statistical Society*, 1961.

17. Goodson, see Agarwala.

18. Harvard Economic Research Project, *List of National Input–output Tables*

19 Hicks, Sir John, Linear Theory, Essay XI *in Surveys of Economic Theory*, Volume III (Resource Allocation), Macmillan, London, 1966

20. Hill, T. P., *Measurement of Real Product* (forthcoming).

21. Johannsen, L., "Exploration in Long-term Projections for the Norwegian Economy", *Economics of Planning*, 1968.

22. Lecomber, J. R. C., *A Critique of Methods of Adjusting, Updating, and Projecting Matrices, together with some New Proposals* (mimeo), Cambridge, Department of Applied Economics, March 1969.

23. Matuszewski, Pitts, and Sawyer, "Interindustry Estimates of Canadian Imports", in, *Proceedings of the Conference of the Candian Political Science Association*, ed. Hood and Sawyer.

24. Neudecker, H., *Aggregation in Input–output Analysis*, Discussion Papers, Series A, No. 93, Feb. 1968, Faculty of Commerce, Birmingham University.

25. Omar, F., "The Projection of Input–output Coefficients with Application to the United Kingdom", Ph.D. thesis, Nottingham University, 1967.

26. O.E.E.C. *A Standardised System of National Accounts*, 1952.

27. Rey, G., see Tilanus.

28. Schiøtz, T., "The Use of Computers in the National Accounts of Norway", *Review of Income and Wealth*, December 1966.

29. Simon, H., see Vaccara.

30. Stephan, F. F., see Deming.

31. Stone, J. R. N. "The Social Accounts from a Consumer's Point of View", *Review of Income and Wealth*, March 1966.

32. Tilanus, C. B., and G. Rey, "Input–output Volume and Value Predictions for the Netherlands, 1948–1958", *International Economic Review*, 1964.

33. United Nations, *Problems of Input–output Tables and Analysis*, United Nations New York, N.Y., 1966.

34. United Nations, *System of National Accounts*, United Nations, New York, N.Y., 1968.

35. Upton, D. C., "An Expanded Provisional Input–output Table for the United Kingdom, 1963", *Economic Trends*, August 1968.

36. Upton, D. C., see Armstrong.

D. SELECTED PAPERS GIVEN TO THE FOURTH INTERNATIONAL CONFERENCE ON INPUT–OUTPUT TECHNIQUES, GENEVA, 1968

1. "Recent Methodological Advances in Input–output in the

United States and Canada," Clopper Almon, Jr., University of Maryland, College Park, Md., U.S.A.

2. "The Use of Input–output Models in Economic Projections and Manpower Analysis by the Federal Interagency Growth Project in the United States", J. Alterman, Bureau of Labor Statistics, Washington D.C., U.S.A.

3. "Methods of Construction of the Regional Dynamic Models of Interindustry Balance," E. F. Baranov.

4. "Dynamic Input–output, Trade and Development," M. Bruno, M. Fraenkel, and C. Dougherty, the Hebrew University, Israel and Harvard University, U.S.A.

5. "Recursive Programming Models of Industrial Development and Technological Change," R. H. Day, University of Wisconsin Madison, Wisc., U.S.A.

6. Dougherty, see Bruno.

7. Duval, see Fontela.

8. "Changes in Relative Prices and Technical Coefficients," Emilio Fontela and A. Duval, Battelle Memorial Institute, Geneva.

9. Fraenkel, see Bruno.

10. "Rectangular Input–output Systems: Taxonomy and Analysis," T. Gigantes, T. I. Matuszewski, and P. R. Pitts, D.B.S., Ottawa, and Université Laval, Quebec, Canada.

11. "Adaptation of Regional Input–output Analysis to Urban Government Decision-Making," Werner Z. Hirsch, University of California, Los Angeles, U.S.A.

12. "The Dynamic Inverse," Wassily W. Leontief, Harvard University, U.S.A.

13. "A Dynamic Input–output Model for India's Fourth and Fifth Plans," Allan S. Manne and T. Weisskopf, Stanford University U.S.A., and Indian Statistical Institute, New Delhi, India.

14. Matuszewski, see Gigantes.

15. "Tests of Marginal Stability of Input–output Coefficients: 1970 Projections of a Coefficient Matrix," A. J. Middelhoek, Centraal Planbureau, The Hague, Holland.

16. "Sampling Techniques in Making Regional Industry Forecasts," W. H. Miernyk, West Virginia University, U.S.A.

17. Murakami, see Tsukui.

18. "Economies of Scale and Input–output Coefficients," Iwao Ozaki, Keio University, Japan.

19. Pitts, see Gigantes.

20. "Empirical Implementation of a Multi-Regional Input–output

Gravity Trade Model," Karen R. Polenske, Harvard University, U.S.A.

21. "The Stability of Input–output Coefficients," Per Sevaldson, Working papers for the Central Bureau of Statistics of Norway, I067/9, Oslo, 1967.

22. "Demographic Input–output: An Extension of Social Accounting," J. R. N. Stone, Cambridge University.

23. Tokoyama, see Tsukui.

24. "The Turnpike of the Japanese Economy: An Application of the Dynamic Leontief Model," J. Tsukui, Y. Murakami and K. Tokoyama, University of Tokyo, Japan.

25. "Changes over Time in Input–output Coefficients," B. Vaccara, United States Department of Commerce, Washington, D.C., U.S.A.

SUBJECT INDEX

Printed in the United States
by Baker & Taylor Publisher Services